HASHISH
AND
MENTAL ILLNESS

Hashish and Mental Illness

Jacques-Joseph Moreau

Editors:

Hélène Peters, Ph.D.
Professor of French
Macalester College, St. Paul, Minnesota

Gabriel G. Nahas, M.D., Ph.D.
Professor of Anesthesiology
College of Physicians & Surgeons
Columbia University, New York City, New York

Translated by
Gordon J. Barnett, Ph.D.

Raven Press, Publishers · New York

To the Memory
of
Esquirol

PUBLISHER'S FOREWORD

Over one hundred and twenty-five years have passed since Moreau de Tours published his pioneering study of hashish intoxication, and in all that time no attempt has been made to reissue it either in the original French or in translation.

It was Professor Bo Holmstedt of the Karolinska Institutet of Stockholm who first brought this book to our attention and urged persuasively that it be reissued in an English translation. Professor Holmstedt's contributions to neuropharmacology and psychopharmacology are well known, but many are not aware that he is also a diligent historian of these areas. For this reason, we have asked him to provide a historical introduction which deals with the life and works of Moreau, a subject which has interested Professor Holmstedt for many years.

Dr. Gordon J. Barnett has undertaken the onerous task of rendering this difficult text into English. Because of the historical importance of the undertaking and the complexities of the author's style, coupled with the changes which have taken place in French medical terminology during the intervening century and a quarter, the entire translation has been completely reviewed and checked for accuracy by Professor Hélène Peters, Chairman of the Department of French of Macalester College, St. Paul, Minnesota. Her task was certainly no less arduous or crucial than that of drafting the initial translation, and to it she brought her unique academic and intellectual gifts. Thanks to her patient efforts the reader can be assured that this classic text has been rendered into English with the utmost possible fidelity.

It was felt that it was necessary to interpret for the modern reader many of the medical concepts and terms used by Moreau which are now archaic, as well as to emphasize those points where modern science has been able to shed light upon the author's work and vice versa. This invaluable service has been rendered by Professor Gabriel G. Nahas of Columbia University. The footnoted commentaries in lower case Roman numerals are the products of Professor Nahas's knowledgeable and painstaking scholarship.

Alan M. Edelson, Ph.D.
Raven Press

TABLE OF CONTENTS

INTRODUCTION TO MOREAU DE TOURS

Bo Holmstedt *

In his famous essay, "Le Club des Hachichins," Théophile Gautier mentions Doctor X who had traveled widely in the Orient. The meetings of this "club" were held in the Hotel Pimodan,[1] the site and setting for the use of hashish that flourished in certain artistic and scientific circles in Paris in the middle of the last century but which never reached any significant proportions outside those circles. Actually, Théophile Gautier first mentioned his use of hashish in his review of theatrical plays under the title of "Vaudeville" in the journal *La Presse* of July 10, 1843. He wrote as follows:

> As you see, the number of plays has been very meager this
> week: a melodrama in five acts and a vaudeville of the

* Department of Toxicology, Swedish Medical Research Council, Karolinska Institutet, S–104 01 Stockholm 60, Sweden.

[1] The baroque palace hotel Lauzun (Pimodan) erected around 1650 can still be visited at 17, quai d'Anjou on the Isle St. Louis. Its inner splendor of paintings and gilt panels has now been restored. The word *hôtel* in French means a privately owned palace and should not be mixed up with the meaning it has now. In the 1840's the mansion was run down and invaded by dyers. Part of it was later rented as apartments. The name at this time had been changed to Hotel Pimodan. Gautier in his writings speaks about "des ors ternis de l'hôtel Pimodan" (the tarnished gold of the Hotel Pimodan). The visitor of today can get an idea of this by looking behind one of the doors where an area of nonrestored gold has been left.

The main banquet hall situated next to the room where the club is supposed to have met has a balcony for the private orchestra of the owner. At the time of the meetings of "Le Club des Hachichins," several people lived in the palace, such as the painter Boissard de Boisdenier. In 1843 the poet Baudelaire rented three small rooms overlooking the Seine River for 350 francs a month from the owner Baron Pichon. Baudelaire, who lived there for two years, was not a regular member of "Le Club des Hachichins." Gautier mentions that he seldom went there and then mostly as an observer of the meetings. Apparently Baudelaire instead took hashish at the house of his friend Louis Ménard.

simplest kind; this is all. For want of sufficient plays we have decided to perform one ourselves, without even having to leave the corner of our sofa. For a long time we have heard rumors of the marvelous effects produced by hashish, although we never attached much credit to them. We already know of the hallucinations caused by opium-smoking, but hashish has been familiar to us only by name. Some Oriental friends had promised us several times to let us taste it but, whether for difficulties in procuring the precious stuff or for some other reason, the plan had not yet been realized. It took place yesterday and the analysis of our sensations will be a substitute for the plays not performed.

We cannot be absolutely sure of the identity of the Doctor X mentioned by Théophile Gautier, but in all likelihood it must have been J.-J. Moreau (de Tours), since he, in his book about hashish, gives an account of Gautier's experiences. We now know, however, that in addition to the poets, painters, sculptors, and architects who frequented the Club at Hotel Pimodan—among them Charles Baudelaire, Gérard de Nerval, J. Pradier, F. Boissard de Boisdenier, Honoré de Balzac, Hector Horeau, and Alexandre Dumas—there were also two medical men, J.-J. Moreau (de Tours) and Louis Aubert-Roche (Pichois, 1964).

Aubert-Roche had been stationed in Cairo from 1834 to 1838 and had traveled extensively throughout the Orient. He published a book in Paris in 1840, entitled "De la Peste ou Typhus d'Orient, documents et observations recueillis pendant les années 1834 à 1838, suivis d'un Essai sur le hachisch," wherein he claimed hashish to be effective in the treatment of plague. Moreau may have derived his interest in hashish partly from his association with Aubert-Roche. Suffice it to say that they were in Egypt at the same time and that they both took part in the strange meetings of "Le Club des Hachichins." Whereas Aubert-Roche's book is only worthy of a footnote in the history of medicine, the works of Moreau (de Tours) form an essential part of the development of psychopharmacology; it is therefore appropriate to give an account of his life and activities.

Jacques-Joseph Moreau (de Tours) was born at Montrésor (Indre et Loire) on June 3, 1804 (Baruk, 1962; Collet, 1962; Ritti, 1887). His

FIG. 1. Present view of Hotel Lauzun, 17 quai d'Anjou, Isle St. Louis, Paris, meeting place of "Le Club des Hachichins."

father, a soldier in the armies of the Republic and the Emperor, traversed all of Europe, taking part in most of the battles, and was finally awarded the Cross of the Legion of Honor. He resigned after the Battle of Waterloo and spent the rest of his life in Belgium, where

FIG. 2. Moreau de Tours in 1845. Portrait executed by N. E. Maurin. Lithography by MM. Grégoire and Deneux, (Library of the Academy of Medicine, Paris).

he devoted all his time to mathematics, for which he had a great passion.

While the father carried on this turbulent life, the son began his studies of the classics at the College of Chinon and later finished them at the College of Tours. Owing to his profoundly brilliant studies, he successfully passed his matriculation examination. Moreau then entered medical school, where he was characterized as a zealous and industrious student with a tremendous appetite for learning. The medical school of the public hospital of Tours was then run by one of the most famous medical men of the period, Bretonneau. Moreau was fortunate in having the opportunity to hear the lectures of this teacher.

After studying two years with this master, Moreau went to Paris to complete his studies and to take his degree. We are not aware of the circumstances concerning his application for the position as assistant physician at the Charenton Hospital, but there is no doubt that on July 6, 1826, the date of his nomination, he found the mission to which he would devote his life, to the benefit of science.

At that time, the psychiatrist Jean Étienne Dominique Esquirol (1772–1840) had recently become head of the mental hospital and, thanks to him, a number of useful reformations had been introduced for the benefit of the patients. Among the various "non-drug" methods of treatment for the mentally ill, traveling had been prescribed even as far back as ancient Greece. Esquirol had a large number of patients from all parts of France and even abroad. Among them were rich persons to whom he could prescribe long travels; he entrusted them to the intelligent care of his young assistants. Moreau was commissioned with such a task and visited Switzerland and Italy with a patient.

Travel then became a necessity for Moreau. He had nothing to keep him in France; he was young and had no desire to settle down, he longed to see foreign countries. Esquirol entrusted him with the care of a new patient, this time for an absence of three years and a journey to the Orient. The young and enthusiastic Moreau wished to learn and profit as much as possible from what he saw and heard, and for

FIG. 3. "Moreau as seen from behind playing the piano, in Turkish dress." Pencil-drawing by Théophile Gautier when under the influence of hashish.

this reason he adopted the dress and the customs of the countries he passed through. He wrote down what he experienced, and it is much to be regretted that he never published his observations. Some of them are, however, contained in his medical books. According to Moreau, it is striking that in the Orient there appear to be fewer mentally ill than in Europe. Is this marked difference to be explained by climate, by race, or by the political and religious institutions? Moreau adhered to the opinion of Montesquieu who suggested the joint responsibility of these various causes. "The heat of the climate can be so excessive that all strength leaves the body. The lack of strength passes on to the spirit no curiosity, no noble sentiments, no generous feelings . . . laziness is happiness . . . resignation. . . ."

During his stay in the Orient, Moreau had noted the common use of hashish, especially among the Arabs. He must also have tried it himself since in his travel reports he writes rather lyrically about "pleasures impossible to interpret" which this "marvelous substance" brings about and which "would be impossible to describe to anybody who had not experienced it."

Hashish had become known in Europe through a publication by the Orientalist Sylvestre de Sacy (1809). Sacy mentioned, among other things, studies by the botanist Clusius (1567) and by the travelers Chardin (1711) and Kaempfer (1712) who wrote about the use of Indian hemp in Persia and East India. He also gave an account of the effects of hashish and proposed "to prepare with our native hemp an alcoholic beverage to be used in medicine at a time when (because of the blockade) the scarcity and the falsifications of exotic drugs encourage us more than ever to find substitutes grown on our own soil."

Owing to the mysterious legend of the "Old Man of the Mountain" and particularly to the imagination of poets and novelists, only the wonderful effects of this substance were known. Moreau wished to contrast poetry with observations and experience, and his experimental research into the psychopharmacological actions of the extract of Indian hemp permitted him to throw light on psychological phenomena which had previously been obscure; they inspired him also with ingenious ideas on the nature of insanity.

No criticism can be made of his investigative procedures. Moreau took hashish himself. It should be mentioned that hashish was then taken in the form of a greenish paste, an electuary, a now abandoned

FIG. 4. Self-portrait from the year 1844 by the poet Baudelaire, drawn during intoxication with hashish. A distortion of perspective has been assumed. Although the Vendôme column appears small in comparison with Baudelaire, this seems to be a questionable case of dysmegalopsia.

form of pharmaceutical preparation (Witschel, 1968). Because of the singular property of hashish to keep intact "consciousness and the innermost feeling" of the user, he could analyze all his impressions and still be aware of the disorganization of his mental faculties. In order to complete this internal self-observation, Moreau also commissioned the persons around him to note carefully his words, acts, gestures, and facial expressions. The results were very characteristic. They fully justified the name *fantasia* which the Oriental imagination gives to the intoxication with *dawamesc,* one of the many names for hashish. Moreau also desired "controls with other people." He turned to his pupils, and with enthusiastic curiosity they lent themselves to experiments with hashish in very varying doses, giving exact accounts of what they experienced. Moreau observed with scrupulous care every (external) symptom during the course of intoxication. The two series were compared, and full conformity was proven. The effect of hashish reveals itself by a series of intellectual disturbances, and Moreau described all the sensations with meticulous care.

When in 1845 Moreau published his extensive book *Hashish and Mental Illness,* its detailed accounts of hashish intoxication aroused the interest of the medical world. Thus, Ch. Lasègue wrote:

> Without accepting as completely as Moreau the identity of the two kinds of madness, the conformity of which has been so well observed by him, I cannot but compliment the talent with which he has presented his opinions and the subtlety of his views. It is certainly an audacity full of novelty and which goes beyond the customary scope of current publications. Moreau has embarked upon an unknown path, and even though his contentions sometimes verge upon incongruities one should not forget that they have this in common with all works of essential originality.

Such factors as the background of the subject, as well as the atmosphere in which hashish is consumed, affect individuals in different ways. Due to the great number and varying nature of the *psychic effects* of hashish intoxication, these cannot be outlined in the same way as the physical effects. However, Moreau enumerated eight main groups of symptoms mentioned in this book.

Moreau pointed out that psychiatry could benefit from these experiments by comparing the symptoms to those in mentally ill people. The illusions produced by hashish—are they not attacks of insanity? These attacks will take on all the characteristics of violent insanity if only the dose of the toxic agent is increased. Moreau had the unfortunate occasion to observe this. His assistant in pharmacy wished to see the effects of the Indian hemp when taken in large quantity, and swallowed sixteen grams of the extract. A very intense delirium broke out, followed by agitation, incoherence, and hallucinations of all kinds. Three days passed before the young man regained his composure and the full use of his powers of reasoning. During the course of the attack he maintained, however, some idea of what was happening to him.

Moreau postulated that there exists in insanity a primary factor which is the source of all symptoms, i.e., excitation, which is the primitive generative power. He attached special importance to this hypothesis and considered it equal to other great scientific laws. Moreau also compared insanity with dreams. The hypothesis is not new; it had preoccupied Aristotle. The learned philosopher from Stagira wrote in his books on *Dreams* that "the reason why we, even awake, deceive ourselves in certain illnesses is the same which produces in us, in our sleep, an impression of a dream."

Even though Moreau cannot be said to be dependent on his countryman, the French materialist and medical man La Mettrie (1709–1751), who said, "Man is what he eats," he still considered a range of causes for insanity. With regard to the concept of an organic origin, he writes; "I am not against the concept of organic damage, but I must *see* the lesion; I only believe in damage which is proven, not in that which is supposed to exist." This certainly was a very wise position to take. Even now, the existence of organic or biochemical lesions in mental illness has been difficult to prove. It may be mentioned here that Théophile Gautier wrote to Moreau only one day after a "fantasia" about an idea that he had had for a long time; "to make a new brain in an idiot (with the aid of hashish) in order to see if the mind could be expanded by development of the rudiments." It has a familiar ring in our time.

When reading Moreau de Tours' contribution to psychopharmacology, one must bear in mind that very few potent drugs were available at the time: opium and alcohol were counted among sedatives and analgesics. Moreau tried to introduce several new ones, mostly of plant origin, and to widen the indications for others, notable among them being hashish.

His perspicacity in drug work is well borne out when one reads the analysis of the effects that can be produced by excessive use of hashish. This was published in a remarkable treatise on transcultural psychiatry (Recherches sur les Aliénés en Orient, *Ann. Méd. Psych.* I, Paris, 1843). The passage is quoted in full here.

One of the determining causes of insanity among the Orientals is the use (that is, excessive use) of a certain botanical preparation by name of *hashish*. In the Memoirs which I published two years ago on the *Treatment of Hallucinations by Datura stramonium* (*Traitement des hallucinations par le Datura stramonium*) I described in detail the truly extraordinary physiological effects of hashish. I also drew attention to the strange effect which in some cases seemed to be the consequence of the prolonged use of this preparation, a sort of combination of madness and reason, a predisposition to hallucinations analogous to no other known type of mental alienation.

Concerning its pathological effects, hashish is no exception to other botanical substances which act specifically upon the nervous system. The misuse of hashish violently disturbs the organ of intellect, exaggerates its action, excites the general awareness to such an extent that it throws the individual under its influence into a world filled with fantasy, transforms in a way his perceptions, his sensations, even his instincts. And yet—and this is remarkable—it never obscures his consciousness or *ego* to the degree that it prevents him from soundly judging and grasping his new situation. But the misuse of hashish, I say, can in the long run bring about disorders which are all the more serious; seemingly, the elasticity of the mental faculties does not snap but a heavy strain is put on it. A state of constant drowsiness, hebetude, mental apathy, and, as a consequence thereof, disappearance of spontaneity of action, willpower and the ability to make decisions. These psychic anomalies are visible by an expressionless physiognomy, a depressed, lax, and languid countenance, dull eyes rolling unsteadily in their orbits, or with a robot-like immobility, drooping lips, slow movements without energy, etc. Such are some of the symptoms characteristic of the *excessive* use of hashish. We have had occasions to observe several examples of this.

I hasten to add, however, and wish to stress that the abuse itself, that is, a lengthy abuse recurring for a great number of years, can lead to the disorders which I have pointed out.

But, from what I have said before, one ought not to form an unfavorable idea about hashish. It is the same with hashish in Egypt as it is with wine and alcoholic beverages in Europe. The use of it is equally common. Almost all Moslems eat hashish, a very great number of them are addicted to it to an unbelievably high degree and, yet, *it is extremely seldom* that one encounters persons upon whom the hashish has had the disastrous effects we have spoken about here. If we disregard opium and other narcotics, wine and liquors are a thousand times more dangerous. Nevertheless, would it not be absurd to prohibit them and deprive us of their benefits because—by misuse of them—one runs the risk of harming one's health? The same can be said, and with a thousand times more reason, with regard to hashish, this marvelous substance to which the Orientals owe *undescribable* delights. In fact, it would be in vain to describe it to anybody who has not experienced it himself.

The present book on hashish is only one of many publications of Moreau. (He regarded as his most important work a publication from 1859 entitled *"Psychologie morbide dans ses rapports avec la philosophie de l'histoire."*) The principal idea of this book is evident on the very first page: "The dispositions of the mind which make a man different from others by the originality of his thoughts and conceptions and by superior intelligence stem from the same organic conditions that may give rise to insanity." As one may imagine, the book attracted great attention from both enthusiastic and sceptical readers.

Moreau worked to the very end of his life. Semelaigne has given a touching description of the aging master's arrival in the hospital of Bicêtre where he signed in and warmed his frozen hands over the fireplace before starting the day's work. He died June 26th, 1884, at the age of 80, after a short illness.

Moreau was undoubtedly the first psychiatrist with an interest in psychopharmacology. It seems that during his lifetime he and his work were never recognized as they should have been. Thus he did not even become a member of the Academy of Medicine. Among those who did not understand his qualities was, regrettably, François Magendie (Collet, 1962). On the other hand, Claude Bernard is said to have

FIG. 5. Moreau de Tours at old age. Portrait by one of his sons.

called hashish a psychopharmacological counterpart of curare. Until recently, people generally have been primarily interested in the literary facts of Théophile Gautier and Charles Baudelaire and in "Le Club des Hachichins" with its strange meetings in the old mansion on the Isle St. Louis in Paris. It is perhaps typical that a very recent collection of papers on the subject of hashish mentions Moreau only in passing (Solomon, 1966). Belatedly, however, the scientific world has begun to recognize his pioneering work, and recently a

"Société Moreau (de Tours)" for the study of biochemistry and psychopharmacology was founded in France.*

REFERENCES

Aubert-Roche, L. (1840), "De la Peste ou Typhus d'Orient, documents et observations recueillis pendant les années 1834 à 1838, suivis d'un Essai sur le hachisch."
Billod, E. (1844), "Observation de Mélancolie, suicide avec hallucination. Guérison de l'hallucination par le Datura Stramonium, et de la mélancolie devenue intermittente par le sulfate de quinine." *Ann. Méd.-Psychol., 3*:308–311.
Baruk, H. (1962), "La vie et l'oeuvre de Moreau de Tours," Annales Moreau de Tours. Presses Universitaires de France, Paris.
Caldwell, A. E. (1970), *Origins of Psychopharmacology,* Charles C Thomas, Springfield, Ill., pp. 12–14, 185–187.
Collet, Cl.-G. (1953), "Un précurseur de la narco-analyse." *Soc. Franc. d'Hist. de la Méd.,* pp. 33–35.
Collet, Cl.-G. (1962), "Candidature de Joseph Moreau (de Tours) au Prix Montyon de l'Acad. des Sciences en 1846," Annales Moreau de Tours, Presses Universitaires de France, Paris.
Dagonet, M., and Ritti, M. (1884), "Nécrologie," *Ann. Méd.-Psychol.,* 6:e Série, *12.*
Desnos, M. (1884), "Nécrologie," *Bull. de la Soc. Méd. des Hop. de Paris, 3,* Série 1.
Gautier, T. (1843), "La Presse," July 10, 1843.
Gautier, T. (1846), "Le Club des Hachichins," *Revue des Deux Mondes,* Année 16:e, Nouvelle série, tome XIII, pp. 520–535.
Holmstedt, B. (1967), Historical Survey. Ethnopharmacologic Search for Psychoactive Drugs. Proceedings of a Symp., San Francisco, Calif., Jan. 28–30, 1967, pp. 3–32.
Kalant, J. (1971), Moreau, Hashish and Hallucinations. *International Journal of Addictions, 6*:553–560.
Kopp, R., and Pichois, C. (1967), "Baudelaire et le haschisch" Expér. et Documentation, *Revue des Sci. Humaines,* Fasc. 125.
Lasègue, E. C. (1846), "Du haschisch et de l'aliénation mentale, Etudes psychologiques," par J. Moreau (de Tours). *Ann. Méd.-Psychol. VII.* P. 459, Bibliographie.

* The information reported in this Introduction is partially based on research supported by grants from the Gustaf and Thyra Svensson Foundation, Karolinska Institutet, Swedish Medical Research Council grant 70E–3743, National Institute of Mental Health grant MH 12007. The author wishes to express his gratitude to his secretary Mrs. Märta Flodén for both library research and technical assistance during many years.

Pichois, C. (1964), Editorial in *Les Paradis Artificiels*, Ch. Baudelaire, Le Libre de Poche Gallimard.

Riese, M. W. (1968), "La structure logique de la Psychologie morbide de Moreau de Tours." *Bull. Acad. Nat. Méd.*, Paris *152*:145–9.

Ritti, M. (1887), "Éloge de J. Moreau (de Tours)," *Ann. Méd. Psych.*, Paris, 7:ème Série, Tome Sixième, 45th year, Paris, G. Masson.

de Sacy, S. (1809), "Des préparations enivrantes faites avec le chanvre, mémoire lu à l'Institut," *C.-R. ou Bulletin des sociétés méd. pub. au nom de la Soc. méd. d'Emulation de Paris*, IV:201–206.

Semelaigne, R. (1930), "Les Pionniers de la Psychiatrie Française avant et après Pinel." Baillière et Fils, Paris.

Solomon, S. H., Ed. (1966), *The Marihuana Papers*, Bobbs-Merrill Co., New York.

Weber, M. (1971), "J.-J. Moreau de Tours (1804–1884) und die experimentelle und therapeutische Verwendung von Haschisch in der Psychiatrie," Inaug. Diss., Juris Druck-Verlag, Zürich.

Witschel, G. (1968), "Rausch und Rauschgift bei Baudelaire, Huxley, Benn und Burroughs," Bouvier u. Co., Bonn.

Chapter 1

HISTORY

As is sufficiently indicated by the title of this work, my efforts in the public's behalf are devoted to the study of *hashish* or, at least, of the influence exercised by this substance on mental faculties.

Knowledge about hashish in the medical world is limited, at most, to recognition of the word for it. Mr. Aubert-Roche, in his book *De la Peste, ou Typhus d'Orient* (1840) (*Concerning the Plague, or Oriental Typhus*), had already called attention to hashish. In 1841 in my treatise on the treatment of hallucinations with *Datura stramonium* (Jimson weed), I applied myself to the task of revealing the psychological effects of this substance. I had become acquainted with the effects of hashish through my own experience, and not merely from the reports of others. Indeed, there is essentially only one valid approach to the study; observation, in such cases, when not focused on the observer himself, touches only on appearances and can lead to grossly fallacious conclusions.

At the outset I must make this point, the verity of which is unquestionable: Personal experience is the criterion of truth here. I challenge the right of anyone to discuss the effects of hashish if he is not speaking for himself and if he has not been in a position to evaluate them in light of sufficient repeated use.

Hopefully no one will be astonished to hear me speak in this manner. Since my travels in the Orient, I have steadfastly pursued a serious study of the effects of hashish. As much as I have been able and by diverse means (a large number of my colleagues, whom I could name here, will bear me witness), I have striven to disseminate such knowl-

EDITORS' NOTE: Footnotes keyed by Arabic numerals are those of the Author. Footnotes keyed with lower case Roman numerals are those of the Editors.

edge within the medical profession. My words have frequently been met with disbelief, but this disbelief would end whenever an individual, overcoming certain fears, and natural ones at that, had the courage to follow my example and try for himself.

Anyone who has visited the Orient knows how widely used hashish is, especially among the Arabs, who have developed no less pressing a need for it than the Turks and Chinese for opium or the Europeans for alcoholic beverages.

Hashish is the name of the plant whose active ingredient provides the basis of a variety of intoxicating preparations used in Egypt, Syria, and generally in almost all the Oriental countries.[i] This plant is quite common in India and in southern Asia, where it grows wild. It is a *species* of hemp similar to our European hemp. Botanists have named it *Cannabis indica*.[ii] Aubert-Roche,[iii] who, like me, has studied hashish in its native location, writes:

> The leaves, the blossoms, and the seeds of this plant seem to belong to hemp that has been grown in poor soil. Hashish comes from the same family and the same genus as hemp. The leaves are opposite each other, petioled, with five deep, sharp divisions. The flowers are hardly visible, and are both male and female as in ordinary hemp. The berry is a little capsule containing a single seed. The male calyx is divided into five layers; the female calyx is in one piece. The plant is taprooted. The difference between hemp and hashish is in the stem, which in hashish reaches a height of two to three feet at the most. Its stem is not single but branches out at the base. The branches alternate, and there are no fibers on the stem as in hemp. The odor emitted by hashish is not as strong as that of hemp and is rather peculiar.[1]

---

[1] In *De la Peste,* p. 217 by Aubert-Roche.

[i] Moreau gives an adequate botanical description of *Cannabis* with its two main variants, the hemp fiber type plant and the drug type plant "hashish." In Arabic "hashish" means herb and it now has come to designate specifically the plant from which the intoxicating substance is prepared. Today the word "hashish" designates the intoxicating substance extracted from the plant rather than the plant itself.

[ii] Moreau uses erroneously the adjective "Indica" (grown in India) to designate the plant *Cannabis sativa* ("sown") as the accepted botanical designation for this Plant. See Appendix.

[iii] See Appendix.

I might add that the fiber of hashish is too coarse to be used by ropemakers.

Hemp is found throughout Eastern Russia as far as its frontier with China in the region of Irkontok. It is believed that the species of hemp now native to Europe was originally imported from China. The plant did not degenerate when spreading to the north of Altai. It is adjusted very well to the summers of Siberia, which were long enough to permit it to grow to full maturity. Since it does not really differ from the plant grown in Europe, one cannot fail to realize that they both come from the same native soil, which can be in China or any southern land.

The most common hashish preparation, the one that is used as the basic ingredient in almost all other preparations, is a greasy extract.[iv] The leaves and the flowers of the plant are boiled in water to which fresh butter has been added. When the mixture has been reduced by evaporation to the consistency of syrup, it is strained through a cloth. This extract contains the active ingredient and has a very nauseating taste. It is used to make various confections, pastes, and certain types of nougats; it is flavored with essence of rose or jasmine to conceal its unpleasant odor.

The substance most commonly used is the one that the Arabs call *dawamesc*. Its color and consistency give it an unsightly appearance, somewhat repulsive to Europeans, who are spoiled by their confectioners. However, it has an agreeable taste, particularly when freshly prepared. With time, unfortunately, it becomes a little rancid, but it loses none of its properties. I own some that was prepared a good ten years ago but has retained all its strength. In order to achieve the effects that the Arabs seek so ardently—because of the excesses they indulge in—cinnamon, ginger, cloves, some aphrodisiacs, and perhaps also, as Aubert-Roche seems to believe, powder of cantharides (*Spanish fly*) are added to this substance. I have heard it said by several people who have traveled in India that one never finds pure hashish there, that it is always mixed with the substances just mentioned, or even with opium, extract of *Datura,* and other narcotics. The addition of these various substances to hashish assuredly modifies its effects to quite an extent.

Hashish leaves can be smoked with tobacco; when they are freshly

---

[iv] Delta-9 tetrahydrocannabinol (THC), the psychoactive substance of cannabis, is most effective when ingested in an oily preparation (Munroe Wall, 1971).

picked, they have a rapid and powerful action. They seem to lose all or nearly all of their properties upon drying. They even serve in the preparation of a kind of beer whose effects are so violent as to be unsafe. Aubert-Roche has seen it provoke an outburst of rage.

I have said that dawamesc is the most common preparation, the one whose effects are the most certain. It is also the easiest to obtain and the one that is least altered during its shipment from the Orient. It is dawamesc that I have used most frequently. It does not have the same effect on everyone. The same dosage can produce extremely different results, at least in intensity, according to individual reports. I cannot say precisely what temperaments or what constitutions are most strongly affected by it. In general, individuals with a "bilious-sanguine" temperament have seemed to me to be the most vulnerable. Nothing can persuade me that hashish has a more pronounced effect on women than on men. I have met several people on whom hashish seemed to have no effect. They resisted dosages that would have deeply affected others. I have become convinced that with some willpower one can stop or at least considerably diminish these effects, much as one controls a burst of anger. We shall see later how these reactions can be affected by external circumstances, by impressions that come from one's surroundings, and by one's state of mind.

Hashish should be taken on an empty stomach or at least several hours after having eaten. If not, its effects are very uncertain or nonexistent. Coffee seems to speed the process, because it shortens the duration and momentarily intensifies the effects.

In general, a dosage at least the size of a walnut, about 30 g, of dawamesc, is necessary to attain some results.[vi] With half or even a quarter of that amount, one feels more or less elated and may be inclined to laughter. It is only with a much larger dose that the results known in the Middle East by the Italian term *fantasia* can be obtained.

(handwritten marginal note: You would be so WASTED if YOU ATE THAT MUCH HASH!)

---

[v] This observation of Moreau explains the uncertain and usual low potency of many unextracted preparations of *Cannabis sativa* such as those presently used in the United States.

[vi] Because such a large dose was necessary, Moreau's extract could not contain more than 0.5% to 1% of delta-9 THC. In 30 g, this would amount to 150 to 300 mg of the drug which is a very large dose, unless one has become tolerant to *Cannabis*. It is recommended that volunteers participating in experiments and who are not habitual users should not be given more than 30 mg THC in sesame oil (Munroe Wall, 1971).

There is no doubt that the effects of hashish have been known since the most remote antiquity. Virey, in a judicious and erudite memoir published in the *Bulletin of Pharmacy* (1803), established that *Cannabis indica* was in reality Homer's *nepenthes*. Diodore of Sicily [2] [vii] tells us that the Egyptians offer various proofs of Homer's stay among them, but in particular they cite the beverage that he had Helen give to Telemachus in Menelaus' home to make him forget his troubles. This *nepenthes,* that the poet claims Helen received from Thoon's wife Polymneste, in Thebes in Egypt, is none other than the famous remedy used among the women of Diospolis to give them their unique ability to dissipate anger and sorrow.

In the Middle Ages, the usage that certain Lebanese princes made of the properties of hashish was astounding. The explorer Marco Polo, according to Sylvestre de Sacy, tells us that the Old Man in the Mountain reared several young people chosen from among the strongest inhabitants in his dominion to carry out his barbaric orders. The purpose of their education was to convince them that, by blindly following their leader's orders, they would secure every sensuous delight in their life after death.

To achieve this end, this prince built delightful gardens next to his palace. There, in pavilions decorated with the most lavish luxury imaginable to the Asian, lived beautiful young women reserved for the pleasures of those to whom these enchanted sites were destined. From time to time, the Ismaelian Princes [3] sent to these places the young men who were to be the blind executioners of their desires. They made them drink a beverage that sent them into a deep sleep and deprived them of the use of their faculties for some time. They were then brought into these pavilions, equal in beauty to the gardens of Armide. When they awoke, everything they saw and heard threw them into such rapture that there was no room for reason in their souls. "This marvelous beverage," says Jourdain, "was none other than hashish, whose virtues the leader knew and whose use increased during the following centuries."

---

[2] Book I, section 2.

[3] According to Jourdan, the Ismaelians were also called Bachemiens, Nazzareans, Molaheds, and Hachishins.

[vii] This claim has not been substantiated and the true nature of nepenthes remains a mystery.

Sylvestre de Sacy has shown, by referring to different Arabic texts, that the word *assassin* is a corruption of the word *Hachishin,* and was given to Ismaelians because they made use of an intoxicating liquor called hashish. Says Michaud:

Intoxication from hashish throws one into an ecstasy similar to that experienced by Orientals through the use of opium. According to the testimony of many travelers, those who fall into that state of delirium imagine themselves enjoying the usual objects of their desires, and taste a happiness that costs little to acquire but whose frequent recurrence changes the biological structure and leads to *marasmus* and death. . . . Those who fall into this habit today are still called Hashishins or Hachaschins, and these two expressions show why the Ismaelians were sometimes called assissine and sometimes assassini by Latin historians of the crusades.[viii]

We know of the fanatic devotion that Ismaelian princes were able to inspire in their subjects by means of the illusions with which they surrounded them. This devotion stopped at no obstacle or sacrifice. As a sign of their subservience to the master, Hashishins threw themselves from the heights of towers, jumped into flames, sank daggers into their hearts, or, ignoring all danger or obstacles, struck at the enemy leaders, who were lying on their sofas, surrounded by their guards in the middle of their palaces.

Sauvages[4] describes as follows the effects produced by a substance used in India and made with Indian hemp:

They say many fabulous things about the virtues of this philtre. They claim, for example, that its effect is to blind a husband when an adulterer is about to enter his bed to seduce his wife. Kempfer has seen several of these things, including the following: In Malabar many beautiful virgins, finely dressed, are led from the temple of the Brahmans and brought among the people to appease the God that watches

---

[4] Nosologie. Paraphrosynie magique. Delirium magicum [see Appendix].

[viii] This etymology linking the word "assassin" to "hashish" is probably incorrect.

over abundant crops and good weather. While the priest reads the set of prayers contained in the sacred books, these girls begin to dance, to leap and shriek, to exhaust their bodies, to whirl their limbs and roll their eyes, to foam at the mouth, and to commit horrendous acts. Then they take the tired Brahmans back to the temple; they put them in bed and, having given them another potion to dull the strength of the first, they bring them before the people an hour later, perfectly sane so that the good people may know that they have been delivered from the genii and that the idol (*Wishnu*) has been appeased.

Kempfer himself shared a bowl of the substance, which had been given to him by some Bengalese at a meal with some friends, who likewise accepted it. When they had swallowed it, they were strangely merry; they started to laugh and hug one another. When night came, they got on their horses and it seemed to them that they were flying through the air on the wings of Pegasus and that they were encircled by the colors of several rainbows. When they arrived home, they ate with voracious appetites, and the next day they found themselves well in body and spirit.

In 1841, when I published my memoir on hallucinations, I had only begun to study the effects of hashish. Since then, I have performed many experiments involving myself and others (among them several physicians whom I persuaded to use hashish—which is not always easy). In the course of this work I will disclose my main conclusions. I can at this point give an account of two *fantasia*, the most complete I have been able to observe in others. First I will transcribe, *word for word*, the notes that were delivered to me by the subject. One will note carelessness of style that I did not want to correct. The notes were written shortly after the *fit*, whose effects were still being felt.

On Thursday, December 5, I had taken hashish, and I knew the effects, not from experience but because a person who had visited the Orient had told me about them, and I quietly awaited the happy delirium that was supposed to seize me. I sat at the table, and I cannot add, as some people do, "after having relished this delicious paste," because to me it tasted horrible. I swallowed it with great effort. As I was eating oysters, I was seized with a fit of laughter, which ceased as soon as I directed my attention to two other people who, like me, had tasted the paste, and who were already seeing a lion's head on their plate. I was calm enough until the end of the dinner; then I took a spoon and stood *en garde* against a compotier of candied fruit with which I was preparing to duel.

Bursting into laughter, I left the dining room. Soon I felt a need to hear and make music; I sat down at the piano, and I began to play an air from *Black Domino*. I interrupted myself after several measures because a truly diabolic spectacle greeted my eyes: I thought I saw the image of my brother standing atop the piano. He stirred and presented a forked tail, all black and ending with three lanterns, one red, one green, and one white. This apparition presented itself to me several times during the course of the evening. I was sitting under a canopy. "Why," I suddenly cried, "do you nail down my limbs? I feel as if I am turning into lead. Oh, I am so heavy!" They took my hands to raise me, and I fell heavily to the ground. I kneeled in the manner of the Moslems, saying, "My father, I accuse myself, etc.," as though I were starting confession. They picked me up and I underwent a sudden change. I picked up a little stove with which to dance the polka; I imitated several actors by voice and gesture, Ravel and Grassot, among others, whom I had seen a few days before in L'Etourneau.[ix] From the theater my thoughts carried me to the Opera Ball. The crowd, the noise, and the lights excited me in the extreme. After a thousand incoherent speeches, gesticulating, shouting like all the masks that I believed I saw, I made my way to an adjoining room that was not lighted.

Then a frightening thing happened to me: I choked, I suffocated, I fell into an immense, bottomless shaft, the well of Bicêtre.[x] Like a drowning man who seeks his salvation in a feeble reed that eludes him, so I wanted to clutch the stones that encircled the well. But they fell with me into that bottomless abyss. This sensation was painful, but it did not last long, because I cried, "I am falling down a shaft," and my friends brought me back to the room I had just left. My first

---

[ix] A popular theater in Paris in the 1840s.

[x] Bicêtre was a "Hospital for the Insane" in the suburbs of Paris where Moreau was an attending psychiatrist. There was a deep well on the grounds of the hospital to supply drinking water.

words were, "How stupid I am." I took that for a shaft, and I am at
the Opera Ball. I stumbled on a stool. I thought it was an actor who,
lying on the ground, writhed in an indecent manner, and I asked a
constable to arrest him. I asked for a drink; they sent for a lemon to
make lemonade, and I asked the maid not to get one as yellow as her
face, which seemed to me to be orange.

I suddenly ran my hands through my hair. I felt millions of insects
eating my head. I sent for an obstetrician, who was then with Madman B., to have him deliver the female of one of the insects who was
having birth pains and had chosen for her "bed of pain" the third
hair from the left on my forehead. After a painful labor, the animal
brought into the world seven little creatures. I spoke about people
whom I had not seen in several years. I recalled a dinner I attended
five years ago in Champagne. I saw the guests. General H. served a
fish surrounded with flowers. He had at his left M. K. They were before
my eyes and, incredible thing, I felt that I was at home, that everything I was seeing had happened in a distant time. However, the people
seemed to me to be there. What was I to believe?

But there was an intoxicating happiness, an ecstasy that only the
heart of a parent can understand when I saw my child, my beloved son
in a blue and silver sky. He had white wings trimmed with pink. He
smiled at me and showed me two pretty white teeth, which I had been
expecting anxiously. He was surrounded by many children who had
wings like his and sailed about in this beautiful sky. But my son was
the most beautiful. Surely there was never a nicer intoxication. He
smiled at me and held out his little arms as if to call me to him. However, this sweet vision faded like the others, and I fell from the heavenly heights to which hashish had led me into the country of lanterns.
This was a country where men, houses, trees and streets were lanterns,
exactly like the colored globes that had lit the Champs-Elysees the
previous July 29th. It also reminded me of the ballet of Chao-Kang,
which I had seen at the nautical theater when I was a child. These
lanterns walked, danced, and shook continuously, and in the center
there appeared, more brilliant than the others, the three lanterns that
ended my brother's imaginary tail. I kept seeing a light that danced
endlessly before my eyes. (It was the flame of the coals that burned in
the fireplace.) They smothered the fire with ashes. "Oh," I said, "you
want to extinguish my lantern, but it will come back." Indeed the fire

flickered once more, and I saw the flame which turned from white to green.

My eyes were constantly closed by a sort of nervous contraction. They burnt a great deal, and I tried to find the cause. I was not long in discovering that my servant had waxed my eyes and that he was polishing them with a brush. That was more than sufficient to explain the discomfort I was feeling.

I drank a glass of lemonade, then suddenly—I cannot say by what fantasy—my gracious fairy carried me along the Seine River to the Ouarnier swimming pool. I wanted to swim and I felt for a moment the painful feeling of sinking under the water. The more I screamed, the more water I swallowed, until a friend came to my rescue and brought me back to the surface. Through the awning I caught a glimpse of my brother crossing the *Pont des Arts*.

Twenty times I was on the verge of indiscretion, but I stopped myself, saying, "I was going to say something, but I must remain quiet." I cannot describe the thousand fantastic ideas that passed through my brain during the three hours that I was under the influence of the hashish. They seemed too bizarre to be credible. The people present questioned me from time to time and asked me if I wasn't making fun of them, since I possessed my reason in the midst of all that madness. My cries, my songs, woke my child who was sleeping in my mother's lap. His little voice, his cries, brought me back to myself, and I came near him. I hugged him as if I were in my natural state. Fearing a crisis, my friends led me away from him. I then declared that he did not belong to me, that he was the child of a woman I knew who was childless and who had always envied me. Then I went visiting; I chatted, I asked questions and gave answers; I went to the café and ordered an ice. I found that the waiters looked stupid. After a long walk during which I met a man, whose nose was enormously elongated, although it was already big enough, I arrived home and said, "Oh, look at that big rat running in B.'s head." At that moment the rat inflated until it became as enormous as the rat in the fairy tale of *The Seven Chateaus of the Devil*.[xi] I saw it! I would have sworn that the rat was walking on top of the head where I had strangely placed him, and I looked at the hat of a lady present. I knew that she

---

[xi] C. Perrault.

was really present, whereas B. was only there in my imagination, but I can swear that I saw him.

One of our most distinguished writers, Theophile Gautier,[xii] had heard about the effects of hashish. He expressed a deep desire to judge it for himself, admitting at the same time that he was little disposed to believe in it. I promptly accommodated him, convinced that a few grams of dawamesc would put a swift end to his doubts. Indeed, the action of hashish was lively and sharp, all the better since the subject was fearless.

Theophile Gautier reported in a journal (*The Press*) the salient and unbiased episodes of the *fantasia* in which he participated. The effects of hashish could not have been better described than by the poetic imagination of Gautier. Need I add that the splendor of his style, or possibly some stylistic exaggeration, need not in the least make me doubt the veracity of the writer, who in the final analysis is describing sensations familiar to hashish users. Says Gautier:

> For many years, Orientals whose religion forbids the use of wine, have sought to satisfy by the use of various preparations their need for mental excitement common to all people, and that people of Western countries gratify by means of spirits and liquors. The aspiration toward an ideal is so strong in man that he tries to release the bonds that keep his soul within his body. Since ecstasy is not within the reach of all, he drinks his merriment, he smokes his oblivion, and eats his madness in the form of wine, tobacco, and hashish. . . . What a strange problem. A little red liquor, a puff of smoke, a spoonful of a greenish paste, and the soul, that intangible essence, is changed in an instant. Serious men do a thousand absurd things; words pour freely from the mouths of the taciturn; Heraclitus laughs heartily, and Democritus weeps.
>
> After a few minutes a general sluggishness overcame me. It seemed that my body was dissolving and becoming transparent. I could clearly see in my chest the hashish I had

---

xii French author and poet (1811–1872) of the Romantic era and member of the "Club des Hachischins."

eaten, in the form of an emerald glowing with a million sparkles.[5] My eyelashes grew to infinity and like golden threads wound around little ivory spindles that spun by themselves with dazzling speed. About me were rivers, nay torrents of gems of all colors, with endlessly changing floral patterns that I can only compare with kaleidoscopic patterns. I still saw my comrades in certain situations, but distorted, half men, half plants, with the pensive air of ibises standing on one leg and flapping their wings. They were so strange that I was convulsed with laughter in my corner. To join the fun, I began tossing my cushions in the air, catching them and throwing them with the dexterity of an Indian juggler. One of the guests addressed me in Italian, which hashish, in its omnipotence, changed into Spanish. The questions and answers were almost reasonable, and touched upon such unimportant subjects as literature of the theater.

After a few minutes I regained my composure, without a headache, without any of the symptoms that accompany intoxication from wine, and quite amazed at what had just happened. Scarcely a half-hour later, I fell again under the influence of hashish. This time the vision was more complicated and more extraordinary. In a strangely lit atmosphere, billions of butterflies swarmed with wings fluttering like fans. Huge flowers with crystal calyces, enormous hollyhocks, streams of gold and silver flowed around me with a crackling like the explosion of fireworks. My hearing was fantastically sharpened. I heard the sound of colors: green, red, blue, and yellow sounds came to me in distinct waves. An overturned glass, a creaking chair, a whispered word, echoed in me like thunder. My own voice seemed so loud that I dared not speak for fear of knocking down the walls or exploding like a bomb. More than five-hundred clocks chimed the hour in their glass, copper, or silver voices. Every object touched made a sound like a harmonica or an Aeolian harp. I swam in an ocean of sound, where themes from *Lucia* and *The Barber*

---

[5] A young physician thought he saw "nervous fluid" circulating in the network of his solar plexus.

of Seville ^{xiii} floated like islets of light. I had never been so overwhelmed with bliss; I dissolved into nothingness; I was freed from my ego, that odious and everpresent witness; for the first time I conceived the existence of elemental spirits—angels and souls separate from bodies. I was like a sponge in the middle of the ocean. At every moment streams of happiness penetrated me, entering and leaving through my pores, since I had become porous. To the last capillary vessel, all my being took on the color of the fantastic environment into which I was plunged. Sounds, perfumes, lights came to me through pipes as thin as hairs, in which I heard magnetic currents humming. By my calculations this state lasted approximately three-hundred years, for the sensations followed one another in such numbers and so rapidly that an accurate appraisal of time was impossible. . . . When the spell was over, I realized it had lasted a quarter hour.

What is different about hashish intoxication is that it is not continuous; it takes you and it leaves you; you rise to heaven and you fall back to earth without transition. As with insanity, there are lucid moments. A third spell, the last and most bizarre, ended my Oriental soirée. In this one I had double vision. Two images of each object registered on my retina in complete symmetry. Soon the magic paste was completely digested and acted with more force on my brain; I became completely mad for an hour. Every kind of gigantic dream-creature passed through my fantasies: goatsuckers, fiddle-faddle beasts, budled goslings, unicorns, griffons, incubi, an entire menagerie of monstrous nightmares fluttered, hopped, skipped, and squeaked through the room. My visions became so strange that I was seized with a desire to sketch them, and in less than five minutes I drew the portrait of the doctor. . . , who, it seemed to me, was seated at the piano, dressed as a Turk, a sun on the back of his waistcoat. Notes were shown escaping from the piano, entwined or capriciously twisted.[6] Another sketch, with the legend *An*

---

[6] It is indeed remarkable how, with hashish, the mind transforms all sensations, gives them palpable tangible shapes, materializes them, so to speak.

xiii Operas by Donizetti and Rossini.

Animal of the Future, showed a live locomotive with the neck of a swan ending in a serpent's mouth that spouted puffs of smoke. It had huge feet made of wheels and pulleys. Each pair of feet was fitted with a pair of wings, and on the tail of the animal one could see Mercury, the ancient god, vanquished in spite of his winged spurs. Thanks to the hashish I was able to sketch an authentic hobgoblin. Up to now I had only heard them moaning and moving at night in my cupboard.

But enough madness. To recall a complete hashish hallucination would require a large volume, and a mere author cannot take the liberty of rewriting the *Book of Revelations.*

Chapter 2

PHYSIOLOGY

INTRODUCTION

At first, curiosity led me to experiment upon myself with hashish. Later, I readily admit, it was difficult to repress the nagging memory of some of the sensations it revealed to me. But from the very outset I was motivated by another reason.

I saw in hashish, or rather in its effect upon the mental faculties, a significant means of exploring the genesis of mental illness. I was convinced that it could solve the enigma of mental illness and lead to the hidden source of the mysterious disorder that we call *"madness."*

I may be accused of being bold and presumptuous for expressing myself with so much assurance on a subject that so-called scientists avoid by relegating to the ill-defined area of metaphysics. This boldness, to which I admit, is justified by the conscientious research that characterizes this project. It will become apparent that it is based not upon arguments or inductions that can be questioned but upon simple, concrete facts derived from self-observation. As one can judge by what follows, I had only to transfer the main characteristics of delirium [1] to those of hashish intoxication and to apply to my study the insights gathered from self-observation.

In this manner and guided solely by the kind of observation that enhances consciousness and self-awareness, I believe I was able to go

---

[1] I use interchangeably the terms delirium, madness, and mental illness to designate mental disorders. I am not unaware of the many differences that distinguish —from the point of view of symptomatology and treatment—delirium, as it is precisely defined, and madness; but from a psychic point of view we have to admit that these differences just do not exist. The causes, the symptoms, or the exterior signs may vary; the intrinsic psychic phenomenon is the same, essentially, in whatever form, acute or chronic, partial or general, the mental illness presents itself.

back to the origin of the phenomenon of delirium. One fact seemed to be basic, seminal, and preliminary to all the others: I have called it the *primary fact*. Secondly, I had to postulate, for delirium in general, a psychological nature not only analogous but *absolutely identical* to a dream state.

This identity, which eludes casual observation since it cannot be seen in others, is definitely confirmed, and even *perceived,* by introspection.

In the studies I am going to report herein, I hope to avoid the aridity and the sterility that one might expect in a psychological study.

Many serious gaps still exist in our knowledge of the causes of mental illness. In their investigations many psychiatrists have examined causes of madness, have sought an organic explanation for the grain of sand that jams the mental apparatus, and have looked ultimately to the brain cells to explain mental disorders. Most of them have carefully studied their patients over a great length of time; but I know of none who, when speaking of madness, has given us the benefit of his own experience, who has described it from the point of view of his own perceptions and sensations.

It still remains for someone to present a report of this kind. Moreover, we all know the uncertainty that prevails in the treatment of mental illness. By revealing the *primary fact,* the primary functional lesion from which flow all the varieties of madness, like so many streams from one source, I hope to point out some useful lessons concerning the best means of treating this illness.

Finally I shall end this work with an account of several attempts at using hashish in therapy.

Physiological Generalities

I

Among our many mental faculties there is only one with which we can study the impact of these very faculties on our own physiological condition: it is reflection, the power of the mind to observe itself. It is a mirror of sorts in which we can contemplate ourselves and detect our most intimate movements.

This power fails us when our faculties are troubled, when there is chaos in their midst, in a word, when there is madness. We know that there may be exceptions to this rule, but patients who can reflect on what is going on within themselves are rare and are found only in certain kinds of mental illness.

In addition, can we be certain we are in a condition to understand these sick people when they tell us of their observations? Do they not speak a language that is foreign to us? How can they communicate the feelings that disturb them? What have we learned when they tell us that an irresistible urge drives them, that some extravagant idea dominates them without their knowledge, and that whatever they do to get rid of it, their thoughts stumble over one another, that they see things and hear sounds and voices that do not exist except, as we say, in their imagination? We see only the surface of things; we cannot proceed further to explore the causes, the succession of mental aberrations they describe to us. Are not mental processes, feelings, or sensations impossible to know and evaluate except through oneself? To understand an ordinary depression, it is necessary to have experienced one; to comprehend the ravings of a madman, it is necessary to have raved oneself, but without having lost the awareness of one's madness, without having lost the power to evaluate the psychic changes occurring in the mind.

II

In the way in which it affects the mental faculties, hashish gives to whoever submits to its influence the power to study in himself the mental disorders that characterize insanity, or at least the intellectual modifications that are the beginning of all forms of mental illness.

When striking and disrupting the various mental states, hashish allows one of them to exist in the midst of the most violent disturbance, namely, consciousness of oneself, that intimate feeling of one's individuality. However incoherent one's ideas, however subject one is to the strangest, most bizarre associations, however deeply affected one's feelings and instincts are, however misled one may be by delusions or hallucinations in the midst of a fantastic world of wild dreams . . . one still remains one's own master. Placed outside its reach, the *ego* dominates and judges the disorders that the *agent provocateur,* hashish, engenders in the lower regions of the mind.

III

There is not a single, elementary manifestation of mental illness that cannot be found in the mental changes caused by hashish, from simple manic excitement to frenzied delirium, from the feeblest impulse, the simplest fixation, to the merest injury to the senses, to the most irresistible drive, the wildest delirium, the most varied disorders of feelings.

When systematically reviewing these diverse phenomena, I will investigate their origins and study the sequence of their development. Then, comparing them with the phenomena of madness observed in the mentally ill, I will examine the extent to which external observation (and above all the remarks of the patients) agree with my own observations.

Through a combination of these two modes of exploration, I have reached the following conclusions.

(1) All forms, all occurrences of delirium or of actual madness, all fixations, hallucinations, irresistible impulses, and so forth, owe their origin to a primary mental change, identical in all cases, that is evidently the essential condition of their existence. It is *manic excitement*.

We use this expression only to conform to conventional language, for otherwise we fail to convey our ideas faithfully. How can we accurately describe that simple yet complex state of uncertainty, oscillation, and flight of ideas often accompanied by a profound incoherence? It is a disintegration, a veritable dissolution of that mental structure known as the mental faculties. Indeed one feels in the manic state that something is happening in the mind similar to what happens when a substance undergoes the solvent action of another substance: the separation, the isolation of ideas and molecules that formed a harmonious and complete whole when they were united.

Nothing is comparable to the almost infinite variations of delirium, unless it be the activity of thought itself. This explains the caution shown by most authors in attributing delirium to an organic lesion, no matter what ideas they may have concerning the nature of this lesion. By reducing all these variations to a basic, elementary form, to mental "excitement," which adapts itself so easily to the exaggerated

molecular movement that occurs in nervous excitement, do we need
to proceed with the caution we just mentioned?

(2) Gradually, under the influence of hashish, the psychic factor I
have just indicated grows; a profound change takes place in the thinking process. Outside of one's awareness and in spite of all efforts to
remain aware, there occurs a state of dream, but of *sleepless dream,*
where sleep and the waking state are mingled and confused. The
clearest, most alert consciousness cannot distinguish between these
two states, nor between the mental operations that characterize either
one.

From this fact, whose importance escapes no one and whose proof
is to be found on every page of this book, we have deducted the true
nature of madness, whose phenomena are included and explained
without exception.

There are various ideas concerning the nature of dreams and their
physiological causes. If we examine the role of the mind in the dream
state, we see that it operates fully. All its faculties are as active as in the
waking state, although under different conditions. In dreams we feel
the same sensations as during the waking state. We perceive; we
judge; we have convictions; we feel desires; we are stirred by our passions. It is wrong to impute what occurs in dreams to imagination,
because it is concerned with only its own purposes. It is not just imagination that reasons, perceives, feels, senses, acts, talks, discusses, is impassioned, and so forth. Its activity seems considerably more restrained
than in the waking state, for one imagines little in dreams, and the
world of sensations, of memories in the midst of which the spirit
moves and which is absolutely foreign to imagination, actually occupies
almost all of its activity.[2]

The experiences that constitute the dream state are purely imaginary, without doubt, but only in a relative sense. For those who dream,
there is nothing but reality. What we see, what we hear, what we
smell in a dream, we are really seeing, hearing, smelling, just as much
as if we were awake. There is a difference only in the source of the im-

---

[2] To imagine necessarily implies a labor of the mind, an effort of the will. How
then can we attribute to the imagination the production of those images that in
dreams appear involuntarily, take shape, frolic before our eyes, take shape and
vanish without involving the will. Try in a waking state to imagine one millionth
of the fantastic creations of dreams, and see if you succeed!

pressions that our mind perceives and elaborates. We do not believe ourselves warranted, for that matter, to agree with one of the most esteemed psychologists of our time [3] that "life may be only an illusion." Function, no matter what its nature, presupposes organs. Outside of the organ I can conceive of nothing that could be called life. If sensations occur during sleep, they must first have occurred during the waking state, and one could hardly assume that a brain that had been closed to all external impressions would create sensations out of nothing, in other words could *dream*. We cannot go that far, but I gladly repeat Dr. Viney's phrase because it depicts so perfectly the mode of action of mental faculties in the state of dream.

Most frequently in dreams a strange confusion, which spares neither things nor people, which disregards time and place, presides over the association of ideas and thus gives rise to the most bizarre productions, to the most monstrous combinations. "A dream," says Viney, with his usual elegance of style, "can be defined as a faulty drama without unity of time or place, comparable to those plays described by Horace as *velut aegri somnia.*" [i]

But it is not always thus. Sometimes the associations of ideas are perfectly regular; a strict logic marks our reasoning, however false, however impossible the point of departure may be. Some object has stirred our passions, excited our anger, roused our pity, filled us with fear, and we obey the impulse that these passions communicate to us and we seek the means of satisfying them.

Moreover, and this fact is of great importance here, in dreams the operations of the mind show at times a regularity that one never encounters in a waking state. Says Nodier: [ii]

It may seem extraordinary but it is certain that sleep is not only the most powerful of all the states of the mind but also the clearest, if not in the fleeting illusions that surround it, at least in the perceptions that derive from it and that it

---

[3] J. J. Viney, *De la physiologie dans ses rapports avec la philosophie* (see Appendix).

[i] "Comparable to mad dreams." Horace is the French name for the Latin poet Quintus Horatius Flaccus.

[ii] Charles Nodier (1783–1844). French poet and author of the Romantic era, who became the protector to many young Romantic authors such as Hugo and Musset.

summons at will in the confused plot of its dreams. The ancients, who had, I believe, little to envy us in experimental philosophy, spiritually represented this mystery by the sign of the transparent door which gives access to morning dreams; and the unanimous wisdom of the people expresses it still more vividly in meaningful phrases found in all languages: *I must sleep on it; the night bears advice.* It seems that the mind never frees itself more easily than in the gentle land of intermittent death where it may rest in freedom, secure from the influence of the conventional personality that society forces upon us. The first perception to catch the morning light through the inexplicable vagueness of a dream is as bright as the first ray of sun through the clouds; and intelligence, briefly suspended between the two states that share our lives, shines brightly, like the flash of lightning that races from the tempests of the heavens to the tempest of the earth. That is when Hesiodus awakens, his lips fragrant from the honey of the Muses; Homer's eyes are unsealed by the nymphs of Meles; and Milton's heart ravished by the last look at a beauty he will never rediscover. Alas, where can one retrieve the passions and the beauties of sleep! Take away from a genius the visions of a world of wonders, and you take away his wings. The map of the imaginable universe is traced only in dreams; the perceptible world is infinitely small.

So it seems that two modes of mental life are known to man. The first results from our relationship with the external world, with that great whole known as the universe; we share it with the creatures that resemble us. The second is only the reflection of the first, and feeds only, in a sense, on materials supplied it by the first, while remaining completely separate.

Sleep is like a barrier raised between these two lives: the physiological point where external life ceases and internal life begins.

So long as this situation exists, mental health prevails, that is, a regularity of the mental functions within given limits. But it happens that under the influence of various factors, physical and mental, these two lives tend to become confused; phenomena characteristic of one or the other blend, unite in the act of consciousness. An imperfect fusion occurs, and the individual, without having completely abandoned reality, belongs, in many ways, according to several mental signals, to false sensations, erroneous beliefs, and so forth, of fantasy.

This individual is the psychotic, especially the monomaniac, who presents such a strange amalgamation of madness and sanity, and who, as has been so often stressed, *dreams while awake,* without otherwise attaching any importance to that phrase, which, in our view, accurately identifies the psychological fact of mental illness.

According to Bichat,[4,iii] dreams are merely partial sleep, "a portion of biological life released from the prison where the remaining portion is trapped." Imagination, memory, and judgment remain active, while sensation, perception, locomotion, and voice are suspended.

It can be conceded that the organic conditions in which sleep places imagination, memory, and judgment can exist to a certain extent when the senses are alert, when speech and locomotion function, when judgment, memory, and imagination operate normally, i.e., as they do outside the circle and limitations of dreams.

This is impossible, we realize, in natural sleep. The dream ends as soon as the mind attends to outer things. But why is it not possible when the mind is under the influence of a cause *other* than sleep, of an analogous but more powerful cause, one more persistent than the law of animal life "that links in its functions periods of activity and inactivity?"

These generalities established, I shall review the principal and in a sense the fundamental phenomena of insanity.

My proposed study takes into account the various classifications that have been attempted up to now by several writers with a measure of success. I am not questioning their usefulness; from the dual point of view of symptomatology and treatment they are indispensable. To grasp, study, and understand a group of phenomena as complex as mental disorders, it is necessary to group them according to their affinities or analogies. Everyone is in agreement on this point. Opinions differ only regarding the nature of the groups and the causes that determine their formation.

Also, there is necessarily more than one opinion on the legitimacy

---

[4] *Recherches sur la vie et la mort* (Studies of Life and Death).
[iii] See Appendix.

of the classifications. I will discuss at least those that are generally accepted. There are such glaring differences among the mentally ill, differences so clear, so striking that it is impossible to confuse them. Manics and monomaniacs are different in many aspects. Both fall under the heading of *dementia*,[iv] while retaining the features that recall their primitive state. However, they might also show new symptoms that are clear signs of a new mental illness so severe, so deep, as to relegate them to a separate class of illness.[5]

While admitting the usefulness of classifications, let us not exaggerate nor forget, by the admission of their authors, that the distinctions are based more on the form than the nature of delirium, or on its external, apparent features than on its essential, intrinsic nature. Let us not forget that, in fact, many patients present a combination of the basic characteristics of the many varieties of mental illness.

Says Esquirol:

The generic characteristics of madness are common to many mental ailments which differ in origin, nature, treatment, termination, and cannot characterize the kinds and varieties

---

[5] The classification devised by Pinel and adopted by Esquirol [v] is in our eyes the least incomplete of all those that have been proposed up to now. It has been modified but without any effective result, and no one has been able to substitute, either in scientific language or in common language, new names for those disorders designated as *mania, monomania*,[vi] and *dementia*. Very recently de Lassiauve, my colleague in the asylum at Bicêtre, has proposed a theory on this subject that deserves mention. According to him, "all madness implies the derangement of the mental faculties. But this derangement is very diverse. It is either idiopathic or symptomatic; it derives from a morbid change in intelligence or is provoked by changes occurring in the other faculties, changes of which it is an indication." In the first case, the seat of the illness is in the intellect; it is actually *mental* illness. In the second, the seat of delirium is outside of the intellect, exclusively in the secondary faculties. From this follow the four categories: (1) perceptive madness, (2) mental madness, (3) emotional madness, and (4) instinctual madness. It is not relevant to my subject to discuss the value of the *Essai de Classification des Maladies Mentales* (A Tentative Classification of Mental Illnesses) . I only want to pay passing tribute to the distinguished talent with which its theories have been developed.

[iv] See Appendix.

[v] Pinel, Esquirol—see Appendix.

[vi] Mania, monomania—see Appendix.

that recur with infinite nuances. Alienation can successively and alternately take all forms; monomania, mania, and dementia alternate and replace one another, in the same individual. This has led some physicians to reject all distinctions in madness and to acknowledge but a single and consistent malady that assumes various forms.

To avoid the danger of prejudice, I have rejected, in my thinking, everything that has been said by other writers about the diverse forms of delirium. I have proceeded analytically and have studied separately the fundamental phenomena that are obvious and acknowledged by all. I have not concerned myself with the extent, the quantity, the type of disorders of the mind, nor with their purely intellectual, emotional, mental, or instinctive origin. I have not wanted to split the indivisible activity of the mental faculties. In all its abnormal manifestations, from the simplest to the most complex, I have never ceased to consider intelligence in its entirety.

Chapter 3

PSYCHOLOGICAL PHENOMENA

I. PHYSICAL CHANGES

I will deal first with the physical changes that ordinarily precede or accompany the mental problems caused by hashish.

(1) With one dose of hashish, weak but still capable of profoundly changing the mind, physical effects are nil, or at least so imperceptible that they will certainly go unrecognized if the user is not alert to the symptoms of their presence. The feeling is comparable to the sensation of well-being generated by a cup of coffee or tea taken on an empty stomach.

(2) By increasing the dosage, this feeling becomes more and more vivid, and invades the entire body, as though it were going to overflow. A light pressure is felt in the temples and the upper part of the skull. Breathing slows down, and the pulse quickens very slightly. A soft, gentle warmth comparable to that felt when taking a bath in winter, spreads throughout the body with the exception of the feet, which ordinarily remain cold. The wrists and the forearms seem to grow numb and to become heavier; they might even shake spontaneously, as if to rid themselves of the weight that presses upon them. Then, mostly in the lower extremities, vague, indefinable sensations begin to spread; they are a sort of muscular shuddering over which there is no control and which are well characterized by their name *"les inquiétudes."* [i]

(3) Finally, if the dose of hashish is considerable, it is not rare to observe nervous phenomena which, according to many reports, resem-

---

[i] In French "inquiétude" means disquiet, restlessness, uneasiness. This word was used to describe muscle twitchings in the legs.

ble choreiform actions. Gusts of warmth suddenly rush to the head in rapid-like jets of steam escaping from a locomotive. As I have heard it reported several times, the brain *seethes* and seems to push against the top of the skull, as if to escape. This sensation, which always causes terror no matter how inured one may be, is analogous to the noise heard when one's head is plunged under water. Dizzy spells are rare; I have never had one; ringing in the ears, on the contrary, is common. Now and then one feels a kind of anguish, a feeling of constriction in the epigastrium, which, after the brain, is the region that seems most affected by hashish. A young physician once said that he believed he could see nervous fluid circulating in the network of his solar plexus. The heartbeats seem to have an unusual intensity and resonance. But if the hand is placed in the precordial region, one can be reassured that the heart is beating no stronger or faster than usual. Spasms in the limbs sometimes become very strong, actually causing convulsions. Activity of the flexor muscles prevails. If one lies down, which one almost always feels like doing, the calves flex involuntarily against the thighs, the forearms against the arms, which hug the sides of the chest; the head tilts and sinks between the shoulders; the strenuous contraction of the pectorals interferes with the expansion of the thorax and stops the breathing. . . . These symptoms are only momentary. They cease abruptly, only to reappear suddenly between intervals of perfect calm, every several seconds at first, then several minutes, half-hours, hour. . . . The muscles of the face, particularly those of the jaw, may be similarly seized with spasms. On one occasion I felt a veritable trismus, or at least something like it. The hands seem to contract by themselves, grasping and tightly squeezing objects.

Such are all, or almost all, the physical disorders caused by hashish, from the weakest to the most intense. One sees that they all relate to the nervous system. As we have already said, they develop much more slowly than the mental disturbance,[1] and the mind can be profoundly changed without affecting the body. It seems that the causal factor

---

[1] Those who are in the habit of using hashish know very well how to avoid the physical disorders. It is easy to graduate the dose, and they can always become initiated to the marvels of *fantasia* without paying for this pleasure at the cost of any disagreeable nervous trouble.

(i.e., the drug) acts directly on the faculties of the mind without the mediation of the organs, as in the case of mental illness.

Is it not true that madness most frequently erupts without warning the patient by any appreciable organic trouble or any physical malfunction? Here is a basic point of similarity between the effects of hashish and mental illness. The cause is evident, but the origin remains undiscovered. Is this not, indeed, what most often happens when that cause, whatever it may be, acts directly, immediately on the mind? We shall see again that when the effects of hashish are revealed in organic troubles, such as those we have just indicated, it transpires that these effects are completely analogous to those reported by mental patients who have been able to study and follow the development of their illness from its inception. Mental patients and users of hashish express themselves similarly when they want to convey what they have experienced. It seems as if they all had been under the same morbid influence.

II. First Phenomenon: Feeling of Happiness

I said in the memoir that I have already cited:

At a certain moment in the intoxication, when an unbelievable effervescence takes possession of all the mental faculties, a psychic phenomenon is evident, the most curious of all perhaps, and one that I despair of conveying appropriately. It is a feeling of physical and mental well-being, of inner contentment, indefinable joy, impossible to understand, to analyze, or to explain. You feel happy; you say it; you proclaim it with exultation; you seek to explain it with all the means that are within your power; you repeat it to the point of satiation. But words fail you to say how and why you are happy. Finding myself in this situation one day, and despairing of being understood by words alone, I uttered cries, or rather veritable howls. Following this happiness, which is so agitated that all your being shakes convulsively, comes a gentle feeling of physical and mental lassitude, a sort of apathy, insouciance, a complete calm, to which your mind abandons itself with delight. It seems that nothing can hurt you in this peace of mind,

that you are inaccessible to sadness. I doubt that the most unfortunate news could draw you out of that imaginary bliss,
which can only be appreciated through experience.

I have just attempted to give an idea of the delights that hashish
produces. I hasten to add that I have presented them here in no more
than raw form, as it were, and at their simplest. It will depend upon
external circumstances to confer upon these feelings of happiness still
greater intensity by directing them toward a determined goal and by
concentrating them on a single point. One imagines what reality can
add to this state of bliss and how much the joys of hashish can be enhanced by external impressions, by direct sensory excitations, or by the
stirring of passions through natural causes. At that time, the rapture
of hashish intoxication, taking shape and form, will assume the dimen-
sions of delirium. This disposition of the mind, linked with another
which I will discuss later, was, I feel, the fertile source from which the
fanatic inhabitants of Lebanon derived that happiness, those ineffable
delights for which they gladly sacrificed their lives.[ii]

It is necessary here to clarify what I have just said. It is really *happiness* that hashish gives, and by that I mean mental joy, not sensual joy
as one might be tempted to believe. This is indeed very curious, and
one can draw strange conclusions—this one among others, that all joy,
all contentment, even though its cause is strictly mental, deeply spiritual, and highly idealistic, could well be in reality a purely physical
sensation, developed physiologically, exactly like those caused by hashish. At least, if one relies on inner feelings, there is no distinction to be
made between these two orders of sensations, in spite of the diversity of
the causes to which they are related—for the hashish user is happy, not
in the manner of the glutton, of the ravenous man who satisfies his
appetite, or even of the hedonist who gratifies his desires, but in the
manner, for example, of the man who hears news that compounds his
joys, of the miser counting his treasures, of the gambler whom luck
favors, or the ambitious man whom success intoxicates.

However, the preceding remarks were not intended to raise a psychological question. I am merely recording observations, and have no

---

[ii] Reference to the young men trained by the Ismaelian princes to assassinate
while under the influence of hashish.

other pretension than that of being the faithful and exact historian of my sensations. Also, I have seen in the phenomena just described a striking description of what occurs so frequently at the beginning of madness. I am speaking of those feelings of happiness, of intimate joy (I cannot use expressions more suitable than these to describe the effects of hashish), which inspire so much hope, so much confidence in the future, and which, alas, are only premonitory symptoms of the most violent delirium. As an example, the loss of a great fortune and countless sorrows threw Madame De . . . into a deep hypochondriac state. This state lasted several years, until the patient was placed in our establishment. Save for a few temporary remissions, her condition remained unchanged, until, a few days ago, when she felt a profound change in her psychic being, a change that gave her a feeling of deep contentment and made her see the future in the most cheerful colors. Her hopes were equal to the depression from which she had just emerged and into which she was plunged for several years. Her face was radiant; a light, rosy tint had replaced her usual palor; the joy in her soul sparkled in her bright, animated eyes. This woman said to me:

I do not know what is happening to me, but I must thank God and you, dear Doctor, because I am deeply convinced that I have reached the end of my illness and of all my pains. Here I am, free at last from those atrocious, unbelievable anxieties that I have so often told you about. No more fears, no more terrors, no more damnations, no more hell. I am finally as I used to be; I can once more be happy; I can take care of my predicament. You can see that I have become reasonable and that I have heeded your good advice.

Scarcely had a few days elapsed when this interesting patient was in the grip of an intense manic excitement.

Here is what another young woman said to me just recently, a woman with a fine, observing mind, recovering from a depression subsequent to childbirth:

Seventeen days after the birth of my child, which, moreover could not have been easier, I felt something extraordinary. It seemed to me that my head was rotating around in a circle

and that, at the same time, my brain was *expanding.* I knew
perfectly well that it was an illusion; however, I could not
help but look in a mirror to reassure myself that my face was
not backwards. I also felt light jerks in my head and in my
neck, something resembling a stiff neck. In the night I awoke
with an indescribable feeling of well-being. I felt happier than
I ever had before. My happiness, my joy, filled me, as it were,
and I felt a need to share it with everyone around me. I waited
impatiently for morning to announce the good news. I felt a
foolish gaiety; I wanted to embrace the whole world, even
my servants.

I shall have occasion to return to the statement of this patient, from
whom I have a curious manuscript in which she detailed all the sensations that she felt in the course of her illness.

Says Esquirol:

A merchant, age forty-five, files for bankruptcy, which in-
conveniences him temporarily without affecting his wealth.
That same day his character changes; he is gayer than usual,
laughs at his misfortune, congratulating himself that he has
learned to understand people better. He makes projects in-
compatible with his fortune and his business. He spends eight
days in a state of joy, of satisfaction, of activity which could
portend a severe illness, something Mr. . . himself suspects.
After this episode, political events that are completely foreign
to his interests but that offend his opinions plunge him into
a psychotic depression from which nothing has brought him
out.

The phenomenon in question is observed principally at the
onset of psychosis, which involves a general impairment of
one's faculties. Seeking to analyze ideas of grandeur, of wealth,
which, as we know, characterize this variety of sickness, we
wrote as follows in another work published in 1840, in the
journal *Esculape* (On Argumentative Madness) : the exercise
of the faculties seems to become easier, the sensitivity more
excitable, the judgment better and quicker, while novel ideas
seem to flow profusely; it is obvious that the subject feels an

inner well-being that causes his mind to expand and to become receptive to ideas and desires that flatter his passions.

The facts that I have just cited suffice, I think, to recall a multitude of others, similar to those observed by our readers in mental patients. However, another observation should be made.

These facts, of great importance from my point of view, have scarcely attracted, or perhaps have not yet attracted, the attention of observers. They are important only because they are frequent, I almost said common, and they have been scarcely noticed in some cases of manic delirium. However, I am convinced (and that conviction is based on the specific acknowledgment of a great number of patients we have interviewed) that the phenomenon in question almost always signals the onset of delirium, partial or general, elated or sad; we accept only those cases where the onset is so abrupt as to exclude all warning. Indeed it is not always easy to detect this delirium. So few patients are in a condition to give a lucid account of what they feel, or to recall the first insidious symptoms, which are more likely to benumb them than to command their attention. Yet some succeed, and they rarely fail to confirm by their statements what I have just described.

In closing this part of the discussion, I add just a word. One of the effects of hashish, the most unbelievable, is precisely the one we have just stressed in detail—the state of fantastic happiness next to which the most alluring reality is just a pale shadow.

This bliss is also generated by numerous and varied factors that cause mental illness. In this area, psychotic and hashish user (or *hashashe,* as the Arabs say) are identical.

III. Second Phenomenon: Excitement, Dissociation of Ideas

When a writer attends the performance of a drama he has written, his concerns and anxieties are focused on a certain portion of the work on which his success depends because it is the cornerstone of the entire edifice. We find ourselves in the same position as we give an account of the psychological phenomenon that is the subject of this section. We know what talent is needed to describe it, but we cannot conceal from ourselves the fact that whatever we do, we will not really convey the great significance attached to it. This phenomenon, in effect, is like the supreme or central point upon which this entire book rests. That is the *basic fact* which I announced at the outset and which is at the heart of all mental disorders.

The slightest occurrence can interfere with the functioning of our mental faculties; Pascal once said that the buzzing of a fly is enough to disturb the deepest cogitations of a genius. In our normal state, when we wish to think of something, to ponder a subject, to contemplate it from various angles, it almost always happens that we are distracted by some extraneous idea. But that idea merely crosses our mind without leaving any traces, and our train of thought is not interrupted.

One of the first measurable effects of hashish is the gradual weakening of the power to direct thoughts at will. We feel slowly overwhelmed by strange ideas unrelated to the subject on which we are trying to focus our attention. These ideas, which we have not willfully summoned in our mind, appear at random and become more and more numerous, lively, and keen. Soon they command more attention and generate bizarre associations and fantastic creations. If by an effort of will we resume the sequence of our ideas, the ones we have rejected still echo in our mind, but as if from a faraway distance muffled like dreams of a restless night.

In the course of this study I will have the occasion to remind the reader of the psychological fact that I have just indicated. I am now content to insist on the expressions I have used to describe them.

These ideas, or rather this series of ideas, are actually dreams, "true" dreams in the strictest sense. One cannot distinguish them from those created by natural sleep. Both come in the same manner and, so to speak, through the same portal: sleep.

In this connection, and in support of this opinion, I recall that Cabanis [iii] made no distinction between artificial sleep and natural sleep, that for him somnolence and sleep were synonymous. He said:

> It is the *ebb of nervous energies back to their source,* or the concentration of the most active existing elements that constitute and characterize these states: whether they derive from the need for sleep in the sensory extremities and in the motor organs, from the simple periodic action of the brain, which

---

[iii] See Appendix.

spontaneously recalls all motor activities either by the application of fresh air, the hearing of a monotonous sound, silence, darkness, tepid baths, refreshing drinks, or by intoxicating drinks whose effect is initially to excite the brain and then to disturb its functions, by recalling the greater part of the sensitive forces destined to the nerve extremities, or by narcotics that immediately paralyze these forces and concomitantly cloud the mental functions by sending a heavy flow of blood to the brain.

Physiology and self observation are in agreement here: natural and artificially induced sleep cause similar organic changes, and the *mental results,* to borrow the expression used by Cabanis, are identical.

To return to the effects specific to hashish, the ideas or series of ideas that occur in the mind during a dream bring together fantasy and reality in a bizarre fashion and draw much more from the past than from the present. You forget those things which at present most excite your interest and stir your passions, which absorb all your attention, to dream only of those which were in the past. Memory is the source upon which these new ideas feed; the brilliance and multiplicity of their imagery greatly excite the imagination, which links them and in its turn gives birth to new productions.

We live in the present by an act of will that directs our attention toward objects that have a current interest for us. Through memory we live in the past; through memory and self-awareness we can, in a sense, start our lives over. Through imagination we live in the future; through imagination we can create for ourselves a new world.

Through this new exteriority, the ego, acting on itself, seems able to transform itself as it changes things, people, time, and places at will.

The action of hashish weakens the will—the mental power that rules ideas and associates and connects them together. Memory and imagination become dominant; present things become foreign to us, and we are concerned entirely with things of the past and the future.

Consciousness appraises these effects in several ways, according to the extent of the mental disturbance. So long as the disorder has not gone beyond certain bounds, one readily recognizes the error in which one is momentarily involved, although not at the very moment that it prevails—which would imply a contradiction, at least as far as errors of the mind or self-deceptions are concerned—but rather immediately after, when, quick as a flash, it crosses the mind. There occurs an uninterrupted succession of true and false ideas, of dreams and realities, which constitutes a composite state of madness and reason and makes a person seem mad and rational at the same time.

As the disorder of the faculties increases, as the storm which perturbs the faculties becomes more violent, consciousness is carried away by the whirlwind and is a toy of one's dreams. *Lucid* moments are increasingly brief. Mental activity seems to withdraw and to restrict itself entirely to the brain. We abandon ourselves to our inner feelings; our eyes and our ears do not cease to function, but they admit only those impressions supplied by memory or imagination. In other words, *we fall asleep while dreaming.*

But then, as if consciousness could never be completely extinguished, here is what happens—I will be better understood if I recall a fact well known to those who dream often without ceasing to sleep—we are sometimes aware that we are dreaming. Better than that, when the dream pleases us, we are afraid to awaken. We force ourselves to prolong the dream, and when we sense that it is going to end, we say to ourselves: "Why is all that only a dream?" This is exactly the same state that is experienced by a person under the influence of hashish in its most potent form.

However, the analogy that we have just drawn between dreams resulting from natural sleep and the mental changes effected by hashish must not allow us to forget that the latter are distinguished by certain characteristics that are theirs exclusively. First, they are far from being disconnected and incoherent like ordinary dreams. The trace of consciousness and of will that, as I have just noted, persists in the most severe mental disorders, seems to restrain the flights of the imagination and prevent the imagination from departing too far from reality. Secondly (and I cannot emphasize this fact too strongly), these mental changes limit themselves most frequently (at least, when the action of hashish is moderate) to errors of sensory perception or of general awareness, or to false beliefs, or to one or more extravagant ideas, without any other alteration of our faculties. Moreover, these convictions, these ideas, do not always relate to imaginary objects. Most often they owe their origin to external impressions, true impressions improperly interpreted, of somewhat specious appearances, products of the imagination drawn from real life.

Before it acts to isolate completely external impressions from the outside world, the action of hashish, working on all the faculties at once, is characterized, as noted in the previously quoted memoir, by, for example, a surplus of mental energy, a brilliance of memories, and a more rapid thought process. Imperceptibly, this produces in the will, in all the instincts, such a relaxation that we become subject to a variety of impressions. The sequence of our thoughts can be broken by the slightest interference; we submit to the most contradictory influences. We go in every direction. By a word, by a gesture, our thoughts can be directed in succession toward a multitude of diverse subjects with a speed and yet with a clearness that are amazing. We are seized by a deep feeling of pride along with the growing exaltation of our faculties and their mounting energy and power. Depending on the circumstances, on the objects we see, and on the words we hear, we will experience the most vivid feelings of happiness or sadness, the most contradictory passions which are at times unusually violent. From irritation one can pass rapidly to fury, from discontent to hate and a desire for vengeance, from the calmest love to the wildest passion. Fear becomes terror, courage a rage that nothing can stop and that defies danger. Groundless suspicions may become certainties. The mind tends to exaggerate everything: the slightest excitation rarely fails to carry it away. Those who use hashish in the Orient, when they want to abandon themselves completely to the raptures of hashish intoxication, take extreme care to ward off anything that might turn their madness into depression, or might arouse anything other than tender, affectionate feelings. They take advantage of all the means offered by the dissolute customs of the Orient. In the midst of their harem, surrounded by their women, under the spell of music and of the lascivious dances performed by the dancing girls, they relish the intoxicating dawamesc and, aided by their beliefs, they are transported into the presence of these countless wonders that the Prophet has assembled in his paradise.

At present I will not specifically relate what has just been said to be mental illness. I will do this when discussing the detailed phenomena that result from the *basic fact* of which I have just drawn a succinct picture. I will limit myself, for the moment, to remarking how much this picture recalls the symptoms of "manic" madness in all its nuances. Although I have not observed this picture in myself, I have seen several persons after they have taken hashish in the same excited state, and I swear that it is impossible to see the slightest difference between them and the patients whom we care for in our asylums.

IV. Third Phenomenon: Errors of Time and Space

Under the influence of hashish, the mind can fall into the strangest errors relative to time and space. Time seems at first to drag slowly: minutes become hours, and hours days. Soon, with more and more exaggeration, all precise concept of time eludes us, the past and the present become confused. The speed with which our thoughts follow one another and the subsequent dream state explain this phenomenon. Time seems longer than when it is measured by terrestrial clocks, because actions or the events confined to that interval extend its limits by virtue of their intensity.

Says A. Delrieu: [iv]

Mohammed, suddenly transported by the fantasies of a vision, upset a jar of water that happened to be near him. The fall had practically emptied the jar at the very beginning of the Prophet's somnambulism. He witnessed wonders of heaven and earth, and when he returned to reality the water in the jar was still not completely emptied.[v]

Time and space are measured by intermediary points that are like so many surveyor's markers placed intentionally between two extreme limits, between the point of departure and the point of arrival. The interval enlarges and can acquire indefinite proportions, according to the number of these markers. Attention must be fixed first on one point, then on another, and then on both at once.

[iv] French historian.

[v] This old anecdote which illustrates the lengthening of time perception induced by hashish should be compared with the more recent one told by West (1970): "Two hippies, high on pot, are sitting in the Golden Gate Park in San Francisco. A jet aircraft goes zooming overhead and is gone; whereupon one hippie turns to the other one and says 'Man, I thought he'd never leave.'" (In *Psychotomimetic Drugs*, p. 325, Raven Press, New York, 1970.)

I was still unfamiliar with the effects of hashish, when, crossing the covered passage of the *Place de l'Opera* one night, I was struck by the length of time it took me to reach the other side. I had taken a few steps at most, but it seemed to me that I had been there two or three hours. I directed my attention to the people, who were numerous as usual. I noticed that some of them were passing me, while I was leaving others behind. I tried in vain to rid myself of the illusion. I hastened my step, but time did not pass more rapidly.

It seemed to me, in other words, that the walk was endlessly long and that the exit toward which I walked was retreating into the distance at the same rate as my speed of walking. I felt this kind of illusion several times when strolling the boulevards. Seen at a certain distance, people and things appeared to me as though I were observing them through the large end of a telescope.

We will remember that Theophile Gauthier, seeking to estimate the duration of a hashish crisis, "calculated that it lasted about three hundred years. Sensations followed one another so numerous and hurried that true appreciation of time was impossible. Once the crisis was over, I saw that it had lasted fifteen minutes."

We can compare the phenomenon we have just described with certain extravagant ideas that are sometimes encountered in psychotic patients. One knows that some of them believe they are a hundred, a thousand years old; some even say they are eternal.

The young woman I mentioned earlier believed that in the first days of her manic illness she had no age. She imagined that she had lived in all the historic periods she could remember.

> I had colossal proportions. Except for God and me, everyone seemed to me to be small, puny, and ugly. I chided those around me for having stolen my measure of time; "for me it no longer exists," I told them. My days and nights passed in an instant, too rapidly for me to be able to carry out the vast plans that filled my brain. I disavowed my mother for the reason that I could not have a mother younger than I.

The action of hashish could not cause distortions such as those I have just indicated. Aware as he is of himself, man easily recognizes the illusions by which mental patients are naturally fooled, and he avoids drawing the ridiculous conclusions that mental patients draw. However, let us not forget that the source of this illusion is the same in both cases, i.e., *excitement*.

V. Fourth Phenomenon: Development of the Sense of Hearing; The Influence of Music

The sense of hearing, like all the other senses, becomes extremely keen under the influence of hashish. I can best illustrate this by quoting the words used by Theophile Gautier (despite their obvious poetic exaggeration). I yield to the pleasure of citing them a second time.

> My hearing was fantastically sharpened. I heard the sound of colors. Green, red, blue, and yellow sounds came to me in perfectly distinct waves.[vi] An overturned glass, a creaking chair, a whispered word, sounded and resounded in me like claps of thunder. My own voice seemed so loud to me that I dared not speak for fear of knocking down the walls or exploding like a bomb. More than five-hundred clocks chimed the hour in their glass, copper, or silver voices. Every object touched made a sound like a harmonica or an Aeolian harp. I swam in an ocean of sound, where several themes from *Lucia* and *The Barber of Seville* floated like islets of light. Never had I been so overwhelmed by radiant bliss.

This excessive development of the sense of hearing must be attributed, at least in part, to the powerful influence that music exerts on those who take hashish. Words fail to portray the variety of emotions that harmony can produce. The crudest music, the simple vibrations of the strings of a harp or a guitar, rouse you to a point of delirium or plunge you into a sweet melancholy. Depending on your state of mind, the mental shock is felt by the organism, the fibers of the muscles and of the soul vibrate in unison, and veritable choreic or hysteriform movements may occur.

I have observed these effects in several people. I have witnessed their

---

[vi] The interchange of sensory modalities (sounds have color and colors are musical), or synesthesia, is one of the symptoms of hashish intoxication and is also experienced with other hallucinogens such as mescaline and LSD.

cries of joy, their songs, their tears and their laments, their deep depression or their frantic elation, depending on the harmonic mode in which the sound reached them. Several months ago *Experience* published an article in which Carriere [vii] described, with the great wit and accuracy of observation for which he is known, the state of excitement in which he saw several medical students to whom I had given hashish:

> A colleague, Dr. . . . , wishing to know for himself the effects of hashish, swallowed several grams of *dawamesc*. The dose was minimal, and some time elapsed before Dr. . . felt anything extraordinary. Then a female voice was heard. It was a maid busy tidying up in the room next to the one we were in. This voice was not disagreeable, which is about all one could say for it. Nevertheless, our colleague paid close attention to it. Soon he approached the door of the room where the songs came from and glued his ear to the keyhole in order not to miss a single note. He remained there, spellbound, for nearly a half-hour and left only when his siren in dustcap and wooden shoes could no longer be heard. Dr. . . was under the influence of hashish without knowing it; and, while admitting that music had never made such an impression on him, he could not convince himself that hashish had anything to do with it. He did not change his mind until much later when all the toxic effect was gone.

As far as I am concerned, I would try in vain to convey the extent to which music affects me in the same circumstances. Agreeable or disagreeable, happy or sad, the emotions that music creates are comparable only to those experienced in a dream. It is not enough to say that these emotions are more vivid than those of the waking state. Their character is transformed, as it were, and it is only upon reaching a hallucinatory state that they reach their full strength and can induce actual paroxysms of pleasure or pain. At that moment the immediate, direct action of harmony and the actual sensations on the ears are combined with the fiery and varied emotions resulting from associations of ideas caused by the combination of sounds.

[vii] Carriere was one of Moreau's assistants at Bicêtre Hospital.

One day I had taken a rather strong dose of hashish. I was surrounded by close friends whose kindness was well known to me. I had asked them to observe me scrupulously, to keep an accurate account of my words and gestures, of the expression on my face, etc. I was not yet quite sure of myself at that time, and I wanted to assure myself of the accuracy of my own observations through the help of others. When I had reached a sufficiently high state of intoxication and in order to subdue the ardor of my ideas and my sensations by giving them a unique twist, I asked a young lady with considerable talent to sit at the piano and to play a sad and melancholy tune. She chose a waltz by Weber. From the first notes of this tune so deeply imprinted with sadness, I felt a chill go through my entire body. My excitement changed abruptly in character. Totally concentrated within me like a burning fire, the waltz evoked in me only sad thoughts, distressing memories. The faces of several of the people surrounding me reflected the sinister mood of my imagination. These people were just serious; others who were laughing at me seemed to be making faces and threatening me. They terrified me, and I nearly accused them of hostility toward me. I closed my eyes so as not to see them and stretched out on a couch in order to collect my thoughts and regain command of my inner thoughts. But then a sadness, a somber melancholy, a painful anxiety overtook me to such an extent that I felt my chest pressed so that I nearly stopped breathing. My tears flowed freely, and, had I been alone, I would have sobbed aloud. I could not stand it any longer and felt an urge to shake off this frightful nightmare. The prayer from the opera *Moise* gradually restored calm in my soul. It seemed that my chest was freed of the weight that was crushing it. I had that physical and mental feeling of well-being experienced upon waking from a bad dream or at the end of a bout of fever.

I had not been fooled for a moment by my illusions, although these illusions had affected me like reality itself. I listened with ecstasy to religious tones that awakened in me memories that I had thought extinct for years, gentle feelings that are known only in childhood and are stifled so quickly by doubt and skepticism as soon as we take our first steps into reality. Then I had the idea to kneel in front of the piano, and there in an attitude of profound meditation, my eyes closed and my hands clasped, I waited for the music to stop. An instant later I arose as if waking with a start. My ears were suddenly struck by rhythms of the waltz and the quadrille. Looking around me, I was astonished to see everyone sitting quietly. "You are not dancing. You can listen to music like that and sit quietly in one spot, like statues!" The expression was appropriate; that was precisely the effect produced in me by the people who surrounded me. Some of them, by their haughty stare, reminded me of that beautiful and frightening automaton that Hoffmann[viii] invented and that Nathaniel saw one day, idle, her hands resting on the table, and her eyes fixed on him. I was not in the least fooled by this odd illusion. I attributed it to the agitated state that was gradually seizing me and the subsequent contrast with their immobility,

It seemed to me that electric currents were running through my limbs and forcing them to move in cadence. It was as if I had been bitten by a tarantula. I asked the lady of the house to waltz with me. I waltzed for more than fifteen minutes in a semi-somnolent state that I can barely describe. I felt, at each moment, as if the floor was disappearing from under my feet. It seemed that my will had nothing to do in the whirlwind that had seized me and that my body irresistibly followed the sound waves coming from the piano, as a child's toy moves when one strikes it. However, I did not miss a beat, and I exchanged a few words with the person with whom I was waltzing.

This rather violent exercise did not cause me the slightest fatigue. Nevertheless, it made me perspire profusely and thus brought a faster end to the crisis, which lasted four or four-and-a-half hours.

To explain the phenomenon that I have just described, it does not suffice to say that hashish excites and heightens the sense of hearing. The causes are much more complicated, and each deserves to be examined in detail.

The action of music on sane mental faculties, free from all foreign influences, can be considered in two distinct manners: (1) from a purely physical or, if you wish, physiological point of view, and (2) from a mental point of view. We will have to consider it from still a third point of view when we account for the changes caused by hashish.

1. In the words of Cabanis:

> The general influence of music on human nature proves that feelings peculiar to the ear are far from being susceptible to comparison with sensations perceived by the mind; there

---

[viii] A reference to the *Tales of Hoffmann* immortalized by Offenbach's opera.

is in these emotions something more direct. Men devoid of any culture are no less fond of songs than those whose social life has rendered their hearing more sensitive and their taste more refined. Without digressing to speak of the winged songster whose wonderful throat is, in this respect, nature's masterpiece, a large number of species of birds fill the air with pleasant harmonies. Several domestic animals and some still undomesticated types seem to listen with pleasure to the songs of man and the artificial voices of instruments that he plays. Certain sound combinations and some simple accents that affect all the senses by the most direct action, immediately engender feelings that the primitive laws of organization seem to have subordinated to them.

We have called this action "organic" because, in fact, it seems entirely concentrated in the organ directly reached by the sounds. It is a sensation and nothing more, and this sensation has no repercussions —a propensity that is in the mind proper, or in the memory, or in the imagination. The organs are more or less apt to feel it, following a propensity that is either instinctive or accidentally acquired and developed. This predisposition can be found even among idiots. We know the taste that some of these unfortunate beings show for music. It certainly does not happen often these days, but music is used at times for the treatment of mental illness. Moreover, the mere exercise of any talent is always accompanied by an enjoyment that ceases, it is true, because of habit, but is no less real and vivid after a momentary halt in this sensation. We know that for Honore Trezel, deaf from birth, the first days that followed the discovery of sound were days of ecstasy. All sounds, noises even, gave him an ineffable pleasure, and he sought them eagerly (Magendie).

The overstimulation caused by hashish throughout the entire nervous system is felt most particularly in the portion of this system concerned with the perception of sounds. Hearing acquires a delicacy, an unbelievable sensitivity. The sounds spread even to the epigastric center; they dilate or compress the chest, accelerate or slacken the heartbeat, and either set in motion the entire muscular system convulsively or numb it.

2. There is another effect of harmony which is responsible for the

influence music exerts upon human beings. Sounds have the power to awaken our memories, to provoke certain associations of ideas that, in their turn, put our feelings in motion. In this way they appeal much more to our mind than to our imagination or feelings. To *feel* music, which is to understand it, sounds must not be dead symbols for us, and the different combinations in which they are placed must be associated with familiar ideas. Therein lies all the secret of the power of harmony. However beautiful the operatic music we first hear, if we do not understand the words, if we do not grasp the situations, the intentions, the thoughts of the actors, we can be only mildly touched. So it is with instrumental music, which can never arouse our enthusiasm if we cannot follow the thought of the composer through the various melodic transformations. In vain will we expose the people whose habits, whose political and religious customs are essentially different from ours to the finest works of our greatest artists; we will find these people to be indifferent because these works speak to them in a language that they do not understand.

I have witnessed several attempts of this kind in the Orient, in Cairo, and in Constantinople, where our military music was introduced several years ago. Nothing could equal the complete indifference with which the Turks and the Arabs listened to it, unless it was the great pleasure, the eagerness, that the same individuals showed upon hearing the discordant sounds of a poor flute and of a kind of Basque drum in use among them. According to circumstances related to time, place, and mood, the simplest tunes, the most common music, can exert a truly marvelous influence for which imagination is largely responsible. A person must have spent several years away from his native land, in countries where nothing recalls the image of people or things among which he has lived, in order to realize fully the kind of impressions that music can make. Then, even the poorest conductor, playing songs from the native land, can take on the greatness of a Paganini. Evidently the harmony plays but a minimal part in the emotions that are felt; memory and imagination do most of the work.

Now if you will recall what I have said concerning the enhancement of the memory and imagination by hashish, the influence of music will already be explained in part. One can imagine that thoughts of mourning and death ally themselves immediately with sad, melancholy songs, happy thoughts with gay songs, religious memories with religious songs, and that these thoughts, these memories, exert an almost unlimited influence upon one's judgment. Thinking being obliterated or nearly so, the mind abandons itself entirely and unreservedly to impressions that cannot be kept in check but which assume an exaggerated importance.

3. The overstimulation of memory and imagination, great enough to leave but little room for external stimuli, combined with the confusion of judgment and the turmoil of ideas results in a certain mental state which I have called a "dream state." This state changes the sensations produced by music in such a way that, although they come from the outside and have their origin in the real world, they resemble those imaginary creations developed in the dream state. They have, in a word, all the characteristics of an hallucination. We shall see later that a pathological condition of judgment may be the source of phenomena of this type.

In this manner we can explain the energy of the sensations, the rapture, the kind of ecstasy that music causes in those who have taken hashish. The overstimulation of the senses of hearing, memory, and imagination that I mentioned at the beginning of this section would be impossible to account for were it not assisted by that mental change just described. It is a fact of self-observation that the sensations and emotions peculiar to the dream state sometimes reach such intensity and power that nothing in waking life can be compared to them.

The strange effect of music on the mental faculties, modified by the action of hashish, naturally draws our attention to a question that has frequently concerned physicians who treat the mentally ill. On many occasions they have tried to treat with music. They have failed, but their failures profited none but those who have tried. New attempts are made with promises of marvelous therapeutic methods that will succeed in good time and that seem to be above reproach.[2]

Music, for a sane mind, is a rich source of feeling. That is undeniable. But is this true when the mental faculties are injured? This

---

[2] Our opinion on this subject arises from several considerations that we will study, but if we must express it now, in all candor, we would have only to quote a modern writer: "Music as a curative method works only at the Opera-Comique. There they cure madness with an aria, fever with a flute solo, cholera with a trombone medley. It is most ingenious, but we have often cursed David's harp and Saul's hypochondria which have evidently produced this nonsense."

question calls for an answer, and no one seems to have pondered it. Another question of equal importance has been no less neglected than the first. If there are psychotics who are affected by music, from what type of madness are they suffering? In our judgment it is less than rational to apply a remedy before knowing its nature or whether it is effective. In so doing, in the great majority of cases, one might as well be talking to the deaf. The meaning and depth of the discourses, the oratorical form, may vary, but in fact one is really talking to people who do not understand, because nature has deprived them of the ability to understand. Moreover, in a few cases all we have done is to supply new nourishment to the excitement that we wished to quiet. Here are the facts upon which these two propositions are based.

Psychotics upon whom music exerts any influence (good or bad, the question is immaterial at this point) are extremely rare. I am speaking here only of "curable" psychotics, from the most to the least curable. I am omitting the truly *demented* (the partially delirious psychotics and the manics) who, unfortunately, constitute the majority. We search in vain among the first for individuals accessible to musical impressions. We find none except among the manics—and only in those whose madness has not gone beyond the point of simple "excitement."

In order to give our ideas all the scope they should have, I add that I do not intend to speak only of the turbulent excitement of the *manic state* but also of the one which sometimes occurs during a mild mental illness.

It must be noted that, among the mentally ill, the ones susceptible to the influence of music are those who, by their state of mind, most resemble individuals who have taken hashish.

For several years, as everyone knows, there has been much music at the hospital of Bicêtre. Several times a week five- or six-hundred psychotics attend fine concerts, where some of them perform when they have regained their health. The principal performers are recruited from among the nonpsychotic epileptics and the older so-called *calm ones,* who are entrusted with the instrumental parts.

Thanks to the judicious selection of pieces that make up the repertory, and above all to the untiring zeal of a young professor (M. F. Ronger, former pupil of Wilhem), whose distinguished talent deserves another audience, these concerts are far from being as defective as one might think, and the music that is performed is meant for the ears of the people to whom the music is directed. Let us look at the results and judge for ourselves: we enter the room prepared for the concert, where arias by Glück and Lully are being heard accompanied by such instruments as violins, cellos, and flutes. The audience is divided into two distinct parts: the first, the larger, is composed of listeners; the second, led by the accordion and headed by the voice instructor, includes only the performers.

Now let us direct our attention to all those faces whose age, nature of illness, and thoughts are so amazingly varied. But pass over the first two or three rows. These are epileptics, and we are not concerned here with them. Are you struck by the immobility of all these faces, by the impassiveness and complete indifference with which they listen to, or rather understand, the music that is being played for them and whose cleverly varied moods appeal to different aspects of their spirit? What! Even the music of *La Parisienne* [ix] and the roll of drums cannot move them! Do not take your eyes off them for one moment and tell me, in good conscience, whether you can perceive, even fleetingly, the slightest sign of the effect of the music on these poor disorganized brains. Have you noticed whether this manic-depressive whom you see in that far corner, his eyes riveted to the ground, his elbows resting on his crossed legs and half of his face hidden in the palm of his hand, resembling *il Penseroso* [x] of Michelangelo, whether this manic-depressive, has abandoned for one moment the black thoughts that preoccupy him; whether this other patient, puffed with pride and paranoia, has ceased to hold his head high and to look around with scorn and disdain; whether that young chronic psychotic has ceased for a single moment to mutter through his teeth, looking hesitantly around him and gesticulating so much that he disturbs his neighbors? I shall not call your attention to that group of expressionless faces, those masks of flesh, so devoid of intelligence. They are the deeply insane, and they are there only to occupy space. However, there are some among them who are listening with a certain amount of attention. You even see them smile when the music is loud and when the *rinforzando* [xi] is at its loudest. But just what does that prove? Who has ever doubted that

---

[ix] A popular musical in the 1840s in Paris.
[x] The Thinker of Michelangelo in Florence.
[xi] The refrain, the burden of the song.

individuals who are insane are yet capable of emotion? Does this mean you can cure them with music? It never occurred to you. That a poor psychotic often listens to your music with pleasure and passion, well and good. So much the better for him. This is a sweet distraction that lightens his burden. But it cannot change the fact of his incurability! No music, no maestro, whether it be Mozart, Beethoven, or Rossini, can help recover a lost intelligence. I conceive the possibility of utilizing the influence of music, so long as the faculties are not weakened or damaged, to restore intellectual harmony through sensory harmony, as advised by the Pythagoreans [xii] and the philosopher of Geneva.[xiii] But we have seen that the psychotics who fall into this category (delusions) are, by virtue of the nature of their illness, completely inaccessible to its influence.

There is another group of psychotics, however, whose faculties, far from being weakened, are actually enhanced. Some of them can be strongly affected by the method that failed with the "delusionals." They are manics in a state of mild "excitement." We have already expressed this opinion, and I mention it here only to reach the facts upon which it is based. These cases are very few in number: I have seen only two in four years. They were in the ward of my esteemed colleague Dr. Voisin. One of the two, totally paralyzed, had ideas of grandeur, of power, of influence. His usual state was an unalterable cheerfulness and a lively excitement which never reached furor. The other (notes on whom are provided at the end of this work) was likewise in a state of habitual excitement, with ambitious ideas but without paralysis. In the case of these two patients, particularly the first, we have been able to verify on several occasions a truly extraordinary impressionability: this has been observed only very occasionally with hashish. Hardly had the first notes struck his ears when L. . . jumped up from the bench on which he was sitting, ran to the middle of the room, and delivered an imitation in accord with the music being played. His extremely mobile face, his eyes, now animated, now downcast or full of tears, his gestures and the varied attitudes of his body appeared to express vividly the feelings in his

---

[xii] The disciples of Pythagoras of Samos, Greek philosopher and mathematician of the Sixth century B.C.

[xiii] Jean-Jacques Rousseau (1712–1778), the social philosopher.

heart. Nothing could depict the energy of his pantomime when a martial air was being played. He was a fearless soldier marching to attack an enemy column or perhaps a horseman mounted on a spirited charger holding at bay the enemy that surrounded him. All this spirit, all this fire died as soon as the songs ceased, and if the patient reverted to a melancholy mood, an indescribable expression of sadness, discouragement, and pain darkened his face, seeming to color all his behavior. The effects that we have observed on the second patient differed little from those we have just described. They were less intense because the patient's excitement was less intense.

As indicated, we have seen only two examples of the influence of music in cases of manic excitement. There could well be more, we are sure, if instead of attempting music therapy by testing the power of sounds and rhythms indiscriminately on everyone whatever their mental condition, as has been done up to now, psychotics had been submitted to some mixed medication that would combine physical and mental effect and would reach those who have been denied access to concert halls because of the disturbance created by their condition.

From what I have just said, I think that everyone will agree with me that it is legitimate to hope for some success in the case that I have just described. From the methods used until now, no good can be expected. The excitement of the manic can only increase, and his condition worsen.

VI. Fifth Phenomenon: Fixed Ideas (Delusions)

This variety of intellectual damage, so frequent in mental illness, affects the largest group of mentally ill, the monomaniacs. It is also caused by hashish, but only when the delirium has progressed to an advanced stage, a stage seldom purposely reached.

Only once have I had occasion to observe it in myself, and not, I confess, deliberately. This was in 1841 when I began to experiment with hashish. The dose of hashish had been slightly increased. I became frightened by what I felt, and the idea occurred to me that I had been poisoned. Three of us had taken *dawamesc,* Mr. H.,[3] Dr. Aubert-

---

[3] Distinguished architect of the city of Paris, who in the interest of art has undertaken trips to various parts of the world, notably in Egypt and in Nubia, about which he is presently publishing a magnificent panorama with text.

Roche, and I. At first I did not accuse anyone. I did notice that my two tyros were considerably less agitated than I. I drew no conclusions unfavorable to them, however. Unwittingly, in my mounting excitement, I persuaded myself that the colleague who had brought the hashish had given me some of a different quality and much more active, and that he had mixed it with pure extract. "He wants to test me," I told myself. "What terrible foolishness! How do I know he doesn't want to poison me?" I shouted then in a loud voice: "Aubert, you are a murderer; you have poisoned me!" The playful way in which he reacted, and the words of consolation he uttered only strengthened my conviction. I struggled for some time with this thought, while realizing its absurdity. However, as the thought repeatedly crossed my mind along with a thousand other thoughts, it ended up dominating me in the most absolute manner.

Soon an illusion, which I shall describe later, triggered another delusion which was much more extravagant and which seemed to be a consequence of the first. I was dead, about to be buried, that is to say, my body was dead and my soul had left it. Probably the residual awareness that I still retained, if not of my personality, at least of my existence, forced me to establish that important distinction. It was difficult to push absurdity farther. One can find similar ideas among the mentally ill, but they are far from common. In a few minutes I had traveled through the best-known stages of delirium. A young man who had taken hashish was overcome with terror and persuaded himself that he was going to die. His friends made fun of him. Someone had the idea of hanging a bolster on the wall and showed it to him. "There you are hanging; you're dead," they told him. "I knew it," cried the poor devil. "Isn't it terrible to die so young and this way!"

When the "excitement" produced by hashish is less intense, delusions are still present, and numerous, but they are fleeting. They appear and disappear. Only with difficulty and in the case of a serious disorder do they penetrate deeply into the mind and remain there for any period of time. At first they are opposed by the inner feeling, by our self-awareness that remains so alert amidst all the disturbance caused by hashish. In the case of madness, delusions, whatever their nature, are essentially characterized by their total and exclusive domination over the mind, as if they had absorbed the individual's personality. And so it is with delusions caused by hashish, which cannot exist

with their distinctive characteristics except insofar as the consciousness, the ego, is warped and involved in the overall disintegration of
the mind.

What does self-observation teach us about the manner in which these
ideas are formed? What happens in our mind in a state of reverie, in
those moments when we let our thoughts go, free from all constraint?
They frolic rapidly through our mind, but they are far from being
uninteresting to us, because they command our attention rather in-
sistently and derive from some dominant passion, some instinct, secret
or acknowledged. An ambitious soldier dreams of battles, rank, honors;
he will become a colonel, a marshal of France. A religious fanatic
dreams of hell, of the torments that await the damned; and if he is
not so fortunate as to be among the select few, he will see the demon
striking his prey, even before his soul has been released from its mortal
bonds; or perhaps paradise and its ineffable joys will capture his
thoughts, and he will encounter the Deity. A lover will be the master,
the mate of the one he adores; all his desires will be fulfilled; her
image will be constantly before his eyes, enhanced by his imagination.
Hateful and full of revenge, he will pursue any rival with invectives
and curses.

In a normal state—that is, in a state of reflective self-control and
perfect independence—those ideas play in our mind, as if they were
in some way alien to us. The slightest impulse of our will makes them
vary endlessly like images in a kaleidoscope that we can stop any
time.

If, as a result of the action of hashish or for other reasons this
intellectual power weakens and completely disappears all at once,
either temporarily or permanently; the fantasy that had only crossed
our mind before, changes into a conviction, a fixed idea, because our
mind is directed by inner consciousness and cannot combat it, accuse
it of falseness, and reject it. With hashish, unless, as we have said, the
intoxication is excessive, the delusions are very short-lived. We find
ourselves imagining the most incredible things, the most bizarre
monstrosities to which we surrender body and soul. Then suddenly in
a flash we regain our power over ourselves, we recognize the extent of
the error. We were mad, in a word, and we have now become reasonable. But we remain convinced that by pushing things a little further,

there would be a good chance that the delusion would dominate us completely and for an indeterminate period of time.

As you see, and there should be no misunderstanding here, I am not offering new psychological theories: I am simply reporting the results of self-observation, and describing phenomena that anyone can verify as well as I. In my eyes they have the same guarantee of certainty as the obvious normal operations of our minds that are easy to appreciate and that no one has ever questioned.

Locke [xiv] has said about the delusions of psychotics: "It does not seem to me that the mentally ill have lost their capacity to reason, but *having improperly associated certain ideas together,* they take them to be true." Elsewhere, "After having converted their own fantasies into realities, *by the force of their imagination,* they subsequently draw reasonable conclusions from them."

So far we have not gone beyond the explanation provided by the English philosopher. Is it necessary for me to demonstrate its inadequacy? Locke evidently limited himself to explaining the fundamental fact of madness by the phrase *having improperly associated certain words together.* He does not even attempt to say why this defective association has taken place or why those it affects permit themselves to be influenced by their false ideas and hold to them tenaciously, so much so that no mental reason or pressure can dissuade them. Do not similar associations occur in our minds all the time without causing us to make incorrect inferences from them? Locke seems to blame our imagination, but he does not indicate the source of this novel, extraordinary ability. What I have just said proves that it resides essentially in the *excitement,* the *basic generator* of all the phenomena of delirium.

In fact, if I am correctly understood, if one recalls the circumstances and the mental conditions that precede delusions, one will recognize first of all the phenomenon of excitement that I am so anxious to explain and that I would readily call a dissolution, a molecular disintegration of intelligence, if I dared express it as I feel it. A delusion is the result of this intellectual disintegration, a result which persists even when the intelligence is more or less restored: it is the theme of a

---

[xiv] John Locke (1632–1704). British philosopher who studied medicine, the father of empiricism, and forerunner of experimental psychology.

dream, surviving the very dream that produced it. The inception of delusions caused by hashish, as it has been described here, can be considered, by the most legitimate induction, as common to the inception of delusions that characterize various types of mental illness known *generically* as *partial delirium*.

Let us see if ordinary observation does not provide us with some new evidence. Let me first repeat what I have said in the preliminaries, being concerned here with a fact of consciousness, of self-observation, which does not reveal itself externally except for symptoms that are usually too fleeting to be observed. Exploration, in this case, must be undertaken by the patients themselves. They will tell us what they feel and, in brief, it is from their very mouths that we must learn what we are seeking. Our part is to state our questions precisely, to put the patients on a track that they would not find by themselves.

I will first investigate the circumstances under which delusions are developed in mental patients.

Physical or mental, morbid causes immediately result in a rather abrupt shock to the mental faculties, exaggerating their action or overexciting them. Prior to any delusion, there is a general state of excitement of the mental faculties, a confused agitation of ideas, a kind of oscillatory movement of the nervous system that characterizes the psychological fact that I have designated the *basic fact*.

Consider, for example, sad feelings, which are the most frequent cause of melancholy ideas. Their action is especially dreaded because it is sudden and rapid. Upon close examination, the action is found to be the same as the first effects of a rather strong shock to the brain, of a congestion of this organ, of a fainting spell, that is, of confusion, more or less rapid and complete impairment of the thought processes, dissociation of ideas, and more or less complete but ephemeral loss of consciousness. Things never happen otherwise, no matter what the nature of the causes that intervene in the creation of delusions.

I cannot cite the testimony of authors who have written about mental illness in support of what I have just said because research on the causes of psychosis, the first symptoms of its appearance, and other related factors has been limited to the physical and mental accidents that seemed directly connected with the manifestations of delirium, or rather with the least significant changes in the character, habits, and feelings of the patient. They go no farther than that. For example,

"Mr. X., having suffered deep sorrows or perhaps following a violent attack of anger or perhaps even following the suppression of hemorrhoidal bleeding, becomes taciturn and bizarre. He is convinced that his life is threatened. His habits have changed completely. He was orderly and thrifty; now he has become wasteful and prodigal, etc."

Such is the formula invariably followed to describe different cases of mental illness. However, from a psychological point of view, one sees that there are important gaps and that only the superficial aspects have been observed.

To penetrate more deeply into the development of the illness, to follow it step by step, not only in its external and observable aspects but also in its internal ones, one must study it in oneself, or perhaps even (although this is infinitely less reliable) by having the patients give an account themselves.

One sometimes finds, unfortunately too rarely, patients of exceptional education who, during intervals of health in which there is some remission or after a total cure, are able to present us with the most valuable information, provided they direct their attention to the subject that occupies us.

As we know, among the psychotics with *partial delirium,* there are a certain number in whom this delirium has been preceded by what, at the outset and during the course of the illness, sums up in its highest expression the *principal* change with which we associate all mental lesions, *manic excitement.* In this case, at least, it is undeniable that, to quote Esquirol describing *mania,* "incoherence of ideas, *confusion of all the elements of intelligence"* precede delusion. These words of the master can be applied to all forms of partial delirium.

I call attention to the observations of physicians who have some experience with psychotics. When their patients were able to understand them, the physicians often asked: "How did your illness begin? How did you ever get such absurd, foolish ideas?" Answer: "I became so sad, I was so deeply upset that I was completely confused; I was no longer normal; I had lost my bearings; my ideas were upside down; I did not know what I was saying or doing, and I imagined that . . ." This is the start of the delusion, the idea that later will dominate the thinking process and will outlive the general confusion, the upheaval of the faculties. Delusions do not always overwhelm the intelligence of mental patients. Sometimes delusions will struggle with the inner consciousness. This is the moment of uncertainty, of indecision, of anxiety, of extreme instability of ideas. In a word, again it is the excitement, less intense perhaps and, if you will permit me the expression, more "watered down" than in the first case. But it is always the same psychological phenomenon. It is the basic fact!

Delusions rarely remain static. Sometimes they even disappear completely, only to reappear later, almost always with renewed intensity. In other words, they undergo phases of alternating remission and recurrence.

Let us study the changes that I have just indicated with scrupulous care, and let us question patients minutely about what they feel when their delusions press them most. To cover the two extremes quickly, with some patients we see simply the external signs of a slight excitement that contrasts with the calm they previously enjoyed; with others, we witness, suddenly or gradually, all the symptoms that characterize intense mania. The majority will offer intermediate symptoms such as restlessness during sleep, agitation, dreams, nightmares, waking with a start. During the waking state, we find indecision, flight of ideas, daydreams, absent-mindedness, vague fears, premonitions, and a feeling of pressure in the precordial regions. Then, along with this disorder, delusions reappear, at first transitory but finally total and complete. Everyone is aware that, in mental institutions, it is necessary to redouble the surveillance of monomaniacs whenever signs of excitement appear so that they do not pose a threat to themselves or to others.

A further proof that the mental changes we have just indicated constitute the basic source of all delusions is that the patients in whom we see them frequently forget their prevailing delusions to adopt new ones more related to their current preoccupations.

Is this not the particular condition of the brain that Esquirol, in his descriptive and accurate style, has termed a *cataleptic state?* [xv] Later I

[xv] This expression usually describes the trance-like state of hysterical or schizophrenic patients who present an apparent loss of voluntary motion and a peculiar plastic rigidity of the muscles. As a result these patients retain for an indefinite time any position in which they are placed. Esquirol applies this condition to brain function which also becomes rigidly fixed in a given pattern as illustrated by the examples he gives.

shall cite a remarkable example. Here, I borrow two examples from Esquirol:

A lady believes that her husband wants to shoot her. She escapes from her manor and throws herself in a well. They tell her that if he did want to kill her, poison would be easier. Henceforth, she is afraid of being poisoned and refuses all nourishment.

A man, in a depression, believes he has lost his honor. After trying in vain to reassure him, his friends offer the comfort of religion, and immediately he is convinced that he is damned.

Once the orderly chain of association of ideas is broken, the most bizarre and extravagant thoughts, the strangest combinations of ideas are formed and take control of the mind. They can be induced by the most insignificant cause, as in the dream state. "The city of Die is dominated by a cliff named U; a young man decides to add the letter *u* to the word Die and makes the word *Dieu* (God), and all the inhabitants of Die are gods in his mind. Soon he recognizes the absurdity of this polytheism, and he concentrates the divinity in the person of his father, the latter being the most respectable individual in the vicinity" (Esquirol). In mania, or simply in manic excitement, these faulty associations come and go with the same speed. The patient is possessed by a wide variety of delusions. In partial delirium, only some of these associations, selected in response to some strong passion from this chaos of ideas, occupy the mind to the exclusion of others.

Mr. X., a retired merchant, was deeply preoccupied with the marriage of an only daughter upon whom he had lavished all his affections. He brought to this important affair all the indecision, the uncertainty, the meticulous and timid prudence that formed the basis of his character, and that, in this instance, derived from the intensity of his paternal love.

This indecisiveness resulted in the rejection of suitors. Regrets followed, and Mr. X. reproached himself bitterly for having compromised the happiness of his daughter. She finally attained an age that hardly permitted her any more delay, and Mr. X. approved of a person who seemed to meet his requirements of fortune and position. The relationship was already far along when Mr. X., falling back into his state of indecision, believed it was his duty to ask for further delays.

Soon after, his mind appeared obviously affected. He believed that he had not fulfilled the simplest demands of integrity and loyalty in proceeding with harmful caution in considering his future son-in-law. This individual would surely wish to avenge himself by attacking and slandering him before the courts. From then on he was a dishonored man; his shame would hurt his whole family. He could see only one way to prevent all these misfortunes: to kill himself. Happily, his fatal plans did not escape the notice of his family, who thwarted his attempts. Mr. X. was brought to our establishment. Such are the symptoms of the malady, drawn from the information provided by the relatives.

But we could not be content with that superficial examination, which revealed to us absolutely nothing about the psychological state of the patient. It was supplied by Mr. X. himself.

Several weeks after his arrival in our establishment, Mr. X. recovered his reason. He was able not only to give an exact account of what happened in the later stages, but also to go back to the beginning of his illness. I will reproduce his words faithfully. I asked him how he got such absurd ideas and whether he could account for them. He said it was difficult, that it was all confused in his mind:

> What I do know is that a few days before, and I cannot explain why, I was dumbfounded. At times I scarcely knew what I was doing. I became unbelievably absent-minded; I was surprised to be thinking of things I would never have wanted to. For the first time, I talked to myself, or rather I muttered meaningless words. I was convinced that my head was in ferment, but it did not hurt and I would not have dreamed of consulting my physician if, exhausted from lack of sleep and tormented by sinister forebodings, I had not finally feared becoming ill. These misgivings were only too justified, since a few days later, my condition worsened, my head felt empty, I felt a weight in my stomach that prevented me from breathing, and suddenly the idea came to me that M., dissatisfied with my behavior, could sue me for libel. From that moment on, this cursed thought never left me.

During your insomnia, were you not constantly tormented by the same ideas, the fear of having offended M.? "God, no. In my crises, in my fits of *mental fever,* as I said, I thought of nothing because I was thinking of too many things at the same time. It was only when I had recovered a little calm that I became preoccupied with all this foolishness."

During the first days at Ivry, Mr. X. seemed little shaken in his delusions, because of the decision that had just been taken regarding him. He spoke of them continually, but with a sort of reserve; it was even easy to call his attention to other subjects. Some time after, upon rising one morning, Mr. X. was overcome with great excitement. A profound anxiety showed on his face. His eyes were animated. His tongue was covered with a yellowish coating. His breath was strong and bad. His skin was dry. His pulse varied from 72 to 76. Mr. X. moved continually. He came and went as if he did not know what to do or what to cling to. He no longer waited to be asked about his troubles and fears. It was a true manic excitement imposed on the partial delirium, for all his thoughts were stamped with his delusions. Soon his convictions acquired an extraordinary strength that called for careful surveillance. For the first time, Mr. X. had an hallucination. He had been suddenly awakened, he said, by a voice that told him several times in a perfectly intelligible manner: "You will no longer be in doubt. There will be a lawsuit. You are lost, and so are your wife and daughter."

In a few days the illness had acquired all the violence of a manic fit, but without the incoherence of ideas. This was the manic passion coupled with the fixed ideas that characterize partial delirium. As most people know, the principal characteristics of manic delirium are (1) looseness, incoherence of thought and (2) irritation, anger, fury, always imminent and ready to explode. In Mr. X. the passions born from his delusions seemed to rumble in his chest, obscuring his self-awareness and carrying away his will; he was too weak from the cerebral shock to resist the slightest stimulus. Very obviously, his delusions had not changed in nature and were still present. But the manic excitement (by that we mean the mobility of ideas, the rapidity of the conception, then the liveliness of subjective sensations, daydreams, etc.) had given him an energy, a violence that was unusual. This state lasted four or five days, after which, under the influence of a very strong medication, Mr. X. gradually regained his usual calm and eventually recovered completely.

Some new symptoms appeared and seem to support what has just been established.

Just as delusions become more intense following an aggravation of the general disorder, so we see them weakening as the disorder lessens. It was easy, in fact, to follow step by step these two series of symptoms in their progressive waning. Having calmed down, Mr. X. was more accessible to our advice, which he understood better and which even led him to reflect. He related more and more to external things. Previously almost entirely self-centered, his mental life now began to expand toward the outer world. He paid more attention to the reasoning with which we were opposing his dominant ideas.

So, and we insist on this point because it is important, as the excitement gradually subsided, so did the delusions, the conviction, the unshakable tenacity upon which they rested. They appeared absolute, irresistible, inevitable as long as the underlying psychocerebral disturbances persisted; then they became more and more like simple misconceptions to which no one is immune, even in a state of perfect mental health.

At this point, Mr. X. who, for a multitude of reasons, some plausible and others obviously absurd, was still a captive of his dominant ideas, declared that if one person in whom he had complete confidence and who was completely informed of his affairs, his brother, came to him and assured him he was in error, he would believe him. His brother was admitted to visit him, and Mr. X. after several hours of conversation with him, announced to us that he no longer believed what he had told us and regarded it all as idle fancy. He was cured.

Anyone who had not followed the delirium as I had, in all its transformations, day by day, hour by hour, most assuredly would have mistaken the character of such a cure and would have credited it to a strictly mental influence. (Writers have noted more than one instance of this nature, and these incidents have been misinterpreted, in my opinion at least, just as this one might have.)

When the patient agreed to talk with his brother, the way had been prepared. The organic cause of the malady had almost entirely disappeared. The patient had ceased to be the victim of a delusion, and fallen under the yoke of a simple error, and there is nothing surprising about the fact that this error disappeared with the statements of a person in whom Mr. X. had confidence.

As I said previously, the improvement in the case of Mr. X. lasted only a short time, forty-eight hours at most. After that, the illness maintained its periodic remissions, with the symptoms indicated above, save, however, for changes in the nature of the delusions. It is important to devote our attention to these for a moment.

With almost every attack, the delusions attached themselves to different subjects. In the beginning, they were related to a supposed lawsuit by which Mr. X. felt threatened. Later, completely reassured on this earlier point, Mr. X. became convinced that a person with whom he had had business differences many years earlier was rekindling old quarrels, yielding to hidden grudges, and was out to ruin him and take the fortune acquired by twenty years of work. Another time he turned his fears to his health. So many emotions, and so many excesses in his diet, he said, had driven him to such a dilapidated state of health that he could not recover. Life was henceforth unbearable. Finally, believing himself guilty of all sorts of evil acts, he decided that the police, who until then had been tolerant because of his state of mental illness, were only waiting for his full recovery to seize him.

These many variations of delusions must surely indicate that, besides these ideas themselves, their primary and essential source lies in the patient's judgment.

Among several other similar cases, the one we just reported is the most important because of its sharply etched features which command attention. It is unusual to meet patients who can analyze their intimate sensations so precisely at a time when their consciousness is ready to fail them. Most often the observer must be content with external signs, and we know that there are many chances for error, considering that these signs can fail, even though the basic psychic disorder is quite intense. That is precisely what happened to Mr. X. at the start of his illness. Already, in effect his ideas were, as he put it, *confused.* At times *he lost his head,* so that one saw nothing in him but a weakness of character that prevented him from making any decisions.

I shall cite again one or two cases which, if they are less complete in some ways than the preceding one, can nevertheless serve to awaken the attention of observers on the subject that occupies us.

Mrs. . . has been tormented for several years by delusions and visual, auditory, gustatory, and olfactory hallucinations. I shall say nothing for the moment about hallucinations, which will be the subject of a special chapter. Mrs. . . is convinced that certain members of her family want to poison her in order to get her fortune. She is also convinced that many other methods have been used in attempts to kill her. These ideas never leave her, but they seldom have the same intensity. Usually Mrs. . . does not seem bothered by them. She speaks about them rarely, even when urged to do so. She behaves quite properly, and absolutely nothing betrays her mental problems.

Episodes of excitement occur at infrequent intervals. Her expression becomes animated, her cheeks are bright, and Mrs. . . becomes talkative and irritable, quarreling with those she blames for her isolation. She speaks endlessly about her prevailing ideas. She wants to know about the persecution she is suffering; she listens to advice with disdain and often with anger. She never ceases to beg for her freedom; she invents a thousand ruses to gain it against the wishes of the doctors of the institution. Sometimes this "excitement" reaches the violence of a manic attack, except that her ideas never become incoherent or go beyond the limits of the delusions.

No one in Mr. N.'s large family has ever had brain damage or a nervous disease. He is forty-eight years of age. In 1831 he suffered a very violent attack of articulatory rheumatism, which lasted six weeks; he was treated with blood-letting and, probably, pain killers. In 1832, shortly after cholera had swept the country, Mr. N., who had been very frightened by the epidemic, had an attack of gastritis that resisted every kind of treatment. Says the patient:

> At the end of about fifteen months my nerves began to be affected, with the exception of those in my head. In my arms, in my legs, I had very painful disturbances, such as quivering or shuddering. My stomach troubles lessened noticeably and, during the three years that followed, they were quite bearable. Starting with this period until 1841, I have rarely experienced them.
>
> For many years I was subject to headaches. Toward the end of 1841 those headaches suddenly became extremely violent, while the stomach pains disappeared completely. My mental illness dates from that moment.

Before going any further, I asked Mr. N. to specify as well as he could what he had felt during that period: "What did you feel in your head? Where did it hurt?" Placing his two hands on either side of his forehead, he said: "It seems to me that I felt pressure on my temples. I felt hot flashes and, as I have often told my wife, I felt as though my skull were going to explode." Was it then that your ideas became disturbed? "I was completely stupefied, I had dizzy spells, I could not think. I would not have understood the simplest question. I had to stop working. I was not sufficiently master of my thoughts to continue. So it was that I fell into the condition in which you see me now."

Here is that condition—thinking is truly in a cataleptic state; the most unimportant ideas can suddenly assume the character of delusions. Mr. N. tries in vain to dismiss them by directing his thoughts to subjects that interest him deeply. These trivial ideas remain, reappear endlessly in his mind as a perpetual nightmare. "These thoughts," he said to me, "are like the songs that we hum involuntarily, although not aloud, nevertheless mentally, and for hours, even days, without being able to stop."

It is worthy of note that in this case the fixed nature of the ideas is completely independent from the emotions. They are, as I have said, completely indifferent; they do not even excite his curiosity. Thus, for example, Mr. N. took a long walk outside the institution one day with his servant. He invited him to drink a little wine and water with him. He said to himself: "This man has accepted my offer, perhaps because he likes wine!" And this thought would not leave him for several days. It tormented him endlessly. Mr. N. said to himself thousands and thousands of times: "But what do I care if this man likes wine or not? What am I going to make of it? Why does it disturb me? Whence comes this notion that haunts me and, worse still, affects me as deeply as the most depressing thought?" Mr. N. confided this new whim to me. He was convinced that the way to get rid of it was to tell it to his servant. But at the same time he feared that a more ridiculous thought would soon replace it. I advised him not to talk about it, and for more than thirty-six hours he was tormented by it. Finally it made way for a thought of another kind: one evening, sitting down at the table, Mr. N. noticed that a lady with whom he frequently dined was wearing a blouse with gold buttons, a departure from her usual style.

Mr. N. asked himself: "Now, why is that lady wearing a blouse today?" From then on there was room in his mind for only this thought. The image of the lady in the blouse never left his mind, and she aroused erotic thoughts that upset him greatly.

Mr. N. was particularly tormented at night by his *fixations,* as he called them. It was then that he felt most intensely a sensation of a peculiar nature that unfailingly signaled the appearance of his extravagant thoughts. Mr. N. described it as follows: "It is like a sheet of electric fluid that envelops me from head to foot, a kind of general trembling. I have dizzy spells, I am light-headed, my head spins. There are moments when I could compare my person to a harp string that has been sharply plucked." All this is characteristic; there is no need for me to stress it.

The illness has followed an obvious course of remission, at least since we have been observing it. Relapses are invariably announced by a strong excitement. The patient's features, which usually are perfectly calm, become mobile and anxious. His eyes brighten. His face pales. Mr. N. cannot stay still and squirms in his chair. His words are rushed; they are not always in harmony with his thoughts, but they are still not incoherent. The *fixations* are numerous then. Mr. N. despairs more and more of being cured. He bemoans his state and accuses himself.

I now summarize the points made above.

(1) Prior to the facts reported, whose number it would have been easy (but tedious) to increase, *self-observation* (observation by the inner consciousness) enabled us to establish that the dissociation of ideas and the dream state that is its natural consequence constituted the primary source, the basic psychic fact of delusions.

(2) We have established that these delusions have an identical source whether one considers them from their origin or at various stages of the illness.

It remains for us to speak of a fact of mental pathology of great importance which supports the thesis I have just developed.

We know that in the great majority of cases, if the partial delirium is prolonged, the individuals who are affected by it end up in total *dementia.* Now, from the psychic point of view, there is little difference between the delirium of the demented and that of the manics. In one case as in the other, the intellectual damage weighs equally on the mental faculties. I am not mistaking the difference in the nature of this damage in both mania and dementia; I certainly do not confuse the abundance of thoughts, the excessive activity, the energy of memories and imagination that one finds in one case, with the weakening of the intellect, of the memory, and of the imagination that is seen in the other case. However, in both cases the psychic result is essentially the same: the incoherence, the dissociation of ideas, the impossibility of making judgments, and so forth.

From these considerations, is it not obvious that delusions which constitute what is conveniently called "partial delirium" or "monomania" have no existence *per se,* but, like the other fundamental phenomena of delirium, depend essentially on a general damage to the faculties? The proof of this lies in the duration of the illness; the damage always becomes evident after having been concealed by the more extravagant ideas which the general disturbance emphasizes.

In closing these considerations on partial delirium, we shall say a few words on the psychic nature of delusions.

Until now, delusions have been only superficially observed, in their external expression rather than their intrinsic nature. By saying that patients hold some strong conviction, it is thought that the whole phenomenon is explained without ever determining what mental combinations have triggered this same phenomenon.

In my opinion, however simple it may seem, whatever appearance of reason surrounds it, the delusion can only be the result of a profound change of the intellect, of a *general* upheaval of the faculties. It is the sign of a total transformation of the thinking process, at least within the limits of certain ideas. Sometimes, especially recently, it has been mistaken for a mere error in thinking. This stands in contradiction to all psychological notions.

An insane man *does not fool himself.* He functions intellectually in a sphere essentially different from ours, from one *in qua movemur et sumus.*[xvi] He holds a conviction against which neither the reasoning of someone else nor his own can prevail, any more than any argument or thought of the waking state can correct the reasoning and thoughts of the dream state.

The same difference exists between the psychotic man and the sane

---

[xvi] "in which we exist and operate"

man (in the same individual) as between the man who dreams and the man who is awake. Delusions are only detached parts, episodic phenomena of a dream state that, within the limits of these ideas, continue into the waking state. Common language has always documented this truth, particularly by designating psychotics who are dominated by these delusions as *dreamers*. And, worthy of note, these patients themselves refer to these ideas by calling them dreams. When they recover, they recall them as portions of a rather bizarre, more or less prolonged, dream.

One cannot easily concede that an individual who is aware of his surroundings can yet be in a dream state when he expresses bizarre thoughts, contrary to common sense. Nevertheless, this partial dream state is real and dominated by a few ideas. To convince oneself of this, one can submit briefly to the influence of hashish, an experience which will prove that one can simultaneously be in a state of dream and yet, because of his surroundings, be in possession of his judgment.

VII. Sixth Phenomenon: Damage to the Emotions

With hashish, the affective faculties reach the same degree of overexcitement as do the intellectual faculties. The emotions have the mobility and, at the same time, the "tyranny of ideas." The individual loses the power to resist his violent feelings until finally the mind itself reaches the point of incoherence.

In order to study these emotions more thoroughly, I will examine them separately: (1) those related to what we recall from the past and (2) those related to what affects us now in the present.

In the second category we include the irascibility that leads us to seize upon any cause capable of exciting our anger, hate, and worst instincts, along with the feeling that causes us to exaggerate our sentiments of friendship and gratitude, our joys, sadness, hopes, fears, terrors. Under these conditions, a fact that ordinarily would at most have aroused our discontent now sends us immediately into a rage. This mounting rage, which is easily controlled in a normal condition, reaches extreme proportions. If something frightens us, we are assailed by fears and irrational anxieties. One day in the middle of a very intense hashish intoxication, my ears were suddenly struck by the sound of bells. This was hardly an hallucination but, being in a sad mood, I interpreted this sound, of which I would not normally have been aware, as the tolling of a funeral bell.

> I fall into a state of panphobia. I am suddenly overtaken by an inexplicable terror from which I seek in vain to escape. I demand that they close the window, not that I want to leap from that window, but I fear that this desire might possess me. I am fearful of various antique guns which I have scarcely noticed until now hanging on the wall. I wonder if they are not meant to hurt me, perhaps to kill me. The presence of several friends does nothing to calm me. With the exception of one, I deeply distrust them; I detest them without knowing why. I ridicule everything they say. In short, every loathsome passion is seething in my soul.
>
> (*Memoire on the Treatment of Hallucinations*)

Like the ideas to which they relate, emotions overpower the intellect because their action is exerted alone, without the discriminating influence of reflective thought. Emotions are blind, instinctive impulses, upon which consciousness has no effect.

I do not believe in any intrinsic damage to the emotions. The damage is only apparent and follows the injury to the intellect. It derives from the pathological state that we have indicated—that is to say, from the drug. As long as the association of ideas is regular, as long as the uncontrollable speed of perception does not trouble the mind, the emotions are not perturbed; they remain under the control of the will. The unthinking state, which is the necessary consequence of the drug, unleashes all the power.

Such is what self-awareness reveals, as does careful observation of mental illness. Nothing equals the mettle and the violence of emotions in manics except the extreme incoherence of their thoughts. Everytime their emotions are openly and forcefully conveyed, it must be attributed to their state of excitement. We presently have under observation a lady who, for several months, has been the victim of delusions and imaginary terrors. She was reasonably calm during her first month in this institution; she had to be questioned a great deal before she would release any information about her dominant thoughts. Then, during a spell of cold weather, a very active state of excitement developed. Her thoughts, usually relevant to the subject of her delirium, were disconnected and rapid, her movements abrupt and jerky. A nervous trembling shook her limbs; the fears, the imaginary terrors of the patient, became overwhelming. She was in the state of one who is suddenly seized by the worst terror, who, in his confusion, does not know what he is saying or doing.

All writers have postulated the existence of a basic trauma of the emotions in certain cases of madness.

Pinel was the first to state the existence of a special delirium bearing *exclusively* upon the emotions:

> One can have a justified admiration for the writings of Locke and yet agree that his notions about mania are incomplete, in that he regards it as inseparable from delirium. I held his opinion at the time I was conducting my research on this malady at Bicêtre, and I was surprised to see several psychotics who never showed an impairment of their judgment but who were tormented by an instinctive rage, *as if the emotional faculties had been damaged.*

Esquirol shares Pinel's opinion, but with reservation. He does not rule out all intellectual damage:

> The signs of reasoning monomania are the alteration of habits, of character, of emotions. In ordinary monomania it is evident that the intellect is damaged and that this damage perturbs the emotions and the actions. In reasoning monomania, the intellect *is not basically damaged,* since it participates in the acts of the patient, inasmuch as he is always ready to justify his feelings and his actions.

Calmeil [xvii] is even more cautious than his master, because he recognizes that "in mental monomania the illness of the intellect is difficult to comprehend and to characterize. Mental illness affects primarily the emotions and the instincts, and its impact on the intellect is not easy to evaluate." (Published in *Dictionary* in 25 vols. Art: Monomania.)

[xvii] See Appendix.

Finally, Dr. Prichard, an English writer noted for his excellent works on mental illness, refers to a mental illness that he describes as "morbid perversion of the feelings, affections, and active powers, *without any illusion or erroneous convictions* impressed upon the understanding."

I regret to disagree with the writers I have just cited, but I believe that without the benefit of self-observation they have given too much importance to simple appearances. Only the intellect is basically damaged in mental illness; the perturbation of the emotions is secondary to the perturbation in thinking. The impairment of judgment and the dissociation of ideas are the primary source of any damage to the emotions. This impairment can disappear in the course of the illness, but it reappears from time to time. When it ceases, the other symptoms disappear rapidly. When the symptoms have disappeared, the patient has recovered.

Esquirol has remarked that the kind of delirium at issue here frequently becomes manic excitement and often ends up as dementia.

The "exciting" action of hashish is exerted on feelings experienced long ago, which have left only slight memories in the mind. A feeling, believed to be completely extinct, suddenly revives or surges with such power that one feels under the influence of some spell. This is particularly true of amorous feelings, probably because of the longing for happiness caused by hashish. The strength of memories, which lends a kind of reality to past events, and the imagination, which embellishes the object of our affections, explain the changes in the emotions of love.

Hashish, in this case, can have the strength of a love potion, so that, while it does not give birth to love, it endows this feeling with such unexpected energy and activity that something will remain, even after the effects of the love potion have disappeared.

Here I could tell many a story that would support what I have just said; it is more fitting that I do not. Stories of this kind have a scandalous quality and would be out of place in a serious work such as this.

I hasten to add, at the risk of disappointing, or perhaps with the certainty of disappointing some, that these effects mentioned are exclusively intellectual. The imagination bears the burden; the senses are not involved. Plato himself could not have dreamed of purer and more spiritual passions than those kindled by hashish.

VIII. Seventh Phenomenon: Irresistible Impulses

Impulses, those instinctive urges which build up in us almost without our knowledge, acquire an extraordinary power under the influence of hashish, one that is practically irresistible if the toxic action is very strong.

Impulses are like passions; they draw their strength from the excitement, from the mental disturbance that impedes regular, free association of ideas. They dominate the intellect all the more if the incoherence is more pronounced and if their action is more isolated and more independent.

Always mobile and fleeting when the toxic action is first felt, impulses can have, as the ideas that give birth to them, their periods of fixity. But they are irresistible only when the basic excitement reappears.

I shall remind you at this time of a fact I have already mentioned. Seeing an open window in my room, I came to believe that, if I wanted to, I could throw myself from that window. I asked that it be closed, though I had no intention of committing such an act; I was afraid that the idea might come to me; behind this fear I already felt a growing impulse, and I had an inner feeling that I might have followed it, given an even stronger excitement.

The action of hashish is not continuous. During the brief period of remission, the same thought was in my mind, but *not* the fear of giving in to the absurd idea of jumping out the window. I had difficulty in explaining even to myself how such a fear had occurred to me. Nevertheless this same fear reappeared with the return of the "excitement."

Using as a guide the facts just revealed, we will see that things occur in the same manner in the morbid impressions of psychotics.

A type of delirium which has recently been of particular concern in medico-legal studies is one in which the patients seem carried away by irresistible impulses without suffering any damage to their judgment. Here, as in many other cases, observation has been superficial and hence incomplete. The observers judged the patient on external signs that could only be insufficient. When the patients spoke, what they said was considered negligible. Only the most obvious and most external symptoms were studied. The alteration of the will, the irresistibility of instinctual drives, is inconceivable without some injury to the intellect.

All philosophers, not only Locke, have posited this truth *a priori*. We have confirmed it by self-observation, which has taught us that impulses become irresistible, that the will is wiped out insofar as there is a disturbance of the judgment when the very foundation of our mental nature is shaken, when the basis of normal activity, the unity of the ego, is destroyed. So long as this unity is preserved, so long as self-awareness is not extinguished, the individual is in complete command of his instinctual drives. Whenever, and however briefly, these drives are not contained, self-awareness has vanished or been damaged.

Listen to the patients whom Esquirol questioned on this subject: "These patients deplored the directions in which they were so irresistibly drawn, but all admitted that they felt something inside them that they could not account for, *that their mind was obscured, that their reasoning was hopelessly confused.*"

The impulses of psychotics are not always compulsive, although they should never be held responsible for following these impulses. The actions of psychotics are often the perfectly logical consequences of false convictions. At other times, a particular disposition of the mind forces the patient to submit to his impulses mechanically, without realizing what he is doing, as if, in fact, he were *in a dream*, to use his favorite expression.

This last fact has a significance that everyone will understand, especially in light of the moral responsibility imposed by the society upon its members. Without entering into a medico-legal discussion, we must at least emphasize the fact itself.

Let me repeat: neither the will nor the instinctive drives become *irresistible* as a result of an injury affecting them alone. There is basic damage to the mental processes, a damage that is profound but in certain cases so transitory that the patients themselves can hardly describe it. And yet this lesion is essentially the same one from which derive all the manifestations of the most obvious and most typical psychoses. This basic lesion is the primary fact of madness, what I call excitement. There are some people who, after having successfully struggled for a long time against certain urges, suddenly surrender to them completely. And yet, neither before nor after is there evidence of any noticeable change of the faculties, however, flashing through as it does without leaving any traces, the excitement violently disturbs the intellect and momentarily annihilates free will. In many aspects this pathological fact is comparable to the "fixities" of epileptics, although less striking.

I have no need to review the thousand and one causes that can bring about this excitement; that would require reviewing well-known etiological details. But I shall speak of a fact identical to the one we are concerned with, that occurs in front of our eyes every day and that we never think to relate to pathological impulses. The most common effect of alcoholic intoxication is to make us submit with an extreme facility and with an often compulsive urge to impulses that, until then, we had controlled and resisted. Does not justice have occasion to punish people who (unable to find in themselves the strength to commit cold-blooded crime) want to borrow from intoxicating drinks the strength they lack? In the Orient, *Cannabis* extract, opium, thorn apple, and other substances are used to produce this "excitement" of the intellect.

We can induce this excitement at will with external agents. Experience has proved for a long time that pathological causes, developed within the very depths of the body, can produce the same excitement, with an even greater intensity and with changes whose secret only nature knows.

It appears then that the most puzzling fact of mental pathology—the irresistibility of urges without apparent intellectual lesion—is no longer a mystery, for it has the same point of departure, the same origin, namely "excitement," as any other. Presented thus, with its own characteristics and in its true light, the mental illness called "reasoning monomania" loses all its strangeness and—to put it bluntly—its *absurdity,* which shocked even those who saw examples of it every day, and it can now be classified among the ordinary, well-known mental illnesses.

The following represent a few cases in support of what I have just said.

An honest shoemaker, a family man, presents himself on his own at the Bicêtre hospital. He asks to be treated for an ailment that he dates back for more than twenty years. There is no obvious cause. There is no mental illness in his family;

none of his relatives is given to drink or suffers from any nervous affliction. He is the father of two children, both of whom enjoy the best of health; he does not recall ever having been seriously ill himself. His stature is small and slender, but he is well built; his open and somewhat animated face, his frank and overt expression, in no way convey the terrible thoughts he has been harboring for so long.

"Since you come to the hospital of your own free will, you must know your illness. What is bothering you?"

"I have bad thoughts. I have heard that there are places where they cure them; that is why I am here."

"Just what are those thoughts?"

"Well, I am a shoemaker by trade; sometimes I work hard, because I have to support my family. In those moments when I have my head bent over my work the thought comes to me to kill my wife and my children. Sometimes this idea is so powerful that I fear I shall give in to it; I throw my cutting tool and my hammer far from me and I leave the room."

"Aren't you warned by anything, by some particular sensation, of the arrival of these bad thoughts?"

"God, no. They come to me just like that, unexpectedly."

"At those moments you feel completely normal, you feel nothing in your head?"

"Ah, yes. I feel something there in the pit of my stomach. And then I choke, I cannot breathe, my head is hot, I have goose bumps, I am dizzy, confused, I cannot see. But not for long. Sometimes I also feel a tingling in my hands, my arms . . . I have always said my blood was plaguing me."

"And your thoughts? How long do they last?"

"That depends. Sometimes, when I get up and go to the window it is all over. But other times it lingers on."

"Is it always like this when these thoughts overtake you?"

"Yes, but not always with such strength. About six months ago, I was ill with a fever. I was very troubled and I wanted very much to get well."

"Do you hear any noises?"

"No, not at the present. But about twelve years ago I recall having felt a breeze, a draft on this side of my head [the right]. It started that way. I was harvesting crops, my head was bare, in an intense heat. I stooped over and felt something like a strong blast of air on that side."

"Couldn't you compare what you felt with something other than a blast of air? That isn't very clear. Did you feel pain?"

"No, but I was confused."

"Did you have to stop working?"

"Ah, yes. I shook myself and it was gone."

"Did you think then of killing your children?"

"No, only when I returned home."

"You are very troubled today; do you know why?"

"No."

Here is another fact no less curious than the preceding—no less conclusive. It was revealed by Mr. Segalas at the April 2, 1844 session of the Medical Society of the Temple.

N. . . had thought several times of committing suicide. The manual labor he was forced to perform in order to live (he was a glovemaker) was a burden to him. He was unhappy about the circumstances in which destiny and the accident of his birth had placed him. He had gradually become disgusted with life, and the only reason he was still alive was that he wanted to find a way of doing away with himself without having to undergo too much pain. Once he tried to drown himself, but he was saved.

His behavior had always been above reproach and he had never been considered eccentric.

Here is how he describes his most recent suicide attempt; I copy verbatim from his manuscript: "Having decided to asphyxiate myself, I closed the doors of my room, and started to plug all the cracks with paper. While gathering my paper, *I was surprised to find myself singing.* It was hardly an act of bravado or cheerfulness, but my preparations took some time, and I have never been able to think of one thing for long *without being distracted.* There were some moments when *I forgot what I was doing and why I was doing it.* . . . This is a strange and unique aspect of my character. . . ."

At the very moment at which his deadly impulses dominate him, when he is coolly preparing to take his own life, N. . . . is surprised (this expression has a marvelous strength) to be singing without knowing why; he is distracted, he thinks of other things.

Is this not *excitement?* Is it not the dissociation of ideas, the intellectual disturbance, brief or long-lasting, that deprives us of our control over ourselves, making us the helpless pawns of our impulses?

As we have seen, N. . . . is scarcely surprised by his condition. He is not inclined to fear it as a symptom of madness, especially since it does not prevent him from carrying out his determination to kill himself.

We have said that N. . . . had already felt the urge to commit suicide several times, that he had even attempted it. But he also said that a state of *distraction* (as he calls it) was peculiar to his character, that he had never been able to concentrate on the same thing for very long.[4]

---

[4] I would like to take this opportunity to mention a problem that has been debated at some length but has not been conclusively resolved.

Is suicide, in most cases, the result of a delirium, a clear act of madness, undistinguishable, in its origin and its nature, from the extravagant actions of most mental patients? Esquirol answered affirmatively, founding his argument on a host of cases he had witnessed. He thus induced conclusions from facts that were interpreted differently from their appearance; he had seen many individuals attempt suicide in a state of unsuspected madness. Esquirol was referring to obvious forms of madness, usually cases of depression. He was still more explicit when, speaking of acute suicide, he declared that the actions caused by a passion that has reached a state of delirium, are equally delirious. "Does the delirium of passions allow reflection? Is not a man acquitted by our laws for committing, in a moment of blind passion, an act that would have otherwise been punished? The actions of a man carried away by a violent passion are not considered as being accomplished by a free agent and are judged as acts of momentary delirium." There is truth in these words that express a generally accepted idea about the delirium of passions; however, in spite of the high authority of the man who pronounced these words, they are not universally accepted. The exaltation of passions is not always an assured sign of madness nor a sufficient reason for relieving the victim of all responsibility for his actions. There are two reasons for this:

(1) Esquirol's statement proves the fact by the fact itself. He establishes a principle that remains to be proven, namely, that when passions reach a certain degree they can be assimilated to madness. It is assuredly insufficient to say that "the mind is strongly affected by a violent and sudden emotion, that the reason is perturbed, that man loses his sense of *ego*, that he is in a state of delirium, etc. . . ." There is nothing so self-evident in this observation that its conclusion must

IX. Eighth Phenomenon: Illusions and Hallucinations

I beg the indulgence of the reader who may tire of my calling his attention so often to the same subject. However, in approaching the important question of illusions and hallucinations, I cannot but repeat again what I have already said.

I am not one of those outside observers who have studied mental illness on the surface and drawn faulty conclusions from what they have gathered on the origin and the development of these phenomena.

---

be accepted on face value: scientific precision demands more. It requires experimental proof of the psychological modification that is claimed as the cause of the act. In other words the illness must be shown, bared, clearly identified before it can be recognized as existing.

(2) One must admit that the facts quoted above are not necessarily identifiable as belonging to the category of those that characterize the overexcitement of passion.

Many suicides cannot be accounted for as results of intense passions. I am referring not only to suicides caused by fixed ideas, but to those committed by individuals whose mental faculties were not affected at any time either before or after their attempts at suicide, who had never been subjected to any passion in their entire lives.

We will now return to our first proposition. Most suicides, including those committed by individuals recognized to be sane in mind and those which appear to be the logical consequence of an untenable, even desperate, situation, are authentic acts of madness. The truth of this proposition, considered from the point of view of our thesis on irresistible impulses and based on information supplied by self-observation, will be challenged by few.

Indeed, what is needed to convert the simple wish, the mere thought of seeking an end to one's miseries in death, into an irresistible impulse, then into an act?

We have just seen it. All that is needed is a small amount of "excitement," namely, that intellectual modification, so serious in reality and so minimal in appearance that those who experience it believe they have been simply *distracted*. The external features of this phenomenon are so unclear, evasive, and fleeting that they can escape even a keen observer.

We know that a multitude of causes can produce a state of excitement; we know the importance and the considerable value of hereditary and acquired *predispositions;* we know that *predisposed* individuals need only an unusual preoccupation, a sudden, unexpected sensation, a light emotion, an irregularity in a body function, (it is impossible in many cases to find other causes for a clearly characterized psychosis) to trigger a state of "excitement."

We can, therefore, declare that the number of individuals who take their own lives without being mentally ill, i.e., those who are in full possession of their mental capabilities and of their free will, is extremely small.

I tell what I have observed in myself, and I say it with the same assurance of being correct as anyone who reports what he thinks, imagines, remembers, and so forth.

To those who, after having read my words, still have considerable doubt, I can only repeat: I understand your doubts because, in the case of psychological matters, I know it is impossible to understand what you have not experienced. With illusions and hallucinations, just as with the phenomena with which we were previously concerned, I can say one thing, and you will be convinced if you follow it. Do what I did: take hashish, experiment on yourself, and see for yourself.

Now, the phenomenon that we still have to study does not escape the basic law that links all the principal phenomena of madness to this "excitement," which is the primary mental alteration, the primordial fact generating all mental illness. "Excitement" carries the seed of all mental pathology as the trunk of a tree, its branches, its leaves, and its flowers are contained in the grain.

Before Esquirol, illusions and hallucinations were treated as a single phenomenon. The distinction established by the master has been adopted by all psychiatrists. We will study them separately.

Illusions

Progressively, as "excitement" grows, our mind shuts itself off from external impressions to concentrate more and more on subjective ones. In brief, as this kind of metamorphosis takes place, drawing us away from real life to throw us into a world where there is no reality except that created by our memory and our imagination; progressively, one becomes the toy, first of simple illusions, and then of true hallucinations, which are like distant sounds coming from an imaginary and fantastic world.

When any object, alive or inanimate, strikes our sight or when a sound, such as the song of a bird, the explosion of a firearm, or the ringing of bells, strikes our ears while the "excitement" is still weak, we feel very strongly that two distinct phenomena are occurring in our minds. (1) We have seen, we have heard, clearly and distinctly, as happens in the ordinary state. (2) Then suddenly, as the result of certain similarities known or unknown to us, the image of another object and the sensation of another sound are awakened within us. As a result of these intracerebral impressions, because of the action of memory and imagination, the mind pauses, soon confusing the two sensations as one, covering the real sensation with the imaginary one and projecting the latter upon the external object. Thus: (1) a sensory impression, (2) following it immediately, a purely cerebral sensation caused solely by the action of the imagination.[5]

The external features of an illusion, with the tremendously varied forms it is likely to assume, will be necessarily borrowed from the particular nature of the preoccupations and habitual thoughts of the individual.

It is conceivable indeed that images or ideas that have made the strongest impression on the mind are the first to be awakened or, as Bonnet would have said, that the cerebral fibers which vibrate most frequently are more readily disturbed than others. A few examples should be given.

The face of a total stranger attracts our attention. In some way this face resembles that of another person whose features are familiar. This resemblance, however slight, suffices to arouse the memory of that person; this memory, with the image from which it is inseparable, has all the vividness of the sensory impression, for the mind perceives it in the same manner as it perceives in the dream state.

From then on, what we have seen with the eyes of the mind replaces what we have seen with the eyes of the body. The creations of our imagination have taken the place of reality. And if all reflective thinking is denied us by the violence of the cerebral disturbance, the two sensations are blended into a single one, and the error is unavoidable.

As I was walking near the Opera one night, I thought I recognized five or six persons of my acquaintance among the strollers; among them stood one whom I had lost track of for many years but whom I had had occasion to speak of often at that particular time. However, no sooner had I focused my attention on the face of the person whom I thought I recognized than the fantasy image vanished.

---

[5] Writers have generally confused these two essential but perfectly distinct conditions of illusions; they have sought the roots of the illusion in the morbid sensations from which the illusion develops. The features of the illusion are variable, as infinite as our memories and the creations of our imagination. Its initial cause, as of all mental disorders, is essentially invariable. I shall return to this subject later.

I have also experienced illusions which differ from the previous one in many respects. Several times during a rather lively state of intoxication, as I gazed at a portrait I saw it come to life suddenly. The head moved slightly and seemed to want to detach itself from the canvas. The entire face assumed an expression that only life can confer. The eyes were especially expressive; I saw them revolve in their orbits in order to follow my movements. The first time this experience happened to me, I could not hold back a cry of fright. I retreated several steps, crying out, "It is fantastic! That portrait is alive! It is magic!" The experience occurred two or three times before I finally could explain the phenomenon and analyze it objectively.

Then I realized that I gradually ceased to see the image in front of my eyes. Imperceptibly I was seeing it only as if it were floating on the clouds of a faint dream. Soon I saw in a dream the very person in the painting and he, like all the products of the imagination, impressed me more forcefully than the portrait.

Here is the strange illusion that I experienced in a *fantasia* from which I have already recounted several incidents. Before I had begun to feel the effects of the hashish, I had stared intently at a very beautiful engraving depicting, as nearly as I can recall, a cavalry battle. We sat down to dine; I found myself sitting with my back to the engraving. After repressing several times the intoxication that was gradually taking hold of me, I stood up, and putting my hand to the back of my head I cried, "I do not like horses that kick, even in a painting. That one [pointing with my finger to one of the horses in the picture] kicked me." My words, as you can well imagine, were greeted with gales of laughter. I laughed with the others; then, reflecting for a moment, I found within me the image of a spirited, rearing horse, but pale and faint like the images of a fading dream. My illusion was nothing more than a dream, but a dream as swift as a thought, and provoked by an external cause, a sensory impression. This last feature, without distinguishing it from an ordinary dream, made it a true manifestation of mental illness.

All these examples of visual illusions have the same character. "Excitement" is the basic, generative fact of the illusion, whose nature will then be modified by a person's particular character, his habitual or dominant ideas. Whatever the condition of our mind, whatever emotions stir us, if no "excitement" occurs, we will not have illusions.

The "excitement" develops illusions, which reflect the nature of the ideas and feelings that are prevalent in us at the time. It is wrong, from both the etiological and the therapeutic points of view, to ascribe too much importance to the nature of illusions that can, at the very most, lead us to the real cause of the trouble.

When, in the features of an old woman, I saw the freshest and most charming face, I was certain that the subjective image which my over-active imagination had made me see in a dream was taking the place of the real image. I told myself there were two explanations for this illusion. (1) In taking hashish, I thought all sensations had to be pleasant, everything had to be beautiful. (2) The image of a pretty woman, by the admiration that it generates and the emotion that it causes, etches itself deeply in our minds and consequently can be reproduced very easily.

When, later, I thought I saw a small, deformed man at my side, I recalled that, at the time, I had been seeing regularly a person whose physical features, without actually being irregular, were far from conforming with the excellent qualities of heart and mind with which he was endowed. It was his image, albeit imperfect, that was summoned by the form sitting near me.[6]

I have reported above, as an example of a delusion, the case of a person who saw himself hanging from the wall of his room. The character of that illusion is explained by the fear which someone had thoughtlessly inspired in him that he would die of poisoning. To change the nature of the illusion and make the hashish user see something other than his dead body in the bolster, it would have sufficed to banish the thought of death that beset him and to direct his mind elsewhere.

One evening in Cairo, several young Europeans were returning home after a hashish party that had taken place at the home of one of them. The hashish was still acting. The long, crooked street they followed was, like all the streets in Cairo at night, deserted and very poorly lit.

---

[6] This illusion had, in many respects, the qualities of an hallucination: the image disappeared when my attention, even briefly, returned to the external object, then it would reappear vividly whenever my eyes were diverted from that object. Thus this image had, at times, its own existence, independent from the cause (the external object) which originally impressed it on the brain. From then on, did not the illusion become an hallucination?

However, our hashish eaters believed that they were participating in a nocturnal celebration and saw a magnificent illumination. Lights were shining through the wooden grillwork of the balconies; a crowd of noisy people, dressed in party clothes, were walking around.

What was the source of this phantasmagoria, of these illusions? . . . colored paper lanterns, hanging from the shops or held by some Arabs who were slowly and silently returning to their homes. But the party had been merry. It had been enlivened chiefly by memories of their homeland, of its brilliant celebrations, and their unique merry-making. These memories, modified by external impressions, had assumed a local color.

Like any other morbid mental phenomena (delusions, irresistible impulses, etc.), illusions are latent in an *excited* brain. They are virtually all there, and the most varied causes will conjure them.

Left to himself, the user of hashish will be influenced by everything that strikes his eyes and his ears. A word, a gesture, a look, a sound, or the slightest noise, by demanding his attention, will confer a special character on his illusions.

I have already said that a few words were sufficient to make me pass from joy, the most exaggerated happiness, to the blackest depression. This depression distorted and mirrored back all the objects that surrounded me: a plaid beret suggested to me the features of a bloody face; in a stove full of glowing coals I saw a glass of lemonade offered to me by one of my friends; in the faces of all close to me I saw pity and the darkest sorrow; finally I saw a light multiplied ten or twelve times around a bier in which I imagined myself lying.

A young lady, after one or two attacks of irrepressible laughter, looked attentively at the face of a gentleman seated beside her. "Well, well," she cried, "I have never told you this! Your eyes are almond-shaped and slanted like those of a Chinese." She laughed at the remark she had just made and added, "Oh my! What is that? Your nose is disproportionately big. How awful! I see little pagodas on it." A few minutes later the lady seemed very eager to sing. The "excitement" increased and I tried to turn her thoughts to a subject that would calm her. I reminded her of the first lines of a romantic song that she knew. She started to sing with intense feeling but suddenly, stopping short, she exclaimed with delight: "Little sheep, little sheep! Don't you see them there in front of me? Oh no, only I can see them! Have you driven me mad?" She was pointing to a red and white checkered mat spread out in front of the couch where she sat.

Illusions of hearing are infrequent with hashish. Rarely are sounds distorted or transformed into other sounds notably different from the original. On the other hand, auditory hallucinations are numerous, but they never develop except at the height of "excitement."

I have already noted that the sense of hearing becomes extremely sensitive, so that the slightest sound sometimes seems deafening and causes a disagreeable feeling. One day, wishing to determine to what extent one could remain master of oneself, even though the faculties were deeply disturbed, I went to visit some close friends with whom I felt at ease. First, I was besieged by many visual illusions. I paid little attention to them, but I found that everyone was talking or rather yelling loudly, which was horribly irritating. After about a half-hour or forty-five minutes, which seemed like a century, I made some excuse and left.

Sometimes sounds are not only magnified but they multiply as though they were repeated by an echo which amplifies them. One evening, in a garden, in 1842, it seemed that I heard, or rather *I did hear very distinctly,* the songs of a vast flock of birds. The garden was small; there was a single bird in it. It was a nightingale, whose song was only intermittent. However, I heard a continual twittering. I covered my ears; I continued to hear it, only less distinctly.

That same evening I heard something like a shooting, followed by the confused buzzing sounds made by large crowds of people. Momentarily overcome by this illusion, I cried out: "Listen! Someone is shooting! There is a riot in the street!" But quickly realizing my error, I sought to discover its cause, and I found that a servant had dropped something while tidying up a room which opened on the garden.

Another time, hearing bells ringing in a nearby church, I asked what it could be. Somebody answered, "Undoubtedly someone has died," and all of a sudden the last word echoed five or six times in my ears, as if each of the people in the room had repeated it in turn, in a rather lugubrious tone. At that time I was not completely sure of the innocuity of hashish. I feared that I had taken an overdose which would explain the nature of the illusion I have just described. This illusion, although only an illusion, was painful, and I must advise those who would experiment with hashish to take every precaution to avoid this experience.

What I have just said concerning auditory illusions shows the psychic phenomenon in its barest simplicity. I have never known myself nor observed in others illusions comparable to those experienced, although rarely, by psychotics. It would require carrying the *excitement* to a degree of intensity capable of destroying all traces of consciousness, and I admit that I have not yet dared go that far.

Be that as it may, the phenomena I have experienced and described present, upon analysis, the same elements as in visual illusions: (1) a sensory impression, which is a true physical sensation; (2) a second sensation that follows immediately, a sensation totally in the mind and purely subjective; and (3) an error in time that merges the two sensations, or rather forgets the first one, and only retains the second, from which results the distorted perception.[xviii]

As rapidly as these three phases of an illusion succeed one another, the mind perceives them distinctly and without confusion, not precisely when the phenomenon occurs but immediately after; consequently an impression of a dream remains and proceeds to repeat itself. In order to give a faithful account of an impression, one would say, *I dreamed that I heard*—a true statement that a psychotic changes to *I heard;* because he is deprived of consciousness (since a greater "excitement" has obliterated all thought in him), he naturally confuses the dream state with the waking state, or rather confuses the phenomena belonging to one or the other.

Illusions of General Sensibility: [xix] I have related several cases of this kind of illusion in my memoir on the treatment of hallucinations. I mentioned an individual who believed that he had been transformed into a steam engine piston, and a young artist who felt such an elasticity in his body that he thought he could enter a bottle and remain there in complete comfort. Once, after taking a very small dose of *dawamesc,* I felt so light that my feet hardly touched the ground when

---

[xviii] This is the first definition of what the psychologists call today "temporal disintegration." This mental condition is characterized by an impairment of immediate memory storage and a disintegration of sequential thought, which is essential for the proper interpretation of sensory perception.

[xix] These are illusions related to self-awareness of body image.

I walked. Another time, under the influence of a much larger dose, I felt my body inflate like a balloon and rise into the air. I spoke earlier of a student in my ward at Bicêtre, today a physician, who felt and saw his nervous fluid circulating in his chest through the network of his solar plexis. Examining his hands with close attention, he saw the skin furrowed with ridges and desiccated like that of certain cadavers.

General sensory illusions seem to defy the analytic study to which we subjected the similar phenomena which relate to the senses of vision and hearing. The psychological reason for the latter phenomena (the simultaneous arousal of two sensations, one external and the other subjective, one true and belonging to reality and the other imaginary and born of a dream state) does not apply, as far as we are qualified to say, to illusions of the general sensorium.

When I felt my body grow in size, inflate like a balloon,[7] this sensation, however unusual, could not be distinguished from ordinary sensation. It was impossible to analyze it, to distinguish the actual sensation from the product of my imagination. Therefore, there is reason to believe that illusions of general sensibility are the result of special sensory alterations, quite as real as those that take place in the most normal sensations. Only the origin of these changes differs.

Nevertheless, an interesting psychic phenomenon cancels, in part, the exceptional nature of illusions of general sensitivity. Contrary to what happens in ordinary sensations, it is not at the periphery of the organs or at the nerve endings that one places the source of the abnormal sensation which constitutes the illusion: this sensation seems to be concentrated entirely in the brain. It develops in the central nervous system, then radiates to the organs.

Thus, when I felt my body inflate, my hands, which I rapidly passed over my body, could not confirm this sensation. They informed me

---

[7] I have not mentioned the point of departure of this illusion. In 1925, as I was convalescing from a grave typhoid fever, my right leg developed an edematous swelling which was extremely slow to subside in spite of the enlightened care of my noble teacher, Mr. Bretonneau. Since then the limb has never recovered its normal form and still is slightly larger than the other leg. Feeling some cramps in the right calf, I touched it with my hand and it was then that my illusion occurred.

that my body had retained its usual size at the very moment I *felt* it increase *inordinately*. This contradiction between my touch and my subjective perception resulted in a strange, ambivalent experience.

I felt light enough to float, my feet barely touching the ground; I distinctly heard in my head, and with some pain, the sound of my steps on the ground. I also felt, feebly, a sensation well known to most hashish users: sudden flashes of pleasant warmth rising to my head. My brain seemed to enlarge, and I thought I was leaving the ground. Such is my own experience with general sensory illusions. The same sensations occur in many normal individuals in the course of their dreams.

These sensations are reported by psychotics in a different form and somewhat more completely, but they are not different in nature; this difference is due to secondary psychological conditions, which I could have produced by increasing the dose of hashish.

Had I reached a degree of intellectual disturbance sufficiently intense to obliterate my consciousness, as happens in psychotics, my illusions could have become the point of departure for delusions similar to those observed in the most severe psychosis. I could have thought I was a bird or a balloon, ready to be carried away by a gust of wind, punctured by the slightest shock, or ignited by a spark. I could have imagined I had the power to fly through the air, to leap through space at top speed—in a word, I could have abandoned myself to the most fantastic notions connected with the dominant illusion.

This is precisely what happened to the young man who thought he had been transformed into a steam engine piston. A morbid sensation and the natural but ridiculous consequence derived from it were the two basic components of his illusion.

Several persons, after taking hashish, have claimed that their brain was boiling and that the top of their skull was rising and falling as though lifted by jets of steam. I myself have felt something similar to this. It is a most frightening sensation for those who are not yet accustomed to hashish.

A young physician, terrified, pressed his head with both hands as if to keep it from bursting, crying: "I am lost; I have lost my head; I am going crazy!" Fortunately, his fears were promptly replaced by the wildest kind of joy.

Therefore, one should not confuse fixed ideas or delusions with the abnormal sensation that constitutes, properly speaking, the basis of an illusion. Delusions are the consequence of illusions, consequences so unnecessary that they can be found linked to totally abnormal sensations. This was the case, for example, to cite one out of a thousand, of that woman who, deeply depressed by a cancer of the stomach, was convinced that some kind of animal was devouring her entrails.

It is obviously wrong to include such cases among general sensory illusions. These are *delusions*, not *illusions*.

One cannot be too circumspect in examining psychic cases. They are easy to confuse with one another, their distinctive qualities being hardly distinguishable. In the case of sensory illusions, one must remain within the category of sensations, abnormal sensations that is, and nothing else.

These sensations rarely give way to absurd beliefs, such as those involving sorcerers, incubi, and succubi. These thoughts and beliefs depend essentially on that general state of the brain which I have called "excitement," as abundantly demonstrated at the beginning of this work.

I now conclude the section on illusions. In the following section, dealing with *hallucinations*, we will again have the opportunity to evaluate the nature of this pathological phenomenon of illusions. I will show that illusions can be considered as true hallucinations. Along with the action of external objects upon our senses, hallucinations develop only on the stimulation of a sensory impression.

In an illusion (to use the word in its abstract sense), the mind is bordering on a dream state. The imagination has not yet shaken off its dependence on external objects; it needs their support to act with the necessary energy when the dream state is complete. This state is complete with hallucinations. The mind has entered right away, so to speak, into the subjective life. The hallucination is only a phenomenon, an accident of this novel life, similar to the fixed ideas and the other phenomena discussed before.

I would like to indicate still another difference between illusions and hallucinations. The illusion is necessarily limited, like the sensation to which it relates. One sees and one hears in a dream because of the effect of external impressions upon the senses of vision and hearing; the imagination acts within the limits of the sensory activity.

The hallucination, at least according to our concept, and as I will describe it later, encompasses all of the faculties of the mind; its only limits are those that nature has placed upon the activity of mental functions. In other words, all mental abilities can be *hallucinated*, and not just certain abilities, such as those connected with the perception, for example, of sounds or images.

Also, there is not, in my opinion, an *hallucinatory state* rather than an *hallucination*. I will use the latter expression, nevertheless, as have other writers, but it will indicate nothing more than the accidental phenomena of a general change in the mental faculties. The hallucinatory state derives from the *essential fact* which is the common source of all the anomalies of the mind. It is a phenomenon of subjective existence, of intracerebral life or dream state.

The "hallucinator" hears his own thoughts, as he sees and hears the creations of his imagination and as he is moved by impressions he finds in his memory. I do not mean to say that the thoughts and memories of the "hallucinator" become *sensations*. This would amount to saying that, with all our mental faculties in their normal state, our thoughts sometimes resound in our mind and we hear them as if our ears were impressed by sounds.

In my opinion there is no transformation other than the one which changes external or real life into the subjective or imaginary life, the waking state into the dream state. There is a general modification involving all the faculties. And only this kind of transformation explains all the phenomena of the hallucinatory state.

I cannot imagine a special state of mind in which one could not say why or how a memory or judgment is changed into a sensory impression—or, in other words, how a memory or judgment can act upon the senses in the manner of an external object.

This theory is based on the manner in which patients express themselves when they give an account of their hallucinations, when they say: *I have seen, heard, or sensed*. I feel this is either a false interpretation of their statements, or an error of the patients themselves, who say and believe, in effect, that they have, for example, seen or sensed, whereas in reality they have only seen with the eyes of imagination, as one sees in a dream, which is just as genuine in certain respects as in the waking state. Unaware of their condition, incapable of really understanding and analyzing their mental condition, they transfer to real life what is imaginary, and believe that they have felt in a waking state what they have felt only in a dream; consequently, they express themselves according to this false conviction.

Hallucinations

Esquirol was the first to make a serious and elaborate study of hallucinations, and he has thrown abundant light on this phenomenon, perhaps the most interesting of all the phenomena of mental illness.

Following in the footsteps of Esquirol, several physicians, most of them his pupils, have turned their attention in the same direction. The field of hallucinations has been thoroughly explored. I have been among the explorers, and in 1840 I broached the question of the treatment of that mental aberration.

Presently we plan to study hallucinations from a new perspective. This does not reflect on the talent and the skill of our predecessors, who did not have the necessary methods of investigation. This point of view, from which we have already considered the principal phenomena of delirium is that of the *pathogenesis* of hallucinations, that is to say, the psychocerebral conditions, the mechanisms which produce this phenomenon.

In the days of pure observation, researchers limited themselves to external facts and, so to speak, the physical, pathological case without delving more deeply into the pathogenic factors, undoubtedly because they thought these factors were inaccessible to direct and positive observation.

These observers related the phenomenon to the physical or mental circumstances with which it appeared for the first time and later developed. From these circumstances they determined the various sources of hallucinations, whose causes thus became infinitely multiplied like the thousands of incidents most frequently associated with them by pure chance.

The primary origin, the basic cause of hallucinations is invariable and identical with itself. It lies in a special state of the intellectual organ. When this state develops, a multitude of objective and subjective physical and mental factors can become the purely fortuitous and indirect cause of hallucinations. Without this special state of the intellectual organ, these agents are powerless.

Do we need to name this essential cause? It is indeed the cause of all the morbid phenomena of the mind, "excitement."

First, I will examine hallucinations from the point of view of the data provided by subjective observation. As the action of hashish is more keenly felt, one passes imperceptibly from the real world into a fictitious world without losing consciousness of oneself. In a way, a fusion takes place between the dream state and the waking state. *One dreams while awake.* I use these words in their most rigorous sense; they are patterned on the very fact that they express repeatedly.

I have spoken of this fusion of two states, which seem to be mutually exclusive, and have carefully shown how this fusion must be understood and what it really was, according to our subjective senses. Unless one exerts an extreme sagacity, developed by habit and attention, one is compelled to believe in the complete identity between the waking state and the dream state, and consequently confuse the phenomena pertaining to *reality* with those pertaining to *fantasy.*

I am not afraid to insist upon this psychological phenomenon because it is the central fact of mental pathology, and sums up all the varieties of delirium, among them the one with which I am concerned here.

Moreover, it would not be difficult to find numerous traces of this phenomenon in the physiological state. Is it not revealed, for example, in that incomplete dream state in which we maintain enough awareness of ourselves to know we are dreaming, in which we submit to the influence of our imagination, although we are not mistaken about its real nature. Are we not like those mental patients who are perfectly aware of their delirium while they give themselves up to the most ridiculous and capricious ideas?

Several days ago I had the opportunity to study a phenomenon of this type in myself. I had worked quite late into the evening. After a few hours of deep, calm sleep, I awoke feeling a little tired. Seeing then what time it was, I felt like going back to sleep; my thoughts, by an association which I was unaware of, turned to a friend who had visited me during the day. I could not keep from having a series of absurd ideas, groundless suspicions, about him. I tried to combat them. Impossible! I became more and more involved in these accusations. I wondered if I were really awake or if I were dreaming. To reassure myself I sat up; I rubbed my eyes; I said several words aloud. All this was useless. I could not get rid of my ridiculous ideas. When daylight came, after having slept an hour or two more, I could not imagine how I had taken seriously what now clearly seemed to be a trick of my imagination.

A lady of my acquaintance told me that she frequently found herself in a peculiar state that was at once waking and sleep. One morning she was in the midst of a dream when two maids entered her room. She was enjoying her dream and did not wish to be interrupted. She thought of dismissing her servants, but she did not, convinced that her dream would stop at once if she spoke. So she returned to her dream, although she heard the maids speaking, opening the shutters, and arranging the furniture.

The causes of the phenomena just illustrated are not very persistent by nature. It takes very little, as one knows, to destroy their effect. The slightest impression from the outside is enough to terminate the state of half-sleep and to dispel its shadowy phantoms.

But let us assume that these causes are more vigorous, more durable, less subject to outside influences. Is it not obvious that the phenomena that result will have an equally longer duration and that the waking state and the dream state will thus be able to exist simultaneously? That is what happens with hashish and, to a greater degree, from the action of the ordinary causes of madness.

One evening I was among close friends. They played some music which greatly stimulated my faculties. There came a moment when my thoughts and my memories carried me back to the Orient. I spoke enthusiastically of countries I had visited; I glibly told of several incidents that had impressed me during my trip. As I was telling of my departure from Cairo for Upper Egypt, I suddenly stopped and shouted, "There, there, I can once more hear the song of the sailors rowing on the Nile: *Al bedaoui, al bedaoui!*" I repeated this refrain, just as in the past.

It was an hallucination in every sense of the word because I *heard,* clearly and distinctly,[8] the songs that so often had reached my ears.

This was the first time that I had experienced this phenomenon in so distinct a manner and, despite the confusion of the thoughts which seemed to be spinning in my head, I applied myself to study it as precisely as I could.

First, I tried to stimulate some new hallucinations by turning my at-

---

[8] Note that I use these expressions only to convey my meaning, in the generally accepted sense and in a language familiar to those who hallucinate. In my opinion, I should say, "I thought I heard" or "I *dreamed* I was hearing."

tention to other thoughts and recalling other memories. It was impossible; I was constantly brought back, in spite of myself, to the same subject; but the hallucination had stopped, although the chain of memories connected to it had been resumed.

It had left nothing in my mind but the fleeting memory of a dream, and I saw only a difference of intensity between that reminiscence and the impression itself. I dreamed I heard; I believed that I was hearing but with that full and total conviction that one has when dreaming. Such was my invariable response when, looking at my innermost thoughts, I sought to account for what I had felt.

So I was dreaming; that conclusion resulted from the clearest, most precise testimony from my inner consciousness. But, at the same time, I remained in touch with my surroundings; I responded with complete presence of mind to the questions I was asked, concerning the songs I said I was hearing.

Several times I have had the occasion to assure myself that other "hallucinators" have experienced impressions of this type. They invariably describe the same impressions: "I dreamed that I saw; I dreamed that I heard; and yet I knew perfectly well where I was, who was around me, etc. It is unbelievable; it is incomprehensible!"

My ideas about the pathogenesis of hallucinations did not at first come to me as clearly and precisely as I have expressed them. Many experiences were necessary to overcome the uncertainties and to dispel the errors, similar to those made by psychotics who have lost all awareness of their condition.

Several times, when the *excitement* was not very pronounced, the voices seemed to *resound in my head,* but it was only a vague impression. At other times, I was inclined to believe that I was talking and that I heard myself. This error corrected itself as soon as I began to speak. Exactly the same thing happens in dreams; we voice our own thoughts and we hold conversations with other people. These are various impressions which we formerly received, which repeat themselves and which we associate and combine in many ways. All these phenomena derive essentially from the dream state, and one should not mistake them for the hearing of voices, when the intellectual faculties have not undergone any change. Between these two kinds of phenomena there is as much distance as between sleep and waking.

One day I had spent nine or ten hours in a rather high state of excitement. There had been numerous illusions and hallucinations, but I was in no mood to evaluate them because of secret terrors (it was my second or third experience with hashish), which interfered to some extent with my judgment. The "fit" came to a close, and I had reached that point of semi-excitement, of calm combined with lassitude, that follows intense excitement. I was quiet and no longer felt the need to pour out in a torrent of words the thoughts that bubbled in my brain. I was, moreover, wide awake, and nothing that happened in the room escaped me. Suddenly I was surprised to hear the muffled sound of voices speaking all at once and in the same tone. At first I thought the noise came from the adjoining room; having assured myself that such was not the case and that I was absolutely alone at the time, I stretched out again on my couch. The noise resumed almost immediately. This time I was not so easily fooled, and I decided that I had been dreaming, but dreaming while wide awake.

This is a phenomenon that occurs frequently in the ordinary waking state. Have we not been suddenly awakened by voices we heard in a dream? And are we not impressed by these voices as vividly as if they were real, to the extent that we have to think about them for several minutes to convince ourselves that we were dreaming?

Let us suppose now that this phenomenon recurs intermittently and that we are perfectly lucid. We then will have an idea of what happens with hashish and with other mental disturbances in which hallucinations occur.

We have spoken only of auditory hallucinations. Our observations apply equally to visual ones. They are identical in nature, namely, mere accidents of a dream state.

A young Frenchman, in the service of the Pasha of Egypt, deeply missed his homeland, and was assailed by nostalgia. He took hashish, which he had been told was a very powerful cure for the boredom that overwhelmed him. The opposite happened. He experienced hallucinations more apt to increase than to lessen his sorrows. His eyes stared at the white bare walls of his room; he saw the house where he lived in the country, the paths, the gardens, and his mother and his sister who strolled there and invited him to join them, reproaching him for his absence. (Data supplied by Aubert-Roche.) xx

---

xx This observation indicates the importance of the mood of the subject on his response to hashish intoxication.

Chapter 4

PSYCHOLOGICAL AND PATHOLOGICAL CONDITIONS FAVORABLE TO THE DEVELOPMENT OF HALLUCINATIONS

From what we have studied so far, it appears that hallucinations, like all the phenomena of delirium without exception, are derived essentially from *excitement,* a cerebral change which, from a psychological point of view, is identical to an ordinary dream state. Through these data, provided by self-observation, we have reached a new vantage point from which we will study the phenomenon of hallucinations in its totality. Without attaching any importance to their external characteristics, to the designations imposed upon them by the prejudices of some methodical writers, we have studied the physiological or pathological conditions in which these phenomena specifically appear. We know of no specialized study on the subject, but the opinions of leading psychiatrists on the matter of hallucinations support our position. We will examine those opinions later.

The results of our studies, recorded in the following pages, will confirm the opinion we held concerning the psychic nature of hallucinations. The hallucinations we observed were increasingly different—in origin and appearance—from those caused by hashish, and closer to those that characterize madness (mental illness?).

We will first study certain factors whose action on our mental faculties is similar to the influence of Indian hemp. We will become convinced that the psychological effects are essentially the same.

I. Action of Various Toxic Substances

We know that several natural substances are endowed with the power to affect the brain and consequently the mental functions. The immediate result can be a well-defined mental illness, usually transitory but sometimes lengthy or even permanent. Illusions and hallucinations are two of the most frequent symptoms.

Numerous authors, among them toxicologists, have noted these effects, but their descriptions have been incomplete because they have only highlighted the main phenomena without accounting for the less obvious nuances. These nuances are very important because they are the links that join these phenomena and enable us to trace them to a common origin.

The experiments we have performed on ourselves have called our attention to a class of symptoms which, until now, have gone unnoticed. We have carefully questioned a great many people who have used toxic substances capable of disturbing the mental faculties. We have always found the mental change that we have identified as the basic, generative factor of disturbances of the mind. Doubtless, this change is not always found with the clear and precise forms that we have ascribed to it on the basis of our own observations. Nevertheless, its features are such that it is impossible not to recognize it or to ignore its presence.

Nitrous Oxide

Let us listen to the chemist Sir Humphrey Davy [1] describing the marvelous results he achieved when he first breathed *nitrous oxide:*

> I felt *all the links in my relationship with the outer world loosen and break.* Trains of vivid, visible images rapidly crossed my mind. Another time I felt with indescribable pleasure the sense of touch increasing in my feet and hands. Dazzling perspectives enthralled me. I distinctly heard the most imperceptible sounds that came from the bell, and no aspect of my condition could escape me. Little by little, the crisis becoming intense, I was completely cut off from my natural perceptions. I felt a physical and involuntary detach-

[1] British chemist (1778–1829). Studied the effects of voltic electricity on chemical compounds and developed the theory of galvanic decomposition; discovered the exhilarating and anesthetic effects of nitrous oxide, among many other basic discoveries.

ment that lifted me from my earthly cares and caused me to pass, through voluptuous transitions, into delicate sensations that, speaking candidly, were completely new to me. It seemed that, in my privileged condition, everything was performed spontaneously and instinctively. Time, in other words, existed only in my memory, and in a flash *the most remote traditions* were revived in all their splendor.

I call attention to the parts we have emphasized. They clearly indicate the sequence of the intellectual change, the point of departure, the origin, and the kind of fantastic drama that was unfolding in Davy's brain and to which he seemed to be a detached witness.

In this rupture of the natural relationships with outer things, this gradual loss of the ordinary input from our perceptions, this physical and involuntary detachment from earthly ties, this rapidity, this instantaneous conception, finally, these vivid images that crossed his mind, it is impossible not to recognize the *basic fact (excitement)*. I would try in vain to describe it better.

Davy did not for a single moment lose consciousness of his condition. However, wishing to give an account of what he had felt after "his imagination, like a becalmed sea [these expressions have an incredible accuracy about them!], had reverted to its normal state," he reported he felt "the same melancholic anxiety as the man who *awakens after a charming dream* [the dream state after *excitement*] and who seeks to recover this ephemeral illusion."

By the sensations that he derived from his heightened imagination and, on the other hand, by the integrity of his subjective sense, and the feeling that he had kept of his own individuality, Davy seemed to belong to two modes of existence, quite distinct and yet joined to each other. He was mad, with an awareness of his madness, precisely as if he had taken hashish.

Opium

Opium seems to possess to a high degree the power to develop that mixed state in which imagination and reason play equal parts. The case we are going to report seems to offer us some interesting data in this respect. You will interrupt the account of the author in order to interject comments as I see fit. The charm of the narration may suffer, but scientific truth can only benefit, which is sufficient compensation.

An Englishman living in India, a daily user of opium for many years, described his feelings:

> The first change that I noticed in myself occurred in the form of visions. It was toward the middle of 1817 that I gained the ability to conjure all sorts of phantoms out of thin air. When the ability to create occurred, I sensed an attraction between the dream state and the waking state. All the objects I happened to summon and retrace voluntarily in the dark were suddenly changed into visions, so much so that I was afraid to use that awful power. I had only to think of something in the darkness, and immediately it appeared before *my eyes* like a phantom.

Such were the consequences of the attraction established between the dream state and the waking state in our opium war! The visions he summoned had all the accuracy and, if I may put it this way, all the *exteriority* of those perceived by the combined cerebral center and the senses. The fusion or, if you wish, the attraction established between the dream state and the waking state is so complete that one who experiences it is hardly aware of it, and when recounting his visions, he explains them as he would ordinary sensations. He thought *his eyes* saw the phantoms whose presence he feared and that he never evoked without trembling.

What difference, not essential but however slight, can one find between this man and an ordinary *madman*, between his language, the expressions he used, and the language, the familiar expressions of hallucinating psychotics? He was cognizant of the disturbances of his mind. But how many "hallucinators" find themselves in the same condition and give an account of their state with the same clarity and precision as Sir . . . ? He vaguely perceived the psychological change, the basic source of his aberrations; he spoke of the attraction between the dream state and the waking state. But are not these the very expressions constantly used by psychotics who want to explain what they feel during the course of their illness and, above all, when they want to convey what their state was like once an authentic cure has restored order to their thoughts?

Among the visions that Sir . . . was pleased to report is the one that follows:

> I always loved Roman history; on the other hand, I was familiar with one period of English history, the war of the Parliament. These two main branches of my knowledge, which in my normal state were the ordinary subjects of my thoughts, became the subjects of my dreams. [We know that the word *dreams* is used by Sir . . . to designate the hallucinatory state induced by opium.] Often, at night, after involuntarily conjuring a gathering of ladies at a party or a dance, *I heard or said to myself:* "These are English ladies from the unhappy times of Charles I. These are the wives and daughters of those who met during peacetime, who sat at the same table, related by marriage or blood." The ladies danced and smiled at the court of George IV. However, I knew they had been dead for almost two centuries. All at once there was a clapping of hands, and I heard the formidable words *Consul Romanus.* Immediately Paulus or Marius appeared, surrounded by a company of centurions in scarlet tunics and followed by ranks of the Roman legions.

As usual the topics that most frequently drew his attention returned in hallucinatory form and were colored with a kind of reality by the prism of *excitement* and the *dream state.*

"I heard or said to myself . . ." These words, which our "hallucinator" says casually, deserve to be noticed. It happens, indeed, that the hallucination is vague enough to lack its principal characteristic, *exteriority.* So it appears in its primitive form and remains as it were, in the brain, where it was born and where it resides until the dream state is completed. Thence, the uncertainty as to whether one sees *in one's head* or *outside of oneself,* whether one hears something said or says it.

We have previously had occasion to indicate this phenomenon after observing it within ourselves.

Alcoholic Beverages

The abuse of alcoholic beverages is, as everyone knows, a frequent cause of insanity. The delirium that ensues takes the most varied forms. Illusions and hallucinations are among the most constant and salient symptoms.

An interesting fact about the subject which concerns us here is that it is not rare to observe in drunkenness (habitual intoxication) those special changes of mentality that stand like a middle ground between the state of madness and the state of reason, that *twilight* state of the mind that is so important and that is so hard to understand. We have often had occasion to present cases in the Section on Legal Medicine which we publish in the "Annales Medico-psychologiques."

In general, in alcoholic psychosis, as in all cases of artificially induced delirium, the onset of the mental disturbance is not so sudden that reason cannot fight it for a certain period of time. During this struggle, the individual is alternately mad and sane, until either madness or sanity takes over; then the crisis resumes or ceases completely.

We have seen people become subject to the strangest hallucinations without any apparent damage to the integrity of their mental faculties. Here are two remarkable examples chosen because they recently provided material for discussions relative to apparitions. It would be hard to find clearer examples of hallucinations without delirium.

(1) Mr. Cassio Burroughs was one of the most handsome men in London, with outstanding qualities, but singularly haughty and something of a swashbuckler. He became the lover of a charming Italian woman who had come to England, where she died. One evening, in an inn some time after the death of his mistress, Mr. Burroughs boasted of his past affair. This was in violation of a promise he had made at the deathbed of the lady, to whom he had sworn never to reveal their indiscretion. Hardly had the secret been told when the beautiful Italian woman appeared before him, a phenomenon which occurred thereafter during his drinking bouts. Mr. Burroughs declared that the sight of the phantom was preceded by a terrible chill, which caught him as he was drinking and

caused the soft and bony tissues of his head to vibrate like a violin string. Subsequently he was killed in a duel; the Italian woman appeared to him on the morning of his death.[1]

(2) The conversion of Colonel Gardiner, in 1719, related by the pious Doddridge, is still alive in the memories of all the "hallucinators" in Scotland. A revelation took place before their eyes that could not possibly be explained by the natural sciences. We know that Colonel Gardiner, having dined in joyous company on the sabbath, left his friends at about 11 o'clock in the evening to keep a rendezvous at midnight with a married woman. To collect himself in his impatient amorousness during the last moments before this sweet encounter, he took a book from his satchel. It was *Soldier of Christ, or the Heavens Taken by Storm* by Thomas Watson. The Colonel's great aunt, either inadvertently or by design, had packed this inspiring work in her grand-nephew's baggage. Several phrases concerning the military profession attracted the Colonel's attention, as he thumbed enthusiastically through the pages of the book. Suddenly a small spark, a sort of wandering flame, fell on the open book. The Colonel thought it came from the wick of his lamp; but, when he raised his eyes, he saw, much to his surprise, a picture of the torture of Jesus suspended in the air in the middle of his room, with the cross surrounded by a halo. A voice, or something that resembled a voice, says Reverend Doddridge, addressed him so movingly that he was converted.[2]

In the following case, which we borrow from Walter Scott, we find the two most favorable psychological conditions for the development of hallucinations: (1) an habitual state of *excitement* resulting from the abuse of strong liquors and an angry, irrascible disposition and (2) a vivid mental impression that seems suddenly to concentrate the mental disturbance exclusively on one series of ideas.

The captain of the slave ship was a moody man, sometimes pleasant and affable with the sailors of his vessel, but more

---

[1] Aubrey.
[2] André Delrieu.

often subject to fits of anger, violence, and rage, during which he paced the bridge roaring like a tiger. The African sun seemed to have been poured into his veins like a fiery liquor, and his eyes became as red as the backs of the blacks bleeding from the whip. The crew never spoke to him without a pistol in their hands.

This captain had conceived a special hatred for a seaman, whose name was probably Bill Jones, an old-timer with a tuft of white hair on his scalp. The crew respected this old sailor, who had never slept away from a ship, but undoubtedly because of this respect, the captain addressed him only with threats and insults. The old-timer, with the license granted to sailors on merchant ships, answered in the same tone. One day Bill Jones was sluggish in climbing to the yard to furl a sail. He was so aged. At that moment, the captain appeared, slightly drunk, at the door of his cabin. "Oh ho," he cried, "you old shark, you cursed buzzard, you bladder full of rum, furl or bust. . . ."

The seaman's reply exasperated the captain, who returned to his cabin and came out with a loaded gun in his hand. He aimed it at the imaginary mutineer and fired. The shot struck the yard like hail. Bill Jones stayed for a moment surrounded by the smoke, then he crashed heavily at the feet of the main mast, holding his intestines, which were spilling out. The other sailors laid him, dying, on the bridge. He raised his eyes to the captain and said to him: "You have done me in, Mister, but *I will never leave you!*" The captain, shrugging his shoulders, contented himself to reply that he would have him thrown in the kitchen boiler, where they prepared the slaves' meals, to see how greasy he was. The poor man died, and his body was actually thrown in the boiler. . .

With terrible curses the captain ordered everyone to keep quiet about what had happened. The sailors, however, were convinced that Bill Jones had not really left the ship. They believed that his spirit was working with the crew in the rigging, particularly when it came to furling a sail, in which case the ghost never failed to be the first to straddle the yard. "I ended up seeing him myself," says one passenger who is the narrator of the tale. "I saw him like the others, and very distinctly, one stormy night near the Azores. I called out "Jones" in a low voice, but he did not answer me and climbed to the top, where he disappeared. Only the captain seemed to pay no attention to this strange thing, and since they dreaded his violent character, no one spoke to him about it. The crew, gloomy and apprehensive, looked with anxious eyes toward the space that still separated us from the coast of England. One night when we had passed the Bay of Biscay, the captain invited me down to his cabin to share a grog with him. His face was concerned; finally he unburdened himself to me in a troubled voice."

"I don't have to tell you, Jack, the kind of companion we have aboard with us."

"Captain," I replied with studied indifference, "it's all a joke. . . ."

"No, no, it is not a joke; he told me that *he would never leave me,* and he is keeping his word."

"How?" I cried with a gesture of surprise.

"*You* only see him from time to time, but he is always at my side. He is never out of my sight . . . Look, Jack . . . At this very moment I see him there behind you! . . ."

The captain became very pale. His face took on an indescribable expression. He arose, very excited.

"I will not tolerate his presence any longer. I must leave you."

I responded calmly to his incoherent words as he paced up and down the cabin floor as if to escape the ghost. I told him the only reasonable course to take was to steer toward the west of France or toward Ireland, to disembark secretly and to leave me with the responsibility of bringing the ship back to Liverpool. But he shook his head dismally and repeated, as if he had not heard me, "I have got to leave you, Jack!"

As he was speaking, he suddenly stopped with the anxiety of a man who hears a distant sound, and asked me if I heard a noise on the bridge. In the extraordinary situation that the ship was in, one was constantly on the alert. I climbed quickly onto the poop deck. My feet had hardly cleared the last rung when the sound of a body falling into the water made me shudder. I stretched my head over the edge of the vessel and saw that the captain had leaped into the sea while we were moving at six knots an hour. At the very moment the poor man went down, he seemed to make a desperate effort, raise himself half out of the water, and stretch out his hand to me, crying "My God! Bill is still with me!"

With that the sea claimed him, and terrified, I dropped to my knees behind the bulwark.

The effects of intoxication have been described too often for us not to limit our recollection of them.

With a little effort, one will easily perceive that these effects are only another manifestation of the *primary* mental change that can be touched off by so many varied causes and that is inevitably found wherever symptoms of delirium occur. Whatever their cause, fortuitous or determinant, all mental illnesses consist of an identical change at their outset. Alcoholic psychosis confirms that law of mental pathogenesis that we posited at the beginning of this work.

Recall, if you will, that feeling of well-being which characterizes the first effects of intoxication, those quickened ideas and perceptions, those easy emotions, that unaccustomed impressionability. Could the signs of *excitement* be clearer? And when this *excitement* acquires a certain intensity when the intellect is carried away in a torrent of thoughts, of memories, and of *imaginations,* then images, hallucinations, delusions, and irresistible chaotic instincts, the fantastic procession of total delirium, surge before a perturbed reason.

At this stage of disturbance and confusion of the mental faculties, observation ceases, because shortly thereafter the drunk falls into a state of torpor and somnolence that cuts him off from the world. If he still appears accessible to external stimuli, the ideas and impressions stirring within him are stamped with the mark of his inner preoccupations and his false convictions.

He belongs entirely to the world of his imagination. Reality no longer has enough effect on him to penetrate consciousness. He is in the condition of the dreamer who, bringing memories of reality to his dreams and being aware of his dream, seeks with the aid of these same memories to correct the rather bizarre products of his imagination.

"In the first stage of intoxication," says Hoffbauer, thoughts succeed one another too rapidly for the drinker to arrange them in the order required to tell them. This rapidity increases more and more; *soon the senses lose their customary delicacy, and imagination gains in proportion to this loss.*" Using the strict and exacting language of self-observation, this German physician means that under the growing pressure of alcoholic *excitement* the drinker passes from the real world into an imaginary one, from a waking state into a dream state. When these two states merge, when the individual cannot distinguish between them, he must be treated as a mental patient.

Narcotics

Narcotics are extremely powerful in inducing an hallucinatory state. Opium falls into this category, as was shown in a case previously reported. We have observed with some attention a few similar substances because they were formerly used in witchcraft to produce hallucinations, for example, thorny apple, belladonna, henbane.

The action of these substances on the mental faculties has been carefully studied, but the researchers have constantly stopped at the external symptoms and the outwardly perceptible signs of this action. They have noted changes in the brain condition, in either its intellectual or emotional aspects, but they have not gone beyond that. The innermost phenomena could be revealed only by a kind of observation rarely employed: self-observation drawn from personal experience.

I have tried most of these substances myself. Furthermore, guided by my own sensations, I have questioned a great many people, mostly "hallucinators" whose mental illnesses had been treated with these substances. Invariably, at least at the beginning, the action of narcotics is identical to that of hashish: dissociation of ideas, reveries which appear to be the prelude to a more complete dream state and in which rather bizarre associations of ideas occur, perceptions without external stimuli, associations and perceptions which form the basis of delusions, hallucinations.

Before feeling the relaxation or the stuporous state that seems to be the most advanced stage of the action of narcotics, one feels very distinctly that one is only passing from one mode of mental life to another. Little by little, the contact with external things is past; the user relates entirely to memories or creations of his own imagination.

Narcotics, therefore, are no exception among the modifying agents of the mind. If madness, with its peculiar characteristics, can result from their slow, prolonged action, it is because of their power to produce *excitement,* to dissolve, so to speak, the mental component, and to induce a state of dream (the highest expression of mental disturbance). Various kinds of madness are only reflections of the dream state merged with the waking state.

In the distant past,[ii] certain people, nowadays conveniently classified as hallucinating madmen, had the idea that through certain practices they could communicate with diabolical powers. In order to go to the sabbaths [iii] and be admitted to Satan's court, it was first necessary to submit to a magical anointing. The senior sorcerers could be exempted from this practice, which was absolutely required from apprentice sorcerers. It is commonly agreed that opium, henbane, datura, belladonna, and other narcotic substances formed the basis of the recipe used to make the infernal paste employed in the *anointing.*

From a psychological point of view, the action of the plants used by the sorcerers must be considered under the double heading: of "immediate effects" and "secondary effects."

The mental change that we have indicated, that general disturbance of the faculties (*excitement*), constitutes the immediate effect. As we have said so many times, *excitement* is the primary generative fact of all mental illness, but it has nothing to do with the specific forms assumed by these illnesses.

The secondary effects derive their origin from the preoccupation prevailing at the time narcotics are used. Passion, desire, curiosity, and general beliefs directed the thinking of those who were to be initiated into the mysteries of the sabbath and gave their delirium its specific character. The narcotic action functions in the same manner as the physiological cause of sleep, which converted preoccupations of the waking state into a dream.

Nowadays, narcotics can still cause the gravest disturbances in our

---

[ii] This is no longer true. The appearance of the drug culture in the United States has been accompanied by a resurgence of witchcraft.

[iii] Nightly revels of witches.

faculties and give birth to visions, hallucinations, and delusions. But they no longer have the power to send us to the witches' sabbath. In Turkey [3] and in Egypt, it is not unusual to find people who have become demented as a result of an abuse of narcotics. Nothing in their delirium is reminiscent of the fantastic visions of the sorcerers of past times.

Furthermore, even in the days of witchcraft, narcotics were not always used for diabolical purposes. "It was mostly [victims of] unrequited or betrayed love that sought their help. Caught up in her passion, a woman would make use of them. Preoccupied with her desires and the yearning to satisfy them, she would go to sleep. It was natural for that object of her desires to occupy her dreams and for her to soon impute to her lover's caresses the voluptuous emotions that the magic sleep produced in her. When she awakened, could she doubt that a charm as powerful as it was delicious had carried her into the arms of her lover or that it had brought an unfaithful lover back to her." [4]

Other ideas and other convictions gave way to hallucinations of another kind. "Two would-be witches, put to sleep by the magic ointment, had announced that they would return flying with their own wings. Both believed that things had happened thus and were astonished when they were told the contrary. One of them, in falling asleep, had even made some flying motions and had sprung up as though she had wanted to take flight." [5]

We are completely in agreement with the author we have just cited. To explain most of the facts recorded in the bloody archives of the civil and religious tribunals and in the voluminous collections on demonology, to explain the confessions of the *madmen* of both sexes who firmly believed they were sorcerers and attended the sabbaths, it suffices to combine the action of the magic ointment with the profound impression produced by the descriptions previously heard of the ceremonies they would be witnessing and the entertainment in which they would participate in the assemblies of the sabbaths. It is known

---

[3] See our *Recherches sur les aliénés en Orient* (Research on Mental Patients in the Middle and Far East) (first issue of *Annales médico-psychologiques*).

[4] E. Salverte, *Des Sciences occultes.*

[5] *Ibid.*

that Pierre Gassendi [iv] tricked some poor peasants by massaging them with narcotics. The peasants fell into a deep slumber. Upon awakening, they declared that they had actually gone to the sabbaths and gave a detailed account of everything they had seen, sensations they had felt, and so on.

The sorcerers were true hallucinating madmen. It is no longer necessary to prove that fact today, now that the torch of science casts a light on all kinds of visions, be they in heavenly places or in hell, at the court of Satan or that of Jehovah.

Nevertheless we believe that some fundamental psychological differences between the sorcerers of yesteryear and the demonists of today have not been mentioned. These differences concern the basic cause of hallucinations and of the false convictions which take hold of their minds.

The sorcerers hallucinated only when they came under the toxic influence of the stupefying ointments. It was mostly at night that they performed their peregrinations and their fantastic dances and that hell held its orgies. When they ceased to see the spectacles they had participated in, the false convictions related to them persisted, because these convictions were echoed in their faith and in their religious convictions, and because their delirious impressions had been so vivid that they could not help believing in them as if they were real.

We know the strength of these beliefs, as deeply rooted as the pathological fact from which they derive, that made these poor fanatics brave the stake and most dreadful tortures.

Moreover, outside the circle drawn by the delirious ideas, the sorcerers, like the actual monomaniacs that they were, maintained the integrity of their faculties. One can imagine, from then on, that it was easy for the crowd to be deceived about the real state of their reason, so persuasive in areas not related to their visions and their imagination of the night. One can still imagine the influence such men must have exerted upon their contemporaries, whose superstitions, whose driving passions, and whose fears and terrors they stirred. The prejudices that prevailed at the time almost justified other men's beliefs in the sorcerer's dream with the same naiveté and the same good faith that justified their own deliria. It was as though there were two distinct men

---

[iv] French philosopher, mathematician, and astronomer (1592–1655).

in them—the rational man who was counsel for the defense and who made himself responsible for the nonsense, and the eccentricities of the disturbed man.

The psychotics of our time who most resemble the sorcerers of the past have been given the name *demonomaniacs* [v] because of the connections they claim to have with the devil. Among them, the delirium is quite extensive and the psychosis complete. One never sees in them those intervals of absolute lucidity which in their predecessors resulted from the cessation of the action of narcotics. The delirium of the demonomaniac is continuous and incessant, like the cause that generates it, a cause whose origins are hidden in the depths of the organism and which, by its spontaneity and its persistence, differs essentially from the ephemeral action of substances introduced into the system.

It is not only in the vague dreams of a more or less prolonged drowsiness, deliberately prepared by means of certain practices, that the demonomaniac enters into a relationship with the infernal spirits; the devil reaches him in all seasons, in all places, at any hour of day or night, in a thousand ways; impels him to extravagant actions, awakens within him depraved ideas, overwhelms him with blows, or sullies him with the filthiest caresses.

One may add that the demonomaniac is always irrational in many ways that have little or no relationship to his dominant idea, that his delirium never confines itself exclusively to the limits of his delusions and his hallucinations.

However, some cases of psychosis have a remarkable similarity to the delirium of the sorcerers. (1) In some cases, madness is only really present during sleep. These cases, of which I will give a remarkable example later, have become extremely rare in our time, when dreams have lost the meaning they once had in the minds of the masses of past centuries. Visions, in the cases we are concerned with, are related to religious subjects and bring with them in the waking state false convictions that are extensions of the nocturnal delirium. (2) In other cases one sees the delirium make its first appearance during sleep and then continue later. Such a person, who falls asleep in perfect health,

---

[v] Before the time of Pinel, all insane people were thought to be possessed by devils. Therefore the therapy was by "exorcism" of the evil spirits according to religious rites or the burning of the unfortunate victim at the stake.

awakens sick, and it is correct to say that he is only continuing his dream in his madness. (3) Finally, it happens that the delirium, born of causes that only our organism knows, offers striking similarities with the delirium caused by external agents; I might add that the latter case, because of its peculiar characteristics, is sometimes completely confused with ordinary psychosis. We know, in fact, that the most typical mental illness, the one that Esquirol defines as a *chronic delirium without fever*, can result from drug poisoning.[vi]

Indeed, as I never tire of pointing out every time the occasion arises, delirium depends essentially upon the psychocerebral change we call *excitement*, identical under all circumstances, whether the causes that seem to have generated it are physical or mental. Whenever a mental anomaly manifests itself, one will find as a primordial, generative fact the disintegration of ideas or, if you will, *excitement*. Madness that is due to the action of narcotics has just given us further proof.

II. Hallucinations Without (Apparent) Mental Disorder

It has been said that hallucinations can appear when the mental faculties are in their normal state. Writers have included many facts of this kind in their books.

Hallucinations are surely one of the morbid phenomena that deviate most from the natural order. To hear, to see, and even to feel without an external impression is a fact of such importance to a certain school of philosophers that they have deemed it the very basis of our mental faculties! That such a phenomenon can occur without our mind's being otherwise disturbed, or injured, is a psychological fact that seems unbelievable.

This fact lends itself beautifully to the thinking of those who want to see in psychosis only a functional disturbance, a psychic change that has nothing to do with lesions of the mental organ. Indeed, it is not repugnant to infer these lesions when one of the principal and most serious symptoms of psychosis can appear without, necessarily, any loss of reason? The psychotic would mainly be an individual with a special point of view, whose thoughts differ *in form* but not in intrinsic nature

---

[vi] This condition is called today "toxic psychosis" or acute brain syndrome (see Appendix).

from those of other men. Why should anyone wish to relate these thoughts to some organic disorder? Does one seek to find what change of cerebral matter might cause the innumerable errors that appear at times in the most organized brains? More than one man of genius has circulated ideas close to those fathered by delirium.

The supporters of *dynamic* or *functional* disturbance cannot, I believe, base their point of view on more specious reasons than those we have just indicated, without repeating *ad nauseam:* "I will not believe at all in your organic lesions, as long as you haven't shown them to me." However, the weakness of these reasons will appear when we demonstrate that hallucinations, even in cases where the integrity of the mental faculties seems intact, are, as in all other cases, the result of a general but rapid and instantaneous disruption of these same faculties.

Hallucinations that seem to coexist with an unquestionable state of mental health must be classified with other phenomena of mental illness.

Before supporting this proposition with direct proof, i.e., self-observation, we could resort to induction. Hallucinations, whatever the mental condition of the person in whom they are observed, invariably constitute a case of mental illness, limited, if you will, but real nevertheless. One could compare the "hallucinator" who is aware of his hallucinations with the *petit mal* epileptic who has only dizzy spells and never *grand mal* seizures. The dizziness passes, and the general health is undisturbed physically and mentally. Because no distinction has been made between the causes which produce the dizzy spells and those which produce the terrible attacks that everyone knows, we must admit a common origin both for hallucinations experienced in a state of apparent sanity and for the most complete sensory psychosis.

Indeed, the fundamental change is the same in both cases, although it is easily overlooked when the hallucination is isolated because it has a short duration, because it has been less intense, or, because its importance has been neglected, the observers being exclusively preoccupied with the obvious, external phenomena: the hallucination on one hand and the opinion of the hallucinator on the other.

Just because the "hallucinator" remains aware of his condition, is it correct to think that no disturbance other than the hallucination has taken place in his faculties? Not at all, because we have seen that with hashish an individual may have hallucinations and yet retain the faculty of rationally judging the position in which he finds himself. He can, moreover, study its psychological cause, trace it back to the mental change from which it originates. Can the same be true in hallucinatory psychosis without delirium? Since our attention was focused on that point of mental pathology, we have had the opportunity to question several "hallucinators" who were able to describe their sensations rather precisely. I would have used the same expressions they employed to convey a condition I have often experienced myself. Later I will cite several of the most remarkable cases I have gathered.

If we reflect for a moment on the nature of *occasional* causes of hallucinations, we will notice, developing under their influence, the psychic fact that we regard as the immediate source of all mental abnormalities. Among the most active of these causes are the violent emotions of the soul, those sudden passions whose explosion abruptly disrupts momentarily but then completely suspends the normal course of the mental faculties, as if these faculties were affected by a cerebral congestion or an epileptic seizure. Held in their terrible clutches of such sudden passions, the individual is stunned, no longer knows what he is doing, momentarily loses consciousness of himself, no longer knows himself, acts mechanically, against his will, his ideas; he becomes the pawn of the dominant impulse, however absurd it may be.

All these expressions, coined by common usage, accurately describe the state in which the mind finds itself when it is deeply disturbed by emotions: a state of confusion, of rapid disorganization, of momentary destruction of the ability to associate.

And do we not have here, at their greatest intensity, the effects derived from the use of hashish, opium, and other narcotics? Does manic excitation at its maximum violence show any other characteristics?

The hallucinations that we are concerned with here are not related to sickness or mental disorder. Therefore, unless they eventually create anxiety by their frequent recurrence and their persistence, one would never resort to regular treatment to cure them. These facts are thus lost to science or, if observers unacquainted with medicine have registered some of them, the details they have recorded cannot satisfy the requirements of science. However, if these details were to be studied carefully, they would not fail to offer proof in support of our point of view concerning hallucinations.

I should like to report an extremely curious fact concerning the hallucinatory state without delirium. I have documents about this fact which are as complete and as precise as if they were personal. The subject is a young lady who is one of my closest relatives.

This lady, endowed with perfect health and a vivid imagination, experienced a deep sadness that caused no apparent change in her physical or mental state. Returning to her home one night with her young sister, suddenly, as she set foot on the first step of the stairs that led to her room, she saw the stairs on fire. After a brief hesitation, certain that it was an illusion, she continued bravely, and it all disappeared. Arriving at her room, and being without a light, she groped for the lighter. She was still trembling with fear at what she had experienced, and she dropped the lighter. She stooped to pick it up, but quickly stood up with a frightened cry. She saw a corpse stretched out at her feet. Her sister, who could understand neither her terror nor her cries, looked for the lighter and lit the taper herself. The entire illusion vanished.

I faithfully transcribed the incident that you have just read from notes I dictated during my first year of internship at Charenton (1826). Since then, I have gone back to question that person several times in order to elicit more details. She is certain of not having been fooled by the first vision, but she does not dare say as much for the second. "I was too frightened," she says, "to really remember what I felt then. I'm sure I saw a corpse, and this time it did not occur to me that it was another illusion like the fire on the stairs."

"You are equally certain that you were in control of all your faculties when you believed that you saw the fire burning?"

"Without question, but at that moment I felt more sorrow than I had ever experienced before. My head was heavy; I felt feverish; I was alternately hot and cold, and when I spoke . . . and I do not know why . . . *my ideas became confused.* Of course, it was not surprising, I was so preoccupied and so sad! At moments like that, *it is so easy to lose one's head.* However, I assure you that I was not mad."

Is it necessary to point out what, in the language used, is characteristic of the primordial fact: this heaviness of the head, this feverish state, and above all this confusion in her thoughts, which she could control, that confused her when she spoke so much so that *she lost her head?* And this would have happened if, as a result of some hereditary or constitutional disposition, the state of which she spoke had lasted instead of occurring with the speed of certain nervous attacks. From the psychic point of view, such a state cannot be distinguished from manic excitement or stupor except by its duration.

Here are several other cases that can be compared with the preceding one. Says E. Salverte:

> A woman mourned a brother whom she had just lost. Suddenly she thought she heard his voice, which someone near her was imitating in a wicked deception. Misled by her fear, she asserted that the ghost of her brother appeared to her glittering with light. . . .

> Jarvis Matcham was paymaster of a regiment. He enjoyed such esteem in his bookkeeping function that it was easy for him to remove a large amount of money from the corps' cashbox. He was sent to a neighboring town some distance from the garrison to do some recruiting. Matcham suspected that this absence was contrived to enable an audit of his papers. He believed the revelation of his misconduct was near at hand, all the more so because his colonel had sent with him a little drummer as a companion during his trip in the country.

> The sergeant saw in this drummer a spy. The poor wretch became confused; he wanted to desert, and, to suppress the sole witness to his flight, he killed the boy.

> The drummer dead, Jarvis, deeply disturbed, made his way cautiously to the road leaving the garrison, changed his clothing, and walked rapidly across the fields. He constantly thought he heard the taunts, the cries, and the sounds of the poor boy's shoes, as the boy struggled with his murderer, kicking the stones on the road. The sergeant finally arrived at an inn, stopped there, and retired, leaving orders that he be awakened early. The boy at the inn did as instructed, and at the appointed time he approached the sergeant's bed and shook him on the shoulder. He was surprised to hear these strange words from the sergeant: "My God, my God, I didn't kill him!"

> Matcham got up, regained his composure, and hastened to Portsmouth by public carriage. There he enlisted aboard a

warship and served as a seaman for several years, always with the proper conduct and docile manner that had earned him his reputation in the infantry. Finally the vessel returned to port. Jarvis and one of the licensed seamen on board decided to go to Salisbury, and set out on the road. It was the first time that Matcham had been on terra firma since he had left England.

The two of them were about three miles from that city when they were surprised by a violent storm, accompanied by lightning so terrible and thunder so frightening that Matcham's conscience was stirred, despite its long rest. He showed an excess of terror that was not natural for a man accustomed to the perils of war and nature. He began to talk in such a strange manner that his traveling companion became aware that something extraordinary was going on in Matcham's mind. By the dim light that glowed in the skies, he could see the former sergeant trembling as though he were cold and glancing to the left and right but not daring to turn around completely. Finally Matcham said to his comrade: "The pavement stones are coming loose and running after me."

Involuntarily, and without stopping to reflect, the seaman turned to see the pavement stones. But Matcham's idea seemed so funny to him that, despite the storm, he burst into laughter. The sergeant made a horrible motion of fear, as if lightning had struck him.

"Don't laugh! Don't laugh! Listen, please walk on the other side of the street. We will see if the stones still follow me when I am alone."

The seaman, who had no desire to laugh anymore, was glad to leave a man who seemed to have lost his reason. He went to the other side of the road and began to whistle. Both of them walked that way for some time. The lightning was becoming very bright.

"You see!" cried Matcham, "the stones are coming after me and leaving you alone. I am the one they want." This time the seaman shrugged his shoulders. Hands in pockets, he sang an old song about the death of Nelson.

"But there is something worse," added Matcham, crossing the road and speaking in a whisper into his companion's ear. His tone was excited and mysterious. "Do you know this little drummer?"

"What drummer?"

"There . . . that boy who is following us so closely."

"I don't see anyone," said the seaman, by now definitely upset at the sergeant's contagious fright.

"What! You don't see the little boy with the bloody jacket? Dragging himself on the stones. Do you hear the stones?"

The murderer's voice was so heartrending that the seaman, finally suspecting the truth, begged Matcham to relieve his conscience and confess his crime. Then the sergeant, at the end of his tether, sighed deeply and declared that he was unable to suffer any longer the anguish that he had endured for several years. A complete confession followed this first outburst of remorse, and since there was a price on his head, he begged his companion to turn him over to the jurisdiction of the magistrate in Salisbury. After a painful struggle with his conscience, the seaman complied. Jarvis Matcham retracted his confession at the beginning of the trial, but because of the testimony of the boy at the inn, who had heard the murderer's words when he talked in his sleep, he was tried, condemned, and hanged.

Count Plater, that illustrious veteran of the Polish rebellion of 1831, reports that in a church located some distance from Warsaw, in the midst of a national festival, a young man, suddenly moved by the religious songs, darted from his pew toward the choir, stopped, and, his arms crossed, his head bowed, he remained motionless for a long time, contemplating the bare floor of the church in an attitude that disturbed the services to the great concern of the congregation. It was precisely a year before the death of the Grand-Duke Constantine; the rebellion had not yet broken out. They gathered around the young man and questioned him about his meditation. The songs ended, and he came out of his somnambulistic dream. "I see the open coffin of Grand-Duke Constantine at my feet," he said. The year passed; the revolution drove the Russians from Warsaw; Constantine died; his funeral rites were held in that church; and his coffin was placed in the center of the choir, at the exact spot where the young man had had the vision.[6]

Webster tells of a Parisian chemist, a very clever man named Lapierre, who had his lodgings near the Temple. Near the end of the sixteenth century he received a small amount of blood in a vial from the hands of a priest with the request that he analyze it. The technician began on Saturday and continued the task during the week that followed. He repeatedly subjected the liquid in the vial to all the states of solvent heat.[7]

The following Friday, six days after the beginning of his work and in the middle of the night, the chemist, who slept in a room located near his laboratory, was awakened at the moment he closed his eyes by a horrible noise resembling the lowing of a cow or the roar of a lion. Once the noise had stopped, the chemist tried to fall back to sleep. At that moment, the moon was full; it shone brightly in the room. The chemist clearly saw a thick cloud gliding between his eyes and the window. He thought he recognized the figure of a man, and he screamed with terror; the cloud disappeared. . . .

In yet another case, an English doctor had secured the body of a hanged man for a scientific autopsy. The body was brought into his laboratory; he started to dissect the limbs and the trunk, which took him several days. When the autopsy of these fragments was completed, he started on the head and directed a young surgeon, who was his assistant in anatomy, to pulverize a certain part of the skull in order to prepare a remedy, well-known in the old school pharmacies: that powder was called *Usnée*.[8]

The young surgeon obeyed his master and scraped the dead man's

---

[6] André Delrieu.

[7] Webster, on Witchcraft, quoted by Delrieu.

[8] *Usnée*, says A. Delrieu, from whom we borrow this account, is a species of human lichen that at one time was believed to grow on the top of the skull of people who had been hanged, and that was regarded to be a moss produced by the juices of the convict's brain following strangulation. According to the theory, the essence of the soul, violently ejected from the cranium, escaped, leaving behind a precipitate or residue, whereas in slow or ordinary deaths the soul retained the time and power to take along all its atoms to the superior regions. It was believed that the vital flame, accidentally held back, concentrated in a particular vegetation, adhered to the top of the skull like a crystallized spangle, at the disposal of the first persons who stole from God the secret of creating a man.

head, although not without repugnance and trembling. This procedure produced a powder which the aide dropped cautiously on a paper that covered the laboratory table, taking care not to touch it. After that he dragged his bed into the laboratory, because hanged men were so rare and so expensive in those days and consequently *Usnée* was so precious that they watched over the skull and the moss as if they were treasures. The poor Englishman went to bed and *tried to sleep.* A lamp burned in the laboratory day and night as a precaution.

But scarcely had he closed his eyes when a strange sound forced him to open them. There was evidently someone in the laboratory. Half dead with fright, the apprentice got up.

"They want to steal the *Usnée,*" he said to himself, as he looked for a weapon to defend his harvest. He took the head of the corpse.

However, the noise continued, and the cause remained unseen. With the skull in one hand and the lamp in the other, the young man looked timidly about the room. The whiteness of the paper spread on the table, gleaming in the dark, drew his attention. . . . His hair stood on end in horror at what he saw. He could not speak or flee. He dropped the lamp when his fingers, loosened by fear, began to shake convulsively at the sight of the terrifying spectacle.

On the paper, in the middle of the powder, moved a small head with its two eyes open, staring at him. From both sides of the head extended two appendages that grew visibly and that seemed to take the place of arms on the emerging ghost. Soon the apprentice could count the exact number of ribs on the skeleton; he saw them being gradually covered with their muscular casing. When this was completed, the extremities appeared in the same order of regeneration. The growth was terminated; the organism was complete. Finally, the man thus created, about the size of a six-month-old child, got to his feet, got off the table very nimbly, and quickly circled the laboratory. His prison clothes, which were hanging on the wall left the hook and draped themselves on the man, as though they were drawn to his body by a mysterious magnet acting as his valet. In a few seconds the hanged man appeared to the surgeon in the costume and with the expression he wore on his way to the gallows.[9]

---

[9] *Philosophical Transactions,* Ferriar.

III. INTERMEDIARY STATE BETWEEN SLEEPING AND WAKING

Between waking and sleeping there is an intermediary state that, without being exactly one or the other, participates equally in both and constitutes a true mixed state; in the case of our present subject, it is of great interest to understand this well.

Not all mental life ceases with sleep. Do not dreams and reveries reveal a sort of inner intracerebral life that feeds itself so to speak, on impressions received earlier, during the waking state, as real life does on impressions from outside sent by the external world?

In the intermediary state that we are discussing, we are equally accessible to these two sorts of impressions. Unable to distinguish between them, we confuse one with the other, from which result the most ridiculous mental combinations, the most heterogeneous associations of ideas—in a word, a true delirium.

A careful study of this state, if one observes it in detail, will reveal all the characteristics that distinguish the primordial change that is the forerunner of the complete dream; as in other cases, it is the forerunner of the hallucinatory state and all the phenomena of delirium.

In fact, it is always the same loosening of the mental ties, the same disintegration of ideas which, as they become more and more vague and random, associate themselves in a bizarre manner, change the convictions, the feelings, and the instincts—in other words, give free rein to the most diverse impulses. To the extent that the *excitement* [10] declares itself, the individual drifts into a state of reverie in which he becomes the victim of his imagination. Soon he exists only in a purely ideal world, wherein everything is new and strange except for customary conceptions. It is the dream with all its bizarreness, its caprices, its monstrosities, and its impossibilities of all kinds. But often we also find the subjects of waking life, the same preoccupations. And then, remarkable thing, our perceptions are often more vivid and lucid, our intelligence clearer, our imagination bolder, our memory surer, our judgment more spontaneous and quicker.

---

[10] I deliberately use this word, as I did previously, to make clearly understood that we attribute to it no other meaning than that of dissociation of ideas, without in any way prejudging the nature of the cause of this dissociation.

It seems that, left on its own, no longer conscious of its ties to outer reality, the mind leaps easily to the high levels of the intellect. Or in other terms, the mental faculties, no longer constricted by self-awareness, become more instinctive in their action and more assured in their conclusions. How many learned men have sought in vain the solution to a problem only to find it in a dream! How many poets, how many artists of all kinds have discovered in their sleep the inspiration which eluded them in waking life!

Similar results are created by the action of hashish, opium, and other drugs, with this minor difference. With hashish the twilight state is persistent, whatever one may do to destroy it, whereas only the lightest external impression is necessary to halt the condition occasioned by the progressive invasion of sleep.

Our self-consciousness becomes imperceptibly dimmer and we endow the products of our imagination with reality. All kinds of hallucinations follow, such as the voices that we have heard (I do not say that we believe we have heard them, because in dreams *we hear, we do not just believe we hear* but we hear differently than when awake), and the people we have seen. We have not really heard these voices or seen these persons except in a dream, but we are convinced we have heard or seen them as though awake, precisely through the merging of these two states.

The more I delve into this strange state of half-sleep, the more I am inclined to regard it as typical of what is commonly called delirium, mental illness. In the state of half-sleep, a purely physiological cause, none other than the organic rule that governs all the phenomena of sleep, is the origin of the same mental changes, which, in other circumstances, are produced by morbid agents.

The hallucinatory phenomena produced by the state of half-sleep appear with various characteristics which must be studied separately, all the more so since they are remarkably similar to the hallucinatory state observed in psychotics.

I shall divide the discussion on this "half-sleep" into four sections.

(1) The beginning of sleep is rarely so sudden that the individual cannot appreciate the state he is in. We are aware of our dreams; we judge, so to speak, the products of sleep with the reason of our waking state. It is true *madness without delirium*, like the one we observe frequently among dreamers of another kind, the psychotics.

In his *Treatise on the Mind, Awake and Asleep*, Opoix says:

> I myself have experienced a kind of dream on two occasions,
> in broad daylight and when walking after dinner in the
> country. I saw bizarre, animated objects. I reasoned with
> myself about the strange state I was in. I was amazed, but I
> firmly believed that what I saw was real.
>
> Some time later, while dining, I was busy trying to recall a
> conversation I had just had, or so I believed. I realized after a
> few minutes that I had not spoken to anyone.

Earlier I reported the case of the woman who, in the midst of a
pleasant dream that she wished to continue, was aware of everything
going on around her.

A young woman several months' pregnant, sanguine in temperament, and subject to headaches that seemed to relate to her condition,
returned home in a carriage one night, sharing the back seat with a
gentleman of her acquaintance. Her husband was seated in front of
her next to the coachman. While thinking of a thousand different
things, she recalled the story of a coachman who had thrown his master
under the wheels of his carriage. Suddenly she became convinced that
the same sort of accident had just happened to her husband. He was no
longer the man sitting in front of her; it was some other person, an ac-
complice of the coachman who had taken his place. This lady was so
upset that she burst into tears, and this painful illusion stopped only
when her husband spoke to her.

This woman told me the incident herself. I tried to convince her
that she had been dreaming. She replied:

> It is possible, but be that as it may, it was an unusually
> powerful dream, because as long as it lasted I never ceased to
> see what was happening, exactly as if I were awake. One can
> dream without being asleep, but I was not dreaming, and what
> I experienced did not resemble my usual dreams. The best
> proof is the fact that M. . . spoke to me two or three times,
> and I replied quite relevantly.

To transform this woman's false impressions into a true state of
madness, does it not suffice to impute to the state of half-sleep, which

was the source of these impressions, a more lasting cause, firmer and more resistant to external impressions, at least up to a point? Had they only lasted longer, would the false impressions not have constituted a true state of mental illness?

A former classmate of mine, presently a professor of philosophy at a small college, attended the dying moments of his beloved father. In the evening of the same day, feeling tired but not really sleepy, though he had not slept for several nights, he lay down fully dressed on his bed. No more than five or six minutes later, as he lay there mourning his father, the latter appeared before him, pale and emaciated from his long illness. My friend said:

> Convinced that this sad apparition was the result of a bad dream, I was not afraid at first, and I attempted to think about something else. But my father's face was constantly in front of me. I was sure I was not sleeping, but my head felt extremely heavy. I was losing control of my thoughts, just as when I struggled to stay awake. Soon I yielded to my fears, although I never doubted that I was the victim of a vision. I leaped from my bed and climbed into the attic, constantly pursued by the phantom, until it eventually disappeared.

This hallucination, by all appearances born in the depths of sleep, continuing with its first intensity into a state of half-sleep and even momentarily into a state of complete alertness, resembles those that are seen in psychotics. Obviously it would have been identical if it had lasted longer, and my friend would have been in an hallucinatory state, with or without delirium.

To complete our etiological data, I must not forget to add that my friend was eminently predisposed to cerebral congestion. I witnessed two attacks that were strong enough to leave him almost totally unconscious for several minutes. Repeated blood lettings and mustard plasters applied near the extremities put an end to these attacks.

This predisposition, the sorrow caused by the death of his father, the lack of sleep, and the ensuing fatigue are sufficient to explain the hallucination experienced by my colleague. These three different causes together produced the dissolution of the mental integrity, the dissolution of thoughts—in a word, the primordial and generative state of all mental abnormalities.

We know that hemorrhages and blood letting can give rise to nervous troubles similar to those produced by cerebral congestion.

(2) There can be no doubt, after what has just been said, that the state of half-sleep is a fertile source of illusions and hallucinations.

Facts such as those we have just cited are far from rare. Surely there are few people who cannot find similar experiences in their memories. These experiences have always been regarded with indifference; no one dreams of relating them to mental disorders. They have received no more attention than dreams, from which they differ, however, by more than one essential feature.

But there is a group of facts similar or even identical to the preceding, which have at all times aroused popular curiosity and which scholars have deigned to ponder. The reason is that they occurred in different circumstances and/or the people concerned found themselves in different mental conditions. *They were not aware* of what they were experiencing, of their visions. They did not have the slightest suspicion that there could be any connection between these visions and the state they were in—hence their unshakable belief in the *apparitions* they experienced. "I am not crazy; I wasn't at the time I saw the phantom any more than I am now. Moreover, I am certain I was not dreaming, because I had not yet fallen asleep. I am sure I saw, heard, felt, what I am saying I saw, heard, and felt."

We must seek the source of the belief—so widespread only a short time ago—in apparitions and ghosts during the peculiar phenomena of the state of half-sleep. In fact, had the apparitions historically been witnessed only by madmen and ordinary dreamers, it is doubtful whether they would have been given such credence. The eccentricities of psychotic "hallucinators" would have inevitably aroused mistrust. On the other hand, whatever pertains manifestly to the dream state is easy to recognize, and, in general, one would hardly confuse fancies of night with reality. This is not true of visions that occur in the twilight zone between waking and sleeping. Those who experience them are sound of mind. Deluded by the nature of the phenomenon, they have been able to convince others on the strength of their unimpaired reason and by the deep conviction with which they tell their story. Among these people are superior, learned individuals, and for that reason it is no longer possible to deny the existence of apparitions. One must believe in ghosts, in the popular sense, grant them form, substance, and even *exteriority,* and admit that their true origin is elsewhere than in the minds of those who say they have witnessed them (for example, in a world unlike ours, an *ethereal* world, to use a common expression). Apparitions have often been considered souls freed from the fetters of physical structure, sometimes endowed with the power to become visible to living people. This is the near consensus that has resulted from the scientific discussions on apparitions and ghosts in various scholarly communities of Germany, Scotland, and France.

The important problem of ghosts is far from being solved even now, as witnessed by the clever and interesting investigations conducted by M. A. Delrieu, an excellent writer, well known for his psychological insight.

According to him, certain apparitions have indeed been linked to a change in the composition of the blood, to illnesses that stem from cerebral exacerbations ranging from ordinary, simple madness all the way to visions and *delirium tremens.* It has been established that the influence of the blood is felt on those features of mental illness that cause what is commonly called an *apparition;* but (and we must quote verbatim) ; "other mental diseases, in the opinion of the physiologists, exist apart from these physical phenomena. Therefore, unable to explain the nature of these phenomena by changes in the bloodstream, the researchers stop short, in awe. Such authenticated, widely known cases do not really permit discussion. Inexplicable in physical terms, but unquestionably documented, they must be approached with the realistic thinking of our times, as the Edinburgh physiologists have done, and left without a plausible interpretation at present." [11]

Is it not curious to see that such an altogether simple and uncomplicated phenemenon of mental pathology, one that is so easy to observe in ourselves when we doze off, is at the origin of so many errors and widespread prejudice among the common people—even among scientists—that such a phenomenon has warranted the most transcendental theories, as nebulous and ephemeral as the ghosts, phantoms, and apparitions they purport to unmask?

Here are two cases that I borrow from Delrieu. They have given rise to endless controversy and are still inexplicable except by a theory of

---

[11] *Revue de Paris,* 1839.

extraterrestrial existence. In my opinion, and in the opinion of those of my readers who are familiar with the phenomenon of hallucinations, I am sure these facts must be attributed to a state of half-sleep.

Delrieu's thoughts on the subject follow the first case. I believe they represent the most advanced opinion of scientists on the nature of apparitions. A candid philosopher [12] writes:

> In 1667 I was in a western English county with several honorable gentlemen in the home of a wealthy land owner whose castle was an old convent. The servants and the people who regularly visited the house had spoken to me of mysterious noises and bizarre apparitions, even during the shortest stay. Because our host had invited many guests, I slept with the majordomo, in a very attractive room known as "milady's bedroom." We lit a roaring fire before retiring and spent the first hours of the evening quite peacefully, reading the old books in the room. Then we climbed into bed and blew out the wick of the lamp. As we were dropping off to sleep, I observed with pleasure that the rays of the moon lit our huge room so brightly that it was possible to decipher a manuscript. M. C. bet that it was impossible. I accepted the wager and, pulling a handwritten paper from the pocket of my robe, I easily won the bet. We had hardly exchanged a few words on the matter, when glancing to the door of the room, which was in front of me and shut tightly, I distinctly saw five women entering. They were quite beautiful and gracious and appeared to have attractive figures, but their faces were covered with long, white veils that swept the floor in flowing folds in the moonlight. They entered in single file, at a measured pace, one after the other, and circled the room along the wall, until the first one had reached and stopped at the edge of the bed I was in. My left hand was on top of the covers and, despite the approach of the first phantom, I resolved not to change my posture. The veiled figure touched this hand with a soft, light caress, but I could not tell if it was cold or warm. Then I asked the women, in the name of the Blessed Trinity, what their purpose was in coming. They

---

[12] Bovet's *Pandemonium.*

did not reply. "Sir," I said to the majordomo, "don't you see the beautiful retinue that is paying us a visit?"

But before a word had left my mouth, and at the mere movement of my lips, they all disappeared. The majordomo was crouching behind me, almost dead from fright, and I was obliged to shake him for some time with my left hand, which had remained on the covers, in order to get him to respond. Finally the poor man acknowledged that he had seen the phantoms and had heard me speak to them and that he had not responded at first to my question because he was utterly terrified at the sight of a monster, half lion, half bear, that was trying to jump on the foot of the bed. . . .

The following night the majordomo did not dare sleep in the same bedroom, where the hero of the episode, the intrepid Bovet, decided to remain.

I brought a Bible and several other books into the room, determined to brave the fatal moment of the vision by reading near the fire and waiting to fall asleep. Having bid my hosts goodnight, I sat down in front of the fireplace, planning to stay up until 1 A.M. At that time I went to bed without having seen anything.

I hadn't been in bed long when I heard something walking around the room, like a woman whose dress swept the floor. This thing was rather noisy, but I couldn't see anything, although the night was bright enough. It came to the foot of the bed, lifted the covers a bit, and entered an adjoining study, although its door was locked. There it proceeded to moan and to move a large armchair in which, as far as my ears could follow its movements, it seemed to sit down and leaf through the pages of an old familiar album.[13] The phantom continued in this manner, moaning, moving the armchair, and turning the pages of the book until dawn.

Here are the observations of Delrieu:

The intermediate spirits of the nuns were impelled by the presence of a living being to return to a room they oc-

---

[13] Bovet was recalling his adventure in a letter to a friend.

cupied for some time and in which fragrant traces of their stay probably still remained. The human infused those vestiges—both concrete and invisible—with a momentary force, a need for temporary condensation persistent enough to partially fill the nothingness of death. The vital radiations of the room's guest summoned up the more noble, more ethereal substances that had followed the souls of the nuns at the hour of the dissolution of their bodies. Finally, the terrestrial appearance of the former inhabitants of the convent, thus reformed, firm, opaque, and tangible, *detached themselves* from the invisible world that surrounds us, for the benefit of the eyes of the person lying in the bed, by an effect of magnetic concordance and superior harmony that enfolded in one unique and instant spell the guest, the nuns, and their ghosts.

The reconstituted nuns, materializing in the darkness of the room, kept close to the wall and seemed to avoid the center of the chamber as they approached the bed. This happened because their earthly vestiges, while gradually gathering the scattered elements of their terrestrial bodies, while slowly coming to life in the magnetic radiations of the guest, had to seek one another out, along the walls of the room which had been impregnated by their tenuous atoms during their evaporation and, had to reach the very seat of their radiations, the bed, which the two living beings had transformed into a pole for the magnetized nuns. It is quite natural that cloisters be the scene of similar phenomena. Monasteries, as a result of the seclusiveness and the longevity of their inhabitants, the perpetuity of the vows, and the strength of the prayers, offer a haven for emanations of human vitality to gather.

Ferriar and Hibbert (adds Delrieu) are convinced that a physiological explanation does not suffice to provide a key to these phenomena. Ferriar asserts that Bovet was not sleeping, whereas Hibbert is inclined to accept a dream theory, but both end up with hopeless misgivings.

Neither of these physiologists was correct but they were actually at the opposite ends of the scale on which the truth lies. They disregarded that intermediary state in which Bovet and his companion experienced their hallucinations.

It was, in fact, as they were falling asleep that the vision took place the first time. The second time it was shortly after retiring, in a room heated by a roaring fire, a condition ideal to produce that drowsy state which is both waking and sleep into which they had fallen as their minds were full of reports about nocturnal visits by ghosts.

The following case is related by Beaumont.[14] It dates back to the close of the eighteenth century, and the bishop of Gloucester received the story in confidence from the father of the young victim:

> In 1662, Sir Charles Lee, an ancestor of Charles Lee, poet, general, participant in the Revolutionary War, and a friend of General Burgoyne, became the father of a daughter by his first wife, who died in childbirth. After the death of Sir Charles's wife, his sister undertook to raise the little orphan, until she became engaged to Sir William Perkins. However, an extraordinary event halted the marriage plans.
>
> One evening, after retiring, the girl thought she saw a light in her room. She called her chambermaid and asked her why she had left a lamp burning in the bedroom. "There is no lamp here except the one in my hand," replied the maid. "Isn't there a fire burning?" asked the dumbfounded girl. "Not any longer," said the maid. "You have been dreaming." "That is possible," replied Miss Lee, and she went back to sleep.
>
> After about two hours of sleep, she was awakened anew by the light, and she saw a rather small woman in her bed, between the pillow and the blanket. She told the girl in a perfectly distinct voice that she was her mother, and that in forty hours they would be reunited. Whereupon Miss Lee called her maid again, got dressed, and locked herself in a study. She stayed there until 9 A.M., when she came out with a sealed letter.
>
> Her aunt, Lady Everard, arrived. She told her calmly what

---

[14] *World of Spirits.*

had happened, and begged her to send the letter to her father when the fatal moment arrived. Lady Everard thought she was mad. She summoned a physician and a surgeon from Chelmsford; the physician could not detect any symptom of mental disease, but yielding to the aunt's wishes, he performed a blood-letting on Miss Lee, who graciously offered her arm.

Having thus satisfied Lady Everard, the young girl asked for a chaplain and recited the last rites with the frightened minister. Accompanied by a guitar, she sang the most touching passages of her psalm book in so charming a way that her music teacher, who was present, burst into tears. When the fortieth hour was about to sound, she sat in a comfortable armchair, arranged her clothing, and breathing two long sighs, she died.

To complete what I have just said with respect to the state of half-sleep and the hallucinations that result from it, I must comment upon a remark made by psychiatrists, namely, that illusions and hallucinations appear most frequently when the patient is falling asleep or awakening.

I cited the story of an "hallucinator" in my memoir on the *Traitement des Hallucinations* (page 29):

In bed in the same room with several comrades, Louis suddenly heard voices that seemed to emanate from all four corners of the room. They accused him of imaginary crimes, told him that he would be hanged, and that his right hand would be cut off like a murderer's. Louis, frozen with terror, was astonished to see everyone around him sleeping soundly. He went back to bed, convinced that he was the victim of an annoying dream. *Hardly had his head touched the pillow* when he heard a loud buzzing in his ear and he heard the voices again, more forcefully than the first time. He awakened his comrades. . . . In the course of his treatment, Louis heard these voices. It was in the evening, just as he was going to sleep. Two days later, buzzing and muffled voices again disturbed the patient, always immediately before going to sleep.

Another "hallucinator" gave this account of his state:

> I felt terrors I could not explain. I heard, usually at night, voices that overwhelmed me with abuse, threatened me, and warned me of misfortunes. Sometimes I felt as if my head rang like a bell, or as if I had plunged it into a bucket of water.

After several days of treatment, the illness seemed to abate. Then new hallucinations occurred, "ephemeral and *only for a few minutes before falling asleep.*" Later, immediately before falling asleep, the patient heard several voices three or four times.

Several incidents of this kind scattered among various writings report this peculiarity of delirium, without recognizing the importance that Baillarger now gives it.

At the Academy of Medicine, on May 14, 1842, Baillarger read a most interesting memoir in which he developed the facts of the above incident in every possible way. I am sorry I cannot analyze its entire contents. The findings were published on May 21 of the same year in the *Gazette Médicale* were numbered from 1 to 14, and I shall reproduce here those that seem related to our subject, adding any commentary I deem necessary.

> 1. Passing from waking to sleep and from sleep to waking is a propitious time for the production of hallucinations in subjects predisposed to madness, in the prodrome, at the start and during the course of this illness.

The facts reported in the two previous articles prove that this predisposition extends much farther and even to individuals in no way suspect of a predisposition to madness. This propensity exists in states of perfect health, but its effects are transitory, like the physiological condition from which they derive. They are, nonetheless, true hallucinations, from the psychological point of view.

> 2. The simple lowering of the eyelids suffices, in some patients, and during the waking state, to produce visual hallucinations.

The lowering of the eyelids produces not only visual but also auditory hallucinations. I shall support this remark, to which I attach great importance, by citing a very curious fact that I observed in Dr. Voisin's ward at Bicêtre.

The closing of the eyes seems to have the purpose of removing the eyes from the effects of external objects. In this sense it must be considered one of the first phenomena of sleep—thus its influence on the creation of hallucinations. Undoubtedly this is the thought contained in Baillarger's proposition.

There is another explanation of this phenomenon that, in our estimation, is more probable. I have conducted and repeated on myself over and over a simple experiment that anyone can duplicate. When an individual feels the beginnings of an intoxication (narcotic, alcoholic, or otherwise), if he will close his eyes slowly and effortlessly, he will suddenly *feel his head going away*. To use a popular expression, he will feel that he is going to pass out. The vertigo, this giddiness makes him fear he is going to fall over backward and forces him to open his eyes to end what has become an intolerable state. These symptoms are still more intense when he closes his eyes more tightly. He then feels malaise, an indescribable anxiety.

It is impossible to miss the striking analogy between these sensations and those you feel when you are falling asleep and are just about to lose consciousness—or better still when you are undergoing a mild cerebral congestion or syncope. The inner senses can perceive no difference. One understands that the closing of the eyelids, in creating effects that, as previously established, best combine all the characteristics of the *primary fact*, eminently predisposes one to hallucinations.

3. Hallucinations occurring in the intermediate state between sleep and waking will, if they persist at all, most often repeat themselves and involve delirium.

In our view, the persistence of hallucinations is only an index, not a cause, of the aggravation of the general psychic disorder from which they originate like all the fundamental factors of delirium. We can conclude from this persistence that the illness is increasing, but not that the increase of the illness is the result of this persistence. Hallucinations are only symptoms or features of the *primary change*. They stand out more clearly and acquire more energy as this modification expands.[15]

4. In people who are already hallucinators, as they fall asleep, madness is principally characterized by hallucinations.

The hallucinatory state that appears in a declared madness is the same as the one which already appeared during sleep. The psychological change to which the phenomenon of hallucinations is related is essentially the same in both cases, although accompanied by new and varied features. Also, hallucinations appear from the outset of delirium. Born in the state of half-sleep, they continue into the waking state.

5. Hallucinations often occur after a hemorrhage that suggests cerebral congestion.

We will soon see that the disposition to congestions and, *a fortiori,* a congestive state of the brain are pathological conditions eminently suitable to the presence of hallucinations and other phenomena of deliria. From a psychological point of view, the effects of cerebral congestion are completely similar to those of sleep.

6. Hallucinations should not be compared with dreams in general, but only with dreams accompanied by hallucinations.

We cannot admit any difference between dreams in general and dreams with hallucinations. In all cases, hallucinations, whatever they be, are one of the phenomena of the dream state. In other words, anyone with hallucinations is, by the simple fact of his hallucinations, in

---

[15] A defective kind of reasoning is frequently used when one has to describe the usual phases of mental illness. Resting on an imagined reciprocity of action of the fundamental phenomena of delirium, it happens too often that when one phenomenon precedes or follows the other, it is assumed that the one is the cause of the other, whereas in reality the appearance or aggravation of both is related to the same and only cause, the aggravation of the *primary change*. One can easily convince oneself of the fact by examining at close hand the general state of the patient, the functional problems that are known and that are all related to manic excitement. If I may be permitted a comparison, this *excitement* is like a source from which one or two streams originate. If it suddenly enlarges, it is no longer one or two streams but ten, or a hundred, that flow.

a dream state, that is to say, in a psychic state that, although brought on by causes unrelated to the state of sleep, is no less identical to the latter state. The basic cause of hallucinations is always the same, whether one calls it *sleep* or *mental illness.*

If I insist on this point, it is because the identity, the homogeneity, of the prime cause of mental illness, whatever form it assumes, is one of the truths that the greater part of this book intends to establish for all time.

7. The propensity of the state between waking and sleeping to create hallucinations proves that, in certain cases at least, it is a purely physical phenomenon, one that calls chiefly for physical activity.

The remote or immediate cause of hallucinations can be either physical or mental, but whichever it is, it can only determine the phenomenon of hallucinations by triggering a physiological or psychocerebral *change* that is exclusively organic. That change is known to us under the name of *primary fact.*

Whatever opinion one may have as to the cause and the mechanism of hallucinations, under no condition can we consider them as anything but a purely physical, or rather *organic,* phenomenon.

Impressions during sleep can be vivid enough to cause physical acts, to make us shed tears, to signal various movements to our body, but, in general, however energetic they may have been, they disappear at the moment of waking leaving scarcely a trace in our minds.

However, it can happen that these same impressions persist into the waking state and that the thoughts and emotions of our dreams, the same joys, the same fears, besiege us in the waking state. We then submit to the influence of delusions and hallucinations whose origins are in the dream and that were basically simple sleep phenomena. In this event it is correct, strictly speaking, to say that delirium is a continued dream. Certainly this is true of sensory impressions. What an individual sees, what he hears in a dream, makes such an impression on him that he believes he is seeing or hearing, even though the end of the dream reestablishes all his relationships with the outer world. He retains his recollection, not as something dreamed but as part of reality itself.

So why not seek the explanation of the phenomenon of hallucinations in this simple fact? Does it not contain the essence of their intimate nature? An hallucination is *a dream of the external senses,* as delusions are *dreams of the intellect.*

Whether one envisages it as activities of natural or artificial sleep, that is, brought on by changes in the nervous system or even by a state of delirium, psychologically speaking the phenomenon is identical. The only causes that produce the mental change where it originates are variable and are distinguished or differentiated by the degree of persistence of their actions.

One of the deepest, most brilliant philosophers of our time told Charles Nodier shortly before his death that in his youth he had dreamed several nights in a row that he had the wonderful power to float and fly through the air and that he could never rid himself of this idea without putting it to a test when he crossed a brook or a ditch.

It is not evident, or probable, that were this impression stronger, it would have eventually surmounted all resistance and that the scholar would have been convinced that he could fly in the air, something that would have quite obviously constituted a state of partial psychosis, that is, his transformation from a dreamer to a psychotic.

We have here a striking example of the persistence of perceptions from sleep into the waking state.

More often the opposite occurs. In some cases, impressions from reality recur during sleep with remarkable persistence. They recur every night, unchanged, in the same circumstances, isolated and free of the phantasmagoria, the jumbled thoughts that one finds in dreams.

Vampires are a striking example of this curious psychological fact, to which I call special attention because it proves that in certain circumstances, with certain predispositions, sleep can convert a perception of waking life into a true delusion, a psychotic idea. Nodier writes:

> Twenty-four years ago I was traveling in Bavaria with a young Italian painter whom I had met in Munich. His company suited my temperament and my imagination at that time because our feelings and our misfortunes were sadly similar. Some time ago a woman whom he loved had died, and the circumstances surrounding that event, as he frequently told me, were of a nature to leave a permanent impression on him. This young woman insisted on accompanying him through the

miseries of a cruel banishment. She concealed from him her weakened condition but finally succumbed, during a halt, to a fatigue so complete that she wished only to die.

They had been without food for two days when they discovered a rocky cave where they could hide. She threw herself on his heart when they sat down, and it seemed as if she were saying: "Eat me if you are hungry." But he lost consciousness, and when he regained sufficient strength to hold her in his arms he discovered that she was dead. He rose, placed her over his shoulder, and carried her to a cemetery in the next village where he dug a grave which he covered with earth and plants, and where he planted a cross made from his walking stick and his sword. After that he was easily arrested since he did not move further. After a while he recovered his freedom but never his happiness.

My traveling companion had preserved at twenty-two only the vestiges of a fine and noble face. He was extremely thin, perhaps because he ate only enough to stay alive. He was pale under a slightly swarthy skin. An Italian's complexion is usually lurid. The activity of his mental life seemed to be confined entirely to his eyes, which were a strange, transparent blue. They sparkled with an inexplicable force, between two red eyelids whose lashes had to all appearances been dissolved by tears. His eyebrows were, nonetheless, quite beautiful.

Since we had told each other that we were subject to nightmares, we were in the habit of sleeping in adjoining bedrooms to be able to wake each other at the sound of moans, which were more like those of a wild beast than of a human. But he had always demanded that I lock the door from my side, and I attributed this precaution to the anxious and suspicious nature of an unhappy man whose freedom had long been threatened and who enjoyed little pleasure in placing himself in the care of a friend.

One evening we had to share a room and a bed for two because the inn was full. He took this news with a more worried look than usual. He arranged the mattress to make two beds, a nicety that would not have occurred to me and that I did not resent at all. Finally he lay on his side of the bed and, throwing me a coil of rope, he said: "Bind my hands and feet," with an expression of bitter despair, "or burn my brain."

I am not making up an episode in a horror story. I shall not reveal my reaction and the details of our talk. You can guess them.

"The poor soul who told me to eat her to save my life," he sobbed, shuddering with horror and covering his eyes with his hands. . . . "There is not a night that I do not disinter her and devour her in my dreams . . . not a night that my abominable fits of sleepwalking do not force me to seek the spot where I left her, when the demon that torments me does not deliver her corpse. Decide now if you can sleep next to me, next to a vampire! . . ."

It would be more painful for me than for the reader to dwell on this account. What I can do is to swear on my honor that all the main points are entirely true, that there is not even that embroidery of the writer that enhances the quality of the thought by lavishing words on it.

Here is another case that Nodier borrows from Fortis (*Voyage en Dalmatie*) and that, forty years later in the same country, he found different enough from his in several details to make him assume that it had been reported more than once:

The belief in vampires is very widespread in the country of the Morlaques. There is hardly a hamlet in which there are not several *vukodlacks,* and in some the *vukodlack* is found in every family, like the cretin in the Alpine valleys. But here the illness is not complicated by a degrading disability that alters the very basis of reason in its most common features. The *vukodlack* suffers from the horror of his recollection. He fears and detests them like my Italian painter. He struggles against them furiously. To get rid of them he resorts to the remedies of medicine, to the prayers of religion, to the severance of a muscle, to the amputation of a leg, and sometimes to suicide. He insists that, upon his death, his children pierce his heart with a stake and nail it to the bottom of his coffin to free his corpse in the sleep of death from the criminal tendencies of sleep in the living man. The *vukodlack* is nevertheless a good man, often the standard and the adviser of the tribe, often its judge and its poet. Through the grim sadness that his recollections impose on him and the apprehension of his nocturnal life, one sees a hospitable, generous soul who wants to love. The sun must set, night must place a lead seal on the eyelids of the poor *vukodlack* for him to scrape graves with his fingernails or upset the vigil of the nurse who sleeps at the crib of a newborn baby, for the *vukodlack* is a vampire, and the efforts of science and the rites of the church can do nothing for his illness. Even death does not cure him, inasmuch as he keeps some traits of life in his coffin. And as his conscience, tortured by the illusion of an involuntary crime, rests for the first time, it is not surprising that he may be found smiling in his tomb. The poor creature had never slept without dreaming! . . .

In Dalmatia, witches or *ujestize* of the country, more refined than the *vukodlacks,* prize the heart of a young lover, and eat it roasted over glowing hot coals. A twenty-year-old fiancé, whom these witches were planning to seize and who had awakened just in time to escape them, decided to sleep with an old priest. The priest had never heard of these awful practices and never dreamed that God would permit such crimes by man's tormentors. He went to sleep quite peacefully after several exorcisms in the room of the youth he was protecting. But hardly had he closed his eyes when he believed that he saw the *ujestize* hovering over his friend's bed. They gamboled and crouched around him with a ferocious laughter, reached into his torn chest, ripped out their prize, and quickly ate it, fighting among themselves for morsels, tossing them into the blazing flame. The priest was kept helpless on his bed by bonds that could not be untied; he tried in vain to utter shouts of horror that died on his lips as the sorcerers, with hideous stares, held him under their spell while wiping their bloody lips with their long, white hair. When the priest awoke, he saw his companion stumble out of bed, take a few uncertain steps, and fall dead at his feet because his heart had stopped beating.

These two men had had the same dream, following a recollection of something in their conversation. What killed the one was seen by the other. Here is an example of reason vanquished by the thoughts of sleep!

Hallucinations of sleep sometimes appear with such realistic features that they convince and drag into their orbit, so to speak, judgment, feelings, and all the faculties of the mind which otherwise keep their own integrity.

This psychological phenomenon has a remarkable quality in that it bridges the gap between sleep and waking and creates what amounts to a veritable merging.

Furthermore we have here a phenomenon that is peculiar to the effects of hashish and that we have repeatedly indicated following the data and the evidence of the inner feelings. Also, we cannot ignore the fact that it is frequently observed in actual psychosis.

Just as hallucinations developed by hashish or any other measurable cause, or even of completely unknown origin, while falsifying the process of judgment, take place in ordinary life, so can hallucinations of sleep falsify the intellect strictly within the range of their action, leaving it intact in all other respects.

Thus, from the point of view of the influence that they exert on the collective mental faculties, there are absolutely no differences among hallucinations, whether they originate in sleep, from the action of toxins, or from the ordinary effects of chronic or acute delirium. Is this not further proof that their psychic condition is the same in these different cases and that only the factors that cause this condition vary?

Cases upon which we base the preceding thoughts are few in number, which is often the way in science. Unwittingly and unknown to us, we have allowed ourselves to be guided in our observations by the theories and systems in vogue. These theories provide us with a ready-made framework within which we confine our attention. It is usually only by accident that we direct our attention outside this framework, which serves so well the natural laziness of our minds.

In the treatment of mental diseases we have, among our predecessors, important authorities who have cleared the road in several directions. It is difficult for us to differ with them and run the risk of losing ourselves in the chaos that we undertake to explore. But, once engaged in a specific course, like common tourists, we explore places we have already visited twenty times, happy if some heretofore unseen feature of the terrain is revealed to us.

If by chance we try a new way of observing, if some as yet unseen fact appears and seems to serve as a foundation for new theoretical concepts, we find ourselves reduced to our bare resources and we find it hard to support these facts with similar ones.

There is no lack of causes of mental illness collected by authors. But these cases, although eloquent on many points, are mute on others. Each observer has accepted them from his particular point of view. He only has seen the aspects in line with his theories; the other facts have completely escaped him or remained in half obscurity, impenetrable and sterile. He has described them as he has seen them, incompletely. The imprint of his convictions is evident in each line. Compare the observations that have been conveyed to us by the partisans of the predominance of mental etiology regarding the dynamic or functional nature of mental change with those observations of the supporters of physical causes, of the organic nature of intellectual lesions: everything that supports the dominant idea is related precisely and in detail; the remainder is hardly indicated or not at all.

I apologize for this digression, and I now come back to the subject that caused it.

We cannot doubt that in many psychotics delirium (in particular the hallucinatory state) has its first and constant point of departure in the state of sleeping.

This fact should have been frequently observed when society was still far from being civilized and when dreams exerted the greatest influence on naive and credulous people. Witchcraft, magic, and lycanthropy, which hardly exist today except in books, had no other origin, at least in many cases.

On this subject, I take great pleasure in citing this passage by Nodier who, as well as saying it with so much modesty and wit, "without climbing to such heights that the Royal Medical Society would never forgive me for being there," develops admirably the thesis that we support here:

> The shepherd, completely isolated from the world, whose thoughts oscillate between flocks of lambs and flocks of stars in the sky; the useless and rejected old woman who maintains

her poor life by gathering tasteless roots in the forest for food
and dry branches to protect her from the cold of winter; the
young girl, painfully amorous, who has not found the heart of
a man to understand the heart of a maiden—these people are
more subject than others to contemplative abberations that
sleep embellishes and transforms into an exaggerated reality
into whose midst the dreamer is thrown like an actor with
a thousand faces and a thousand voices to act out alone and
unwittingly an extraordinary drama that leaves all the caprices of imagination far behind.

Consider this ignorant, impressionable, thoughtful person.
He is a sleepwalker who sees things unknown to his peers. He
is having a nightmare. He awakens to the freshness of the
morning dew with the first rays of the sun that pierce the fog,
two miles from the spot where he went to sleep. He is, if you
please, in a clearing in the forest, where three tall trees stand,
crowded by the boughs of other trees. Deformed by lightning,
they dangle from their branches the noisy bones of some
truant. When he opens his eyes, a terrible laugh still rings in
his ears. A slowly disappearing trail of flame and smoke marks
the path of the demon's coach. The circle of trampled grass
around him retains the imprint of a nocturnal dance. Where
did he spend this night of terror if not at a midnight sabbath?
He is found with his face to the ground, his teeth chattering,
his limbs paralyzed with cold. He is dragged before the judge
and questioned: he has come from the sabbath; he has seen his
friends and neighbors there; the devil attended in person in
the form of a goat, a gigantic goat with fiery eyes and radiant
hooves, who spoke a human tongue, because such are the ways
of animals in a nightmare. The tribunal announces its ver-
dict; flames consume the poor unfortunate who has confessed
a crime without understanding it, and his ashes are thrown to
the wind. . . .

What man accustomed to the hideous visits of nightmares
will not understand perfectly that all the idols in China and
India come from dreams? The shepherd, afraid of wolves, frequently will dream that he becomes a wolf himself, and in his
sleep he will acquire the bloody instincts that are so fatal to

his flock. He hungers for living flesh, he thirsts for blood, he crawls around the shed on all fours, uttering that kind of savage growl that is typical of the nightmare and that reminds us of starving hyenas. And if by some grim chance he meets a poor stray animal, too young to flee, you may find him with his hands fastened to its fleece, baring his teeth at his favorite lamb. Lycanthropy is one of the phenomena of sleep, and this horrible illusion, more likely to perpetuate itself than the majority of ordinary nightmare illusions, has passed into real life under the name of a disease, known to physicians. . . .

To the details you have just read, in which you found the physiological truths that Nodier adorned with his poetic descriptions I would like to add a few facts whose intrinsic value, I hope, will not be attenuated by the dry simplicity of my presentation.

During the 1830's I traveled to Italy with a patient who had been entrusted to me by my worthy teacher Esquirol. During the entire year that this trip lasted, I never lost sight of this patient for a single day, or even for more than a few hours.

Mr. . . had been afflicted for several years with an intermittent delirium, whose principal symptoms were a manic excitement, sometimes quite intense, delusions of a religious nature, ideas of damnation, fear of hell, and so on. The attacks came irregularly, daily or every two or three days, and lasted from five or six hours to twenty-four to thirty-six hours. They invariably struck at the moment of waking, and they were especially violent and enduring when sleep had been prolonged.

On intermittent days, it frequently happened that Mr. . . developed a fever and, tired by the journey, he would lie down at my side in our carriage. After having gone to sleep in a perfectly sane condition, he would awaken delirious. But he was less ill than after a separated slack period.

Quite obviously the delirium originated during sleep. From the deepest sleep, Mr. . . passed to a state of drowsiness that was followed rather rapidly by a sort of reverie. It frequently happened that he would utter several words in a low and almost unintelligible voice, always in his native tongue (Mr. . . was Irish), never in French. This was the prelude to waking. Soon incoherent words gushed out, frequently including: "My God, my God! The devil is here!"

In the periods of relief his fits were generally of short duration. It even happened that they went no farther than a few words that could be the last whisper, the feeble echo of the nocturnal delirium.

Mr. . . , who was aware of his condition, could never satisfactorily account for this phenomenon so worthy of study. He retained only a vague memory, a very imperfect recollection. However, he was in the habit of using very appropriate expressions, in my opinion, to explain the manner in which the phenomenon occurred. He continued to dream, he said, even during the fit. I objected that he answered when I spoke to him, that he himself spontaneously remarked on what he had seen, and that I therefore had to believe that he was wide awake. "That is possible," he replied, "but nevertheless it seems to me that I am dreaming, except perhaps at the moment that I am answering your questions and when I speak to you myself. Don't you think I am a sleepwalker? My eldest brother certainly is. . . ."

Nothing could be more curious, surely, than this rapprochement between the dream state and the delirium, a rapprochement so close that all differences between these two conditions were completely erased. The dream of the awakened man was evidently the continuation of the dream of the sleeping man, and they did not differ except for the labels applied to them. Delirium is still the dream, but the individual who feels it has passed from a state of sleep to a waking state. Mr. . . was delirious while he had dreamed, and had he been able never to fall asleep, he would never have been delirious.

I tried several times to verify this natural conclusion by experience, at least as much as it could conform to the laws of the organism. The occasion arose several times during the course of our voyage. Whenever I could delay his bedtime by deliberate distractions, I prolonged the normal exercise of his mental faculties and, at the moment he awakened, I postponed the explosion of the delirium. Mr. . . , who appreciated his condition as well as I did, helped me in these experiments with all the power of his will.

One day in Rome we were invited to spend the evening with Cardinal W. who had known Mr. . . for a long time and was well aware of his illness. At first Mr. . . refused the invitation for fear of a mishap. However, I was aware of his deep desire to attend this gathering and I knew of the brilliant entertainment that he would find there. Knowing his motives, and somewhat reassured by the former relationship between my patient and the master of the house, I persuaded him to accept the invitation. I insisted that we go there together. As a further precaution I permitted him to depart from his usual habits and have a cup of weak coffee after dinner. We rode to the *Pincio* in a carriage, and at about 9 o'clock we arrived at the Cardinal's home. I had to come to his assistance a bit at first, in view of his considerable anxiety at being in the midst of a large gathering for the first time in several years, a group composed of serious, dignified men such as princes of the church, prelates, high-ranking officers, and foreign ambassadors.

After an hour or two of music whose effects on my patient I feared, not because it was not exquisite and executed by performers of great distinction, led by the Cardinal himself, playing a harmonica, but because we were forced to remain quiet and silent. Different groups formed, and Mr. . . took part in the conversation. The Cardinal, whom I had made partially aware of the scheme, was courteous with him and kindly attentive.

Thus happily and discreetly fortified, Mr. . . struggled successfully against sleep until almost 2 o'clock in the morning. He was at least four hours ahead of the game, because he usually retired between 9 and 10 o'clock.

However, I deemed it prudent not to push the experiment further, especially as a profound feeling of fatigue told me that it was time to retire.

In fact, we were hardly in our carriage when Mr. . . fell asleep, despite all my efforts, and when it was necessary to awaken him to enter the hotel, the delirium exploded with such violence that I vowed for some time to forego any further experiments.

A young man in Bicêtre Hospital (February 24), admitted in January 1845 for the fourth or fifth time, was deeply annoyed at not being able to win the hand of a young woman with whom he was desperately in love. He came from a family that included several psychotic members, most of them fairly well educated. He became morose, taciturn, and aloof. Life in his native country became insufferable, and he went to Paris with the hope of finding a diversion. Endowed with a vivid imagination and an eagerness to learn, he went to the public lessons of the most popular hypnotists and phrenologists of the day.

However, B. . . could not forget the sorrows that beset him; his nights became more and more disturbed. He was harassed by dreams that gradually dominated his mind. In these dreams he believed he saw timely secret warnings, the language surely "of a superior mentality specifically in charge of watching over him."

I let B. . . record his thoughts himself, and I transcribe *verbatim* certain parts of the voluminous manuscript that he sent me when he was convalescent:

> I believed in destiny, in a star, in a fate that governs the world and forces all animated beings, men, animals, birds, and insects to behave in a certain manner. Then I read the works of Fourier (which have already made many men of my acquaintance become mad and blow their brains), of Gall, of Mesmer, of Lavater, and of Spurzheim, things that comforted me in my unfortunate sorrows. The course in Magnetism that I studied under Doctor F. . . together with a course in phrenology comforted me most in my unhappy fallacies. I had also read certain notes dictated by Napoleon to Mr. Lascases in the Memoire de Sainte-Hélène, in which he said that he was seized with a gentle warmth, following which his mind joined an invincible mind which caused him to fall into an ecstasy and to see supernatural things that often changed his decisions in his grand operations. I read, I still know not where, that several days before his decapitation Louis XVI had had extraordinary visions, that he had seen monsters tearing his face apart in his palace, and all his soldiers, heads down, feet in the air, and the point of their bayonets at the ends of their rifles stuck in the ground. Finally, the result of all this was that I believed that the fate of everyone was governed by an invisible spirit, which I called providence or God; that what the pen of this God or destiny had traced, all the skill of man could not erase; that our misfortunes, our accomplishments, were not our doing; that it was He who managed our blind courage according to His will; that the duration of our emotions was not determined by us any more than the length of our life; that God, finally, or the above-named superior spirit, was master of all of us and managed everything through inspiration, dreams, visions, and premonitions. Consequently, convinced, like all human beings that I had a special destiny and an important

role to play in the grand drama of humanity, I believed that a superior spirit guided and directed me by the above-mentioned methods and in the following conditions, all of which were signs of good or bad omen for me.

All these manifestations, supposed to be under the direction of the spirit in question, fell into several classes:

1. Small dreams.
2. Large dreams.
3. Small visions.
4. Large visions.
5. Signs of good and bad omens, which consisted of encounters with things, objects, men, animals, and birds that I saw on my path and caused me to advance or to retreat, to continue or to change my direction, according to their significance.

In this manner I traveled for a long time in my illness, without passport, without papers, without being arrested, and I took such long trips that they called me Mr. Providence.

1. The small dreams were marked by the appearance in plain sleep of one or two subjects that indicated what I thought I had to do on the following day. Thus if I saw a hand writing, then it was urgent that I write the next day. If I saw a lion or a tiger or an oak tree or a flight of pigeons or crows or one or more snakes or an eagle or magpie or a column or a bumpy road or a maze or a broken iron bar or, in short, billions of other objects, there seemed to be, or so I thought, a direct relationship with what I saw and what I had to do during the course of the day.

2. The large dreams beset me during a deep, calm sleep. They were extraordinary stories, complicated comedies, that I sought to recall as soon as I awoke. I believed I had to do seven or eight different things, according to the significance of everything I had seen. [I skip the numerous details that follow.]

Small and large dreams were closely related to the small and large visions with respect to what affected their meaning. But the latter differed greatly in the manner in which they were manifested, particularly by the kind of clearness, the strong impression, and *the suffering that they left in my head after they were over.*

3. The small visions appeared in a complete waking state, *when I was tired,* whether walking or sitting or standing, *by the communication of a magnetic fluid* ⱽⁱⁱ *that disturbed my vision.* At the moment it appeared I saw all kinds of scenes before my eyes—tiny little men, huge men, cripples, dogs, lions, tigers, bears, elephants, soldiers, weddings, musicians whose music I clearly heard, an infinity of things like those in the small dreams but which appeared only when I was awake and when there was sufficient time to produce an extremely strong impression on my mind, that I felt I was obliged to follow.

4. The large visions manifested themselves in more or less the same way as the small ones, except that a *gentle warmth combined with the magnetic fluid and spread through all my limbs, leaving me totally unable to help myself as I wished, even depriving me of the freedom of my mind so that I could no longer direct my thoughts, my body, my limbs.*

I have limited the lengthy account of excesses, which could become monotonous. It suffices to say that it was almost always following "a rather violent headache which dazed him," after having felt *warmth,* an infallible prelude to his visions, or *a feeling of fatigue that tired his limbs* that his hallucinations appeared.

The woman he loved appeared frequently:

One day I was in bed at four in the morning and wide awake. I was seized all at once by the soft warmth announcing my large visions . . . One day, following a great fatigue, I went into my study to read the newspaper at seven or eight in the morning. I had hardly begun to read when a large vision appeared with the inexplicable *warmth* that momentarily paralyzes all my limbs. I quickly found myself on a mountain trip, pursued by an endless number of people, especially my parents, who wanted to have me committed. I leaped over all

---

ⱽⁱⁱ The occultists referred to a "magnetic fluid" to designate unperceptible influences, similar to the "waves" of the parapsychologists.

obstacles with an astonishing agility and, after having eluded my pursuers, I hid on the top of a mountain, in a large hole. Upon entering I heard a large heavy stone fall noisily in front of the cave and seal it. I found myself in a sort of tomb four meters square, where I discovered a stone to sit on. No sooner was I seated than I saw phantoms, specters with faces like those one sees in the costume shops at carnival time. Then a flash of smoke and fire caused them to disappear. This vision warned me that my freedom was threatened. By a strange coincidence, that same day I went to sleep on the grass of the Champs-Elysées and was awakened by a policeman who questioned me and took me to the station and then to Bicêtre.

The point of departure of B. . .'s madness and of the extremes to which he went rested in the visions that beset him, principally in his sleep.

These visions, by the regular progression of their subjects, the order that reigned in the depths of the worst disorders of the mind, had something strange about them. I doubt that such visions can occur except in the brain of someone hereditarily predisposed to madness, as was B. . . , who dreamed as only a madman can dream. The delirium would start during his sleep and continue later when he was awake.

As far as we can see in certain passages that I have emphasized, many of the visions took place in a state of half-sleep, or somnolence, caused by fatigue and announced by a gentle warmth, a general numbness. And these visions were identical to those that so often disturbed his deepest sleep.

These same visions recurred, but were less numerous, less extraordinary, in a state that the patient called *a state of being completely awake.*

So in the final analysis, the hallucinatory phenomenon was the same, whether B. . . was completely asleep, half-asleep, or even awake.

Sauvet (of Marseilles), a student in my ward at Bicêtre, published in *Annales Medico-Psychologiques* (March 1844) an extremely curious observation that resembles B. . .'s case in more than one way.

First there are simple dreams to which the patient attaches no importance. Little by little these dreams acquire vividness and recur so consistently that A. . . accepts them as visions to which he is obliged to give a mysterious meaning. Soon they are no longer dreams. A. . .

was mistaken about the real nature of the strange phenomena that took place for some time during his sleep. They are warnings from heaven. What he sees, what he hears is real, not (and these are the patient's expressions) "coming from an ordinary normal reality, but from a reality ordained by God." What he saw or heard was beyond the power of man and happened by order of the divinity. His senses were not in error; he had visions, but these visions did not imply that he was psychotic. Are not similar visions (the patient is speaking) in the holy Scripture, inspired by God?

Thus the basic mental disturbance in the case in point rests solely in the visions or hallucinations of sleep. In the waking state, the patient did not experience any phenomenon of this type, but the disorders of sleep carried over in A. . . .'s belief in his hallucinations, in the conviction that he had to adapt his behavior to the orders that came to him from above. From being purely *sensory*, the madness became *intellectual* by the transition from sleep to waking.

A. . . , a painter on glass, was born in Paris in 1808 to parents healthy in body and mind, of average wealth, whose business satisfied their needs. His education was not religious, and his father devoted himself to providing him with a general knowledge that might later make his son fit to enter the line of work that pleased him. At a very tender age, A. . . was noted for his extreme vivacity, together with an extreme sensitivity, and he already showed that imagination, that enthusiasm for beauty, that was to increase with age and bring such disastrous results. He was scarcely twelve years old when the sight of a beautiful woman filled him with admiration, and without really understanding what he was doing, he fell in love with her and was so impassioned that he was about to leave his family to live with someone he had only seen once.

It should be noted in passing that this precocious enthusiasm, this exaggeration of imagination in a child is almost always an infallible forerunner of genius, or more often, of madness.

Soon A. . . was orphaned and, feeling the need for an occupation, he entered an artists' studio. But his comrades laughed at his ideas. They joked at the rigidity of his ways because, entranced with mental beauty, A. . . ignored sensual pleasures, and only after much urging, did he consent to go to a woman of ill repute. The crudeness of the pleasure disgusted him, and he went three whole years without the slightest desire. At that time he fell in love with a woman whom he addressed in the language of the heart. He soon stopped because, he said, she did not understand him. From then on he was never alone. He felt an irresistible need to love, and he offered to share this love with his mistresses. But they all laughed at him and forsook him in turn. "My sentimentality bored them," he said. However, a married woman, who understood him, offered herself to him, and he loved this woman more than all the others, because theirs was a shared love.

One night while asleep he heard a voice that said: "You must not take your neighbor's wife." He heard the same thing several times, and despite the pain, he soon gave up this woman.

In 1840, never having been concerned with politics but perhaps encouraged by circumstances, he hung a sign in his window upon which he had written four verses expressing his contempt for the government and his admiration for Napoleon.

At this time, A. . . began to feel remorse over the life he was leading, and soon he saw his remorse confirmed, as it were, by apparitions during his sleep.

One night he believed that he was transported to the Pont-Neuf. There he saw Moses in the clouds, holding the Tablet of Commandments in his hand. Behind Moses were St. John and Christ carrying his cross.

Another time, he felt carried through the air by a spirit of whom he saw only one arm, holding a lamp, and every time the spirit breathed on the lamp, sparks fell from it, setting on fire everything they touched. A. . . believed that this phenomenon revealed to him the cause of unexplained fires that had occurred in the past several years.

Another night A. . . found himself in front of Nôtre Dame. He saw the moon crossing the sky and uttering in a sepulchral

voice the words "death! death! death!" Everywhere around
him he saw houses crumbling and men and animals dying of
fright. Soon the river united its two arms, sweeping everything
away in its waters. A. . . stood alone presiding over this uni-
versal cataclysm.

Shortly after, A. . . was so struck by what he had seen, that
looking for explanations, he decided for the first time to read
the gospel. He was astonished to find in it the scenes he had
witnessed, and even his interpretations of them. No doubt
about it, he was a protégé of heaven; his visions were most
certainly celestial warnings. From then on he was constantly
reading books about saints, interpreting them in his own way.
The visions occurred more frequently and more explicitly,
and finally an apparition ordered him to marry the woman he
lived with at the time and by whom he had a child. He felt
compelled to obey, and a few days later he was married. Soon
he saw the supreme Being once more in a dream. This time
he had the face of a venerable old man and was surrounded
by a multitude of angels, resplendent with joy and beauty.
Then underneath him there were innumerable men, women,
and children of all ages who were dancing and appeared quite
happy. A. . . saw in this scene the image of happiness mortals
would enjoy once he had announced the truth to them. "I
found them so beautiful, so happy that if I had not been
afraid to commit a crime I should have committed suicide to
share their happiness immediately."

However, poor A. . . shared everything he had seen with
his wife and his family and, far from treating him as a vision-
ary, everything indicates that they regarded him as a man
inspired by God; in such a manner that his ideas, thus encouraged, pursued him everywhere and nearly caused him to
commit a public act of madness.

One night he saw the Gospel, flying through the air with
wings of fire. It touched several people and burned them upon
contact. All fled and tried to protect themselves from its reach
and, as they struggled, burning leaves fell from the book,
fluttered about and ignited everything they touched. A. . .

alone, who ran after them and gathered them, was completely unharmed.

At last there was a final vision, the most meaningful for A. . . In the middle of his sleep he heard a voice that said to him, "Get up, take your shirt off and put on your overcoat." Then, after a moment of quiet, he distinctly heard the word "work" repeated twice. The poor man woke up with a start. He believed more firmly than ever that he was sent from heaven to preach to men. Moreover, had he not just heard the formal order to work, that is, to acquaint men with the truth? He got up, dressed, and prepared to leave. He did not know how to go about spreading the light, but what of it? . . . He was going out to repeat what he had seen. He knew very well that he probably would be arrested, incarcerated perhaps, and then what would happen to his wife and his child, whom he saw sleeping peacefully before him? He hesitated for a moment. . . , but the voice had spoken and he had to obey. With a last loving glance toward the two people whom he loved so tenderly, he left the house. He walked until it was light, and soon, finding a convenient place, he wrote about his vision on a wall. A few moments later he was arrested and taken to Bicêtre.

Except for his ideas, A. . . is an educated and intelligent young man, expressing himself eloquently and pleasantly. His religion and his morals are those of a perfectly honest man; he is not a religious fanatic and is quite rational. In short, on one hand he has an unshakable faith in the truth of his apparitions; on the other, he is endowed with every good mental and moral quality. Such is the bizarre character of the patient whose history we have just reported.

IV. CEREBRAL CONGESTION

We will not concern ourselves here with those cases where a disastrous and rapid action strikes down the individual, partially or totally obliterating the mental faculties and inflicting serious damage on the motility. These cases are rather infrequent. In general, cerebral con-

gestion is limited to simple dizziness, to the partial suspension of cere
bral activity, and its effects are rarely followed by unfortunate conse
quences.

Simple congestion is a common pathological case. Few persons have
not had occasion to observe it. But too little importance is attached
to it for pathologists believe they should examine it closely, and give
a detailed account of what goes on in the mental faculties.

Andral [viii] writes in *Clinique Médicale:*

> The dizzy spells are more or less intense; at the same time,
> patients may have cephalalgia, dizziness, ringing in the ears,
> momentary aberrations of vision, temporary speech impedi-
> ment, tingling in the extremities, and sometimes in the face;
> the eyes are bloodshot; the pulse is ordinarily slow and erratic.

On the basis of careful reports gathered from various individuals
subject to dizziness, and from my own experience, because I have them
in common with several members of my family, I would add that when
the dizzy spells (which usually do not arrive suddenly or unannounced)
appear, it is with hot flashes in the head, a feeling of pressure on the
temples, blankness of thought, inability to concentrate, and isolated
distractions. Sometimes it seems as if a cloud is passing before the eyes
but so rapidly that you are hardly aware that the logical association of
ideas is interrupted. Often, also, there has been an interruption, nearly
a stoppage of thought, to the point that it seems that existence is sus
pended, such as happens when one falls abruptly into a deep, brief
sleep.

Let us note that completely identical phenomena are created, in
termittently, by the action of narcotics, particularly high doses of
hashish. Those hot flashes, that lifting of the top of the skull, that en
largement of the bony cavity, that flowering of the brain, and so forth
are all *congestive* sensations, so to speak. A young physician who had
taken hashish told me, as he tried to explain the nature of his sensa
tions: "I am undergoing a rapid succession of congestions."

Thus we find in cerebral congestions, as in the above cases, the pri
mordial psychic change that we have identified as the basic, necessary

---

[viii] See Appendix.

source of all mental aberrations, particularly hallucinations, or the hallucinatory state.

From then on we cannot be surprised if cerebral congestions constitute, in a great many cases, the preliminary state of madness and, furthermore, if they are immediately followed by manic delirium and a total incoherence of the mental processes.

We will shortly see that in certain individuals hallucinations are always announced by symptoms that closely resemble cerebral congestions.

Cases where cerebral congestions are evidently the point of departure of the hallucinatory state are not rare in science. I will be content to cite the following.

J.M. is a man of good reputation, of sanguine temperament. In his youth he was subject to *dizziness* (these are his words) that he had had treated several times by bloodletting. At times he lost consciousness, and he avoided a fall by leaning either against a piece of furniture or against the wall. By his own statement, he would suddenly be affected and would feel a sensation "like boiling water being injected in my head." One evening he was picked up on Rue des Fossés-Saint-Victor, unconscious and, apparently intoxicated, he was taken to the police station at Maubert Place.

When J.M. came to, he seemed terrified. He said, not without some confusion in his ideas, that he had been the victim of a frightful ambush, that he had suddenly been attacked by four men dressed in white, their faces painted white, who threw themselves on him and hit him hard on the head with sticks.

There was no question that J.M. had been seized with one of the cerebral accidents to which he was subject and that this time his mental faculties had been affected. It was impossible to dissuade him from believing that his hallucination was born in his mind, and his ideas are just the same to this day, after a stay of several years at Bicêtre.

In Lelut's *The Demon of Socrates,* I find a case similar to the one I have just cited. The hallucinatory state is unquestionably linked with a habitual predisposition to congestions:

> G. . . was an elderly man of sixty-five, with gentle manners
> and an ordinary intelligence, working as a shoemaker. He was
> admitted to the mental ward on May 1, 1828. . . .

He had returned from military service with chills that rapidly made him ill and left him with a lumbago that forced him to walk bent over.

In 1820 he returned from Montsouris. He was, he said, in good health, and had not been drinking. He saw eight or ten men following him. He heard them singing and stepped aside to let them pass. He fell and woke up in a police station with a deep wound over his left eyebrow, where there still is a scar. He was taken home. Several days later he was told that undoubtedly he had been struck by the men he saw following him on the plain of Montsouris. He believed it all the more because one of his friends and his wife had recently been attacked and injured, only elsewhere. To this day, G. . . is convinced that he was followed and attacked by a party of robbers who had committed many crimes without having been punished. Following his fall and injury, he felt a pain on the right side of his head for some time. He added that for two or three years it often happened that he saw "red or green" on the edges of brooks, and that this often coincided with violent dizzy spells.

In August 1827, entering his house one evening, he suddenly "began for the first time to hear noises, voices" that threatened him and frightened him to the point that he called a neighbor and asked him to search the attic. The search was fruitless. G. . . persuaded his neighbor to sleep with him. During the night he "heard the same voices", but his companion heard nothing. During the following days and nights G. . . was subject to the same perceptions. This lasted four months. At the end of that time he had not only "heard the voices but he saw, whether in total or in part, the people who spoke to him. . . ."

We must also relate to a congestive state of the brain the delirium with hallucinations experienced by some Arabs when they pray.

The ways in which Moslems fulfill this important obligation of their religion cannot fail to have a harmful influence on the mental faculties. It results, as I have said previously, in a rush of blood to the brain, which immediately results in a stupor and convulsions. At the same time, the imagination, by now quite wild, is thrown off its course and indulges temporarily in manic delirium.

In this connection I cite the following facts:

One evening I asked the sailors who sailed the boat in which I was going up the Nile to recite a chorus in honor of the Prophet. There were seven of them, including the captain. Sitting close to one another, legs crossed, they began by repeating the refrain of the hymn that one of them was chanting. I saw their heads move imperceptibly from right to left and from front to back. This movement became faster and faster, and the rest of the body soon followed. *Allah, la, la, lah!* This invocation, uttered at first in a firm, clear voice, soon degenerated into a kind of growl, a hollow, irregular sound that was painful to the ear. Finally, after more than a half-hour devoted to this increasingly violent and disorderly agitation, one of them, a young man of twenty-three or twenty-four, more excited than his companions, beat his head against the boards of the boat with such force that I thought he would break it. Two other sailors tried to restrain him. The fanatic quickly stood up, as if he had been propelled by a lever. Light convulsive movements appeared, and then he fell exhausted. His face was red and inflamed, the veins of his neck enlarged and bluish, as if ready to burst. His expression was dazed, his head leaned sharply backwards. His eyes were constantly lifted toward the sky. This state lasted nearly two hours! . . . I made some observations on this man. He was gentle, laborious and not at all irritable. He had never had convulsions and had never indulged in any excesses.

The next day a child of ten or twelve, a relative of the captain, participated in the prayers. After a few moments this child's excitement reached an extraordinary degree. He had to be restrained for fear he would jump in the Nile or would crack his head against the boat. He was very agitated, making some kind of cry and uttering volubly words that no one could understand, since they were neither Arabic nor Turkish and, said my interpreter, belonged to *no known language.* After about fifteen minutes, he fell, unconscious, among his comrades, who formed a circle around him. They seemed to worship this child and were convinced he would be a saint some day.

When the future saint had calmed down, I asked him if he could describe what happened to him when he prayed with such fervor. "I saw the sky open," he replied, "and I heard words that I cannot recall. Then I saw a saint who called me to him and held out his arms to me. I also saw a human head that soared above me and frightened me a great deal. I do not know what it means; God is great! Allah! Allah!"

Not long ago in the commune of Kuenheim, three miles from Colmar, there was a sect of convulsive fanatics who indulged in religious practices that have a certain similarity to those of the Moslems and to whom our reflexions about the latter apply:

The leader was a farmer noted for his exaggerated piety. In the room where the society (composed of thirty or forty men, women, and children) met, there was an open Bible on a table. The leader read aloud from this Bible to the members, who were seated on benches or standing around him. This sermon was delivered in solemn tones, first in German, the only language that the congregation understood. Then he spoke in a jargon unbeknown to all, *even to the orator*. If, after the meeting, you asked the leader what language he had spoken, he would reply that it was sometimes Latin, sometimes Hebrew, that he did not know either tongue, but that in those moments he was inspired by God, who made him speak in the language He chose.

As the jargon of the orator became more forceful, more rapid, more unintelligible, the congregation murmured, stirred, spoke aloud, and finally began to roar, to howl in so terrible a manner that they could be heard in the neighboring forest, more than a quarter of a mile away.

In the middle of this uproar, the women (almost always the youngest) got up, waved their arms over their heads, and turned on their heels, uttering piercing cries that rose above this savage sound. Then a convulsive movement seized their bodies, and they fell as though exhausted. When they rose, after ten or twelve minutes, they began to dance, to sing and to laugh, with the nervous laugh of someone drunk or mad. The dance and the song were incoherent, lascivious, the eyes glowed and tears trickled down the cheeks of these unfortunate creatures.

During this horrible uproar, the orator maintained the calm of an inspired chieftain. He stepped into the midst of his disciples just when the excitement was about to subside. Then those who were somewhat calmed by fatigue approached him. Some of them bent forward and touched his body with their heads or hands. Some succeeded only in touching him with their fingertips. Surrounded in this way, the chief resumed his talk and his violent gesticulations, spinning around and causing all of his disciples to revolve about him. After five minutes, the paroxysms redoubled, new convulsions seized the women, etc. . . . .[16]

A predisposition to cerebral congestions can cause hallucinations without otherwise occasioning a derangement in the mental faculties.

According to all appearances, it is to a cause of this nature that we must attribute a case that created a commotion among the distinguished psychologists of Germany in 1791. I quote Delrieu (*Revue de Paris*) :

In February 1791, Mr. Nicolai, a wealthy bookseller of Berlin, a strong and mentally healthy man, neglected his customary spring bloodletting. He was seized with a strange illness: every day he was visited by one or more ghosts endowed with the features of dead people who gathered without ceremony in the shop of the sick man, climbed on his bed, and even followed him into the street and into the homes of his friends.

Despite the enormity of such a crisis, Mr. Nicolai had the presence of mind to study the ghosts with the sophistication of a man of the world, the imagination of a poet, and the curiosity of a scholar. After several weeks, thanks to a blood-

---

[16] *Gazette des Magistrats,* October, 1844.

letting, the specters appeared less distinctly. Their colors faded and the patient recovered his own color and health. When he was completely well, they had disappeared.

The bookseller had the moral courage to submit the chronicle of his suffering to the Philosophical Society of Berlin at a time when the appearance of the ghost of Maupertuis to Mr. Gleditsch, a famous Prussian botanist in the Institute of Natural History, predisposed the members of this erudite body to serious reflection on extraterrestrial life.

They noted the following details in the bookseller's presentation:

"My ghosts seemed to be the size of an ordinary living man. The uncovered portions of their bodies, their faces and hands, had the complexion of the living. Their clothing had the color of materials used for toweling, but their tones were paler than in real life. Their faces were neither terrible nor funny nor repulsive. Their appearance was extremely courteous. I heard them speak distinctly; sometimes they chatted without me, sometimes they admitted me to their conversation. Their discourse was brief, rapid, a bit dry, but always pleasant. The ghosts of my friends evidently concerned themselves with my sorrows; their comforting presence followed me especially when I was alone. It happened, however, that I would hear them in the midst of a crowd, in a salon, even when real people were speaking to me. And, since I was deeply embarrassed for fear of appearing foolish by replying to my ghost and to my company at the same time, I remained silent and hesitant, which made me appear how I wished not to."

Considerable time had elapsed since the cure of the bookseller. One day, at his desk, as he was thumbing through a bundle of papers related to his illness, the ghosts tried to appear. He sensed it because of a peculiar sensation that stole all over him, but he hastened to put the papers back in the drawer, shut the desk, slipped away full of terror, and the apparitions disappeared.[17]

---

[17] Nicolai, *Memoire à la Société royale de Berlin,* cited by A. Delrieu.

The *Société philosophique de Berlin*, sceptical but cautious, ordered that the bookseller's memoir be deposited in the Bureau of Inquiries. It would be difficult, we must admit, to say precisely what state Nicolai was in when he was visited by the ghosts. But I will venture that the consequences of neglecting the customary bloodletting, the domestic problems that had preceded it, and finally the disappearance of the ghosts upon resuming the bleeding probably established a cerebral condition similar if not identical to the state resulting from congestions.

V. FEBRILE EXCITEMENT

All febrile excitement, whatever its origin when it reaches a certain intensity or simply by virtue of its very nature,[18] is likely to cause changes or, rather, perturbances in the mental faculties.[ix]

These disturbances can appear at the beginning of the fever, during the incubation period so that the individual who is threatened can hardly explain what he is experiencing. The same is true with the decline of the illness, when convalescence begins.

Among other symptoms that open the scene, as it were, especially when the nervous system seems most exposed to the strains of the incipient illness, we note a heaviness in the head, pressure on the temples, hot flashes, dizziness, blurred perceptions and thoughts, propensity to daydreaming, and partial or total deprivation of sleep. Sleep is replaced at times by an abundant activity of aimless and uncontrolled thoughts that wander from one subject to the other or else are irresistibly attracted to a particular subject, at times by continual, bizarre and absurd dreams.

The same symptoms, at least those connected with the mental facul-

---

[18] We know that the contagious fevers such as yellow fever and the plague are frequently accompanied by varied cerebral symptoms, that the delirium that follows includes the characteristics of the most identifiable madness. To cite only one example, in the plague that devastated Carthage in the fourth century B.C., most patients, in a frenzied state of excitement, sallied forth in arms to push back the enemy whom they believed had invaded the town.

[ix] Such episodes are known as acute brain syndromes.

ties, can recur upon the decline of a serious fever. Such symptoms are like the last spasms of the intense delirium that preceded them. They appear mainly when the pain has required bloodlettings which resulted in a state of anemia.

It has long been known that excessive bloodletting can give rise to the same nervous accidents and mental anomalies such as those caused by congestive failure or by the introduction of toxic substances in the blood stream.

From the preceding, one may conclude that febrile excitement causes the same psychocerebral changes that have been the subject of our studies up to now, changes that inevitably occur every time the mind undergoes some alteration, at the outset of partial or total disturbances of the mental faculties, disturbances that are the natural and necessary precursors of delirium, whatever its form or type.

Here are several examples of hallucinations that occurred in the circumstances just mentioned:

> A friend of Ross's went upstairs to his bedroom. As he entered the room he was embraced by a woman dressed in white. He protested in vain against this display of tenderness, but received no answer. After the disappearance of the ghost whose caresses had been as swift and rapid as lightning, he felt a malaise in all his limbs. He went to bed and was *seized by a fever;* ten days later, he died.[19]

Nicolai wrote:

> At the end of a *nervous fever,* when his convalescence was still uncertain, one of my friends, in bed but wide awake, saw the door of his room opening. At the same time the figure or the semblance of a woman moved toward the foot of his bed. He watched the ghosts for several minutes and, as his eyes began to tire from contemplating this form, he turned over to wake his wife. But when he looked around, the phantom was no longer there.[20]

The Marquis of Rambouillet, elder brother of the Duchess

---

[19] Rose's *Arcana.*
[20] Nicolai, *Nicholson's Journal.*

of Montausier, and the Marquis of Précy, eldest son of the house of Nantouillet,[x] both between twenty-five and thirty years of age, were close friends and went to war, as did all persons of quality in France. They were chatting together one day about the other world; after several remarks that testified to their lack of conviction in common beliefs on the subject, they made a mutual promise that the first one to die would appear to his friend with some information. After three months, the Marquis of Rambouillet left for the wars in Flanders, and de Précy, seized by a severe fever, remained in Paris. Six weeks later, still recovering, de Précy heard a rustle in the curtains of his bed at five o'clock in the morning and, turning around, he saw the Marquis of Rambouillet in battle dress. He got out of bed to embrace de Rambouillet and to express his joy at his return. But Rambouillet, stepping back, told him that his caresses were untimely, that he had come to live up to his pledge, because he had been killed that evening in the trenches. He added that everything that was said about the other world was quite correct, that his friend had to think about changing his life habits, and that he had little time to lose because he would be killed in the first encounter in which he fought.

De Précy's surprise at this conversation was indescribable. Disbelieving what he had heard, he tried anew to embrace his friend, who he thought was deluding him, but he embraced empty air. Rambouillet, seeing his friend's scepticism, showed him his wounds, from which blood still seemed to be flowing.

At this point the phantom disappeared, leaving de Précy in a state of terror easier to understand than to describe. He told everyone in his house what he had just seen, but it was attributed to the *intensity of the fever,* which could have affected his imagination.[21]

In the state of depression that followed an inflammatory illness, a man equally distinguished for his intelligence and

---

[21] *Memoires de Rochefont.*

[x] Members of the French nobility attached to the retinue of Louis XIV (1632–1715). The War of Flanders took place in 1672–73.

for his military abilities was besieged by visions all the more strange since he was in possession of all his faculties and none of his senses was altered. Nevertheless, fantastic objects beset him which he knew full well did not exist. They were as vivid and easy to enumerate and describe as the actual objects around him.[22]

VI. Convulsive Diseases

We know that convulsive disorders, the primary ones being epilepsy and hysteria, frequently accompany hallucinations of the senses, that is, a partial or general hallucinatory state. Let me add that in no case is the hallucinatory phenomenon, particularly as it relates to the general sensibility, more varied or stranger than with convulsive illnesses.

These facts have been noted by writers with relative accuracy. One cannot say this of the symptoms or psychocerebral accidents from which the hallucinatory state develops and that are none other than the *primary fact.*

If you question patients carefully, with appropriate questions which help their judgment and their uncertain and confused inner awareness, it will be easy to get a clear, definitive idea of the phenomena that occur in the case we are studying.

Many patients do not develop their disease with such suddenness that it is impossible to see it developing. They are warned of its approach; certain physical and mental accidents alert them and put them on their guard.

Sometimes in advance, several days or only a few hours or even a few minutes, they feel a peculiar sensation in the head that they most frequently compare to *dizzy spells* or to momentary *vapors.* They are absent-minded and distracted, and their vision is blurred. They find themselves having the most bizarre and incoherent thoughts, and they even utter words that have no meaning they are aware of.

Some of them, principally hysterics, combine the mental disturbances that we have just indicated with others that are related to the feelings; these include panics, baseless fears, and acute anxieties.

---

[22] E. Salverte, *Sciences occultes.*

When hallucinations appear, the fit is imminent, and it takes place shortly.

For several months I had in my ward at Bicêtre an epileptic whose seizures were almost always preceded by hallucinations. As he felt certain pains in his joints and his fingers became cold and stiff, this man, who was ordinarily quite calm, diligent, and gentle, gradually became wild, garrulous, and unruly. He continued to work, but in an absent-minded way. As he said himself: "There is no use in doing it; I am not interested any longer; I don't have my head with me any more."

Imperceptibly L. . . became somber and quiet; he avoided his friends and expressed fears that he would be poisoned. He showed a marked defiance toward all those who lived with him. Finally he heard threatening voices and believed that he was being followed by spies. One evening he left the house where he lived, in the suburbs of Saint-Antoine, shouting that he was going to be murdered. He fled at top speed along the Saint-Martin Canal, convinced that he was being pursued by three armed men who wanted to kill him. He did not return home until the next day, having spent the night crouched behind a pile of wood on the embankment.

Approximately three months ago I was consulted by a young man who provided these details concerning his illness:

> I do not know what I feel, but since I have lived for a long time with S. . . , whom you treated for epileptic seizures, I am afraid I have caught his illness. I perform my religious duties in a Jewish temple. When my illness comes, I no longer know what I am doing, and I am forced to interrupt what I am doing, lest everything go wrong. I never have a headache; I do not feel any unusual warmth; my vision is never blurred. Sometimes, without being cold, without feeling ill, I have chills throughout my body and at the same time I involuntarily blink my eyes. It seems that the chills affect my brain. . .

For several years S. . . had been afflicted with a convulsive disorder presenting the clearest characteristics of hysteria. S. . . never lost consciousness, even at the height of his attacks, which were nevertheless of frightening intensity. During the almost two years that he spent in my ward I was often able to get from him a complete accounting of what he felt at the beginning of the attack.

As far as the mental features were concerned, it was almost the same as the disorder that I have just described. However, it lasted less long and yet was much more serious. S. . . compared the state in which he found himself at those times with a temporary intoxication. "It is exactly as if I had drunk a bottle of strong wine in one gulp," he would tell me. "I feel something going to my head; my ears ring; I cannot think. Sometimes I want to speak and I cannot. At other times I speak in spite of myself. It seems as if I am leaving for another world."

At this point of the illness, sometimes before convulsions appeared, S. . . would throw himself on his bed, after warning the attendants or some of his fellow patients, and he would wait until the attack was over. Often he could still answer in gestures the questions that were asked of him; at other times he seemed unaware of what was said. This was not true, however, because when the attack was over he would tell us everything that was said or done during his "lethargy."

I could easily offer further illustrations, but those I have given suffice to call attention to the fact of psychological morbidity that we are investigating and to establish that mental disturbances, particularly the hallucinatory state, that accompany certain nervous diseases, flow from the same psychic change or, if you will, begin with that same psychic change that we are trying to present in every portion of this work.

VII. Debilitating Factors—Privations: Hunger, Thirst, Cold

The most indispensable physiological function is nutrition, or the act by which solid and liquid substances are introduced into the body's economy to contribute to the growth of organs and to replace materials that have been expelled by peristaltic movement.

When nutrition fails, the organs of the mental functions show their state of deprivation by strange symptoms that have always amazed observers. We will soon see that, from our point of view, far from being peculiar, these symptoms are expected to be such and the mental changes should have the characteristics which we know.

I will not concern myself with the mode of action of the causes enumerated above or the manner in which the deprivation of solid or liquid nourishment affects the nervous system. The answers to these questions are of no interest whatever here. It is important that we direct our attention to the nature of the mental disturbances that appear in the circumstances in question.

As always, the scene opens with the best-known signs of manic excitement, or of gradual dissociation of ideas, of transformation of reality that feeds on sensations from outside, into a completely imaginary existence nourished by inner sensations or by the merging of these two lives.

If I list these phenomena with such assurance (observation in this case is limited and difficult), it is because I rely on my personal experience and my own sensations.

In July 1837, I was crossing that part of the African desert that extends along the Mediterranean coast from Damiette, or rather Lake Menzale, to El-Arich. A French servant, a Turkish interpreter, and three camel drivers made up the caravan. After eight days of travel through the sand at a temperature of 36 to 38° C, our water supply was exhausted. We had to use the briny water which is found by digging into the sand to a certain depth. This distasteful drink was so repugnant to us that we swallowed a few sips with great reluctance to quench our burning thirst.

J . . . (the servant), a man of about fifty, healthy but destined to die shortly thereafter from dysentery, was the first to suffer from being deprived of liquids. His strength, which had not been lowered by travel, fatigue, high temperatures, nor the Kamsin winds, seemed gradually to weaken. He became strangely apathetic, and I attempted to encourage him, which had never been necessary previously. As he rode his camel, he was overcome by an irresistible urge to sleep. He did not sleep, but he was preoccupied with memories that took him back to his native land.

"It is amazing," he told me, "I have tried to stay away from these memories. I kept thinking I was over there, and I was not sleeping nor dreaming, any more than I am now as I talk to you. I saw our mountains, their forests, their crystal-clear brooks. . . . How sad that all that is not any more real than the water and the trees over there, before us, which keep receding as we think we are coming closer to them." J. . . . was speaking of the effects of a mirage.

Once he started talking, J. . . . exhausted the subject. It was impossible to direct his thoughts elsewhere.

Toward the end of the eleventh day of travel, we arrived at El-Arich, where we found fresh water, just in time for poor J. . . . , whose *excitement* was about to degenerate into a veritable mania.

Since I had experienced something similar to the symptoms of my servant, I was able to study them in myself. Besides, I had been able to swallow a few mouthfuls of water from time to time; and it was undoubtedly because of this that I felt only mild stomach pains and a little dryness of the throat.

However, I gradually felt overcome by a strong desire to sleep. The bright sunlight reflected by the burning sands tired my vision. Weary of the monotony of the desert and the endless expanse of plains of sand touching the horizon, I had gotten into the habit of reading as I went. I found myself so distracted that it was most difficult for me to focus on a single thought. My attention wavered and seemed to weaken. The more I tried to fool time and especially my thirst, that worsened by the minute, the more helpless I felt. Soon I could only think of the moment when, having reached El-Arich, we would have all the water we wanted, and the great happiness I would feel upon quenching my thrist drinking as much as I desired. I tried to fight these thoughts by thinking about other things and summoning memories of past sensations, or by evoking in my imagination scenes that could distract me. Impossible! The matchless pleasure and delight that obsessed me without end and absorbed me completely was the thought of quenching my thirst, and I would have forfeited all worldly pleasures for the ineffable delight of a glass of water. I dreamed only of cold drinks and sherbets. I especially pictured, with great delight and such a vivid imagery that I was on the verge of hallucinating, a certain café at del Castelle in Naples, where I had been going in the evening during the August heat to drink delicious wine. It was a veritable monomania of my imagination, encircled by a train of thoughts and memories relating to my thirst, that instinctive need which was in distress.

The primary fact and the psychic consequences that it entails are no less obvious in what has just been said than in the considerations I have dealt with in the preceding sections.

The normal association of ideas gradually escapes the influence of the will. Certain thoughts, those that occurred to the mind at the very moment it lost its freedom and its spontaneity of action, become more and more preponderant as the general disturbance increases and the mental upset is more extensive.

For the same reasons, the ties that bind us to the external world relax and let go. Our self-awareness weakens, and we pass from real life to an imaginary one. Gradually, objects which exist only in the imagination appear to be real, as happens in a dream. Let me repeat: we dream while wide awake. We confuse perceptions of reality with those of our imagination.

When we are thirsty, it is natural that we should think of the best means of satisfying our thirst. This thought, the first to arise in the mind initiates a host of other thoughts, more or less related to it. This happens by virtue of the principle of association of ideas, which in the case under discussion, functions with all its native energy, as in manic excitement and in dreams, without being restricted by the free, deliberate will.

Thus tormented by an awful thirst in the middle of the burning sands of the desert, our imaginations chose to dwell upon memories of limpid waters, of places where lush vegetation provides coolness and shade. We know that the unfortunate victims of a famous shipwreck, beset with the tortures of hunger and thirst, by the anguish of despair, ready to descend into the abyss at any instant, experienced visions whose charm contrasted sharply with their situation.

Prolonged intense cold can induce delirium and the development of an hallucinatory state. Should these effects be attributed to numbness of the senses and of the nervous functions? We believe they are more probably due to a flow of blood from the periphery of the body to the center, a flow that produces a congestive state of the inner organs, particularly the brain. We find in these effects, as in the other delirious states I have reviewed, the most obvious symptoms of mental excitement: that state of half-sleep or the merging of the dream state with the waking state which betrays the primordial state.

Dr. Prus, whom we all know to be an authority on nervous ailments, experienced the influence of extreme cold himself when, in 1814, he left the army post where he was stationed to travel two miles to see his family:

> I had hardly gone one mile in the most intense cold, when I noticed that I was not in my normal state. I was walking from habit rather than by will-power. My body felt extremely light. Aware of the reason for and the seriousness of this state, I wanted to make haste, but in vain. What troubled me most was that my eyes kept closing involuntarily. I was then assailed by a host of pleasant images; I thought I had been carried into a delightful garden; I saw trees, meadows, streams.[23]

[23] Report presented to the *Société de Médecine,* November 1843.

Chapter 5

I. HALLUCINATIONS IN THE MENTALLY ILL

In the preceding chapters I have demonstrated experimentally that whenever we observe the phenomenon of hallucinations mingling with the activities of real life, we inevitably find the psychic conditions, the mental changes, in other words the dynamic nervous lesion, that the action of extract of Indian hemp taught us to recognize. We have identified this lesion as the basic source, the primary, generative fact of all the other pathological phenomena of the mental faculties.

This lesion has been observed: (1) in the hallucinatory states produced by toxic substances; (2) in states which develop under physiological conditions where no mental faculty seems to be coincidentally injured and, since it is impossible to relate these states to any morbid factor, which have merely been noted as bizarre coincidences between hallucinations and a state of sanity; (3) in the intermediate state between waking and sleeping and in total sleep; and (4) finally in certain pathological conditions other than madness that are capable of creating the hallucinatory state, such as (a) cerebral congestions, (b) fever, at its onset and its decline, (c) neuroses, and finally (d) deprivation of food and drink or prolonged, intense cold.

The continued studies we have reported have led us to the opinion, suggested by self-observation, that an hallucination is the most frequent symptom and the fundamental fact of delirium, mental illness, and madness.

And first, from what has been said, we are led to declare *a priori* that mental excitement, the sudden or gradual dissociation of ideas, the weakening or the complete discontinuance of the balance between the various mental powers, in a word what we have designated under the collective name of *primary fact,* is the source of hallucinations specific to madness.

Now we will look at the facts and relate them to what we know concerning hashish and the psychological nature of the hallucinatory state.

To throw some light on our task I will first direct our attention to the most well-known facts, and then turn to those less accessible, by their nature, to investigation. Where we cannot observe directly, induction will provide the way—induction, that precious guide we must use every time facts are incomplete, a frequent occurrence, because how can it be said that facts have been studied from every angle, and drained of all their substance?

We shall examine only those cases of madness in which the hallucinatory state attains its highest degree of development. Although madness caused by drunkenness is surely one of the mental illnesses in which hallucinations appear in the most varied forms, we will not concern ourselves with it here: because in Chapter IV are reported the pathological phenomena that are peculiar to it, and because we discovered the *primary fact,* that by the nature of its determining cause it coincides, up to a certain point, with the mental disturbances caused by hashish.

There is no form of mental illness in which the hallucinatory state is as developed as in *stupidity.* It is also in *stupidity* that the primary fact appears most conspicuously.

Baillarger,[i] in an excellent memoir in the first issue of *Annales médico-psychologiques,* has called attention to the real nature of delirium in certain psychotics (from a symptomatological point of view), who have until now been confused with those whom authors have called *stupid*[ii] and whose state Esquirol has referred to as *acute dementia.*[iii]

If you read carefully Baillarger's observations you will see that the psychotics called *stupid* live in the midst of illusions and hallucinations of all kinds; according to him, their external impressions have undergone a transformation of sorts to the extent that they seem only to exist in an imaginary world.

---

[i] See Appendix.
[ii] See Appendix.
[iii] See Appendix.

Grouping the principal characteristics of delirium observed in the *stupid,* Baillarger summarized them as follows:

> The "stupid" psychotic never ceased to be the victim of terrible illusions and hallucinations. He was in a desert or on a galley, in a house of prostitution, in a foreign country, or in prison. He mistook a bathroom for hell, bathtubs for boats, a blister for a convict's brand, psychotics for revived dead people, prostitutes or soldiers in disguise. The faces he saw were hideous and menacing. It seemed that everyone was drunk. He saw carriages loaded with coffins, his brother being tortured, a ghost at the foot of his bed, volcanic craters, bottomless chasms which were going to swallow him, traps to underground tunnels. Of everything he heard, only these words stood out: You must kill him, burn him, etc. He was insulted. His head was full of the sound of bells of the detonation of guns firing around him. His parents, struggling with murderers, begged for his help. He was questioned about the activities of his entire life, and he answered. He heard a machine used to torture his children. His body was pierced by bullets, and his blood flowed on the ground. Someone was choking him. He accused himself of all his misfortunes.
>
> Most frequently he understood the questions he was asked. But he could not say why he did not reply, why he did not yell in the midst of the imaginary dangers that threatened him. Who was restraining his will? Who was paralyzing his voice and his limbs? He did not know. However much he wanted to shout or move, he could not do so. When this state was over, the patient seemed to come out of a prolonged slumber. He asked where he was and how long he had been there. The best description he could give of what happened to him, he said, was that it felt like a bad dream.

The similarities between the psychotic state of *stupidity* and the dream state are numerous and could not escape the sharp attention of Baillarger, who observed that:

> The man who dreams, like the psychotic afflicted with *stupidity,* loses his awareness of time, of place, of people; he

has numerous hallucinations, and if he perceives external stimuli, they become the source of illusions. The will is suspended, and the mind wanders, just as when it drifts into a state of reverie.

One patient whom Baillarger observed and who gave him a very accurate account of her condition told him that she could best describe her condition by comparing it to a bad dream!

If you will recall what I have said about the dream state which precedes or follows sleep and which is equally a part of waking and of sleep, and how I insisted on the identity between that state and what I call the *primary fact,* do we not have the proof that this fact is the essential source of the state of psychotic *stupidity?*

Baillarger notes in all psychotic *stupid* patients "the loss of awareness of time, of place;" these are precisely the basic symptoms of the mental change produced by hashish. Such is what we observed at the beginning of this work, as well as four years ago in my memoir on the treatment of hallucinations. New proof is supplied by observation, new facts establish the consanguinity between the mental disturbances in *stupid* psychotics and those caused by the action of hashish, and consequently, from the standpoint of their psychic origin, their connection with the primary fact.

The similarity between *stupidity* and the dream state does not alone betray the existence of the primary fact.

Certain early symptoms of the illness, certain circumstances surrounding its outbreak bear the unmistakable stamp of the primary fact. So it is with the six observations cited by Baillarger (excepting only the second, which reveals nothing about the antecedents of the illness). These observations contain some of the active causes of the primary fact, such as intense cephalalgia, cerebral fever, convulsions (first observation), chronic migraine, amenorrhea, uterine discharge, excessive use of black coffee (third observation), superorbital pain, dizzy spells, suppression of habitual hemorrhages (fourth observation), post-partum effects (fifth observation), and abrupt ending of a copious hemorrhoidal flow (sixth observation).

These data, incomplete as they may be, leave no doubt that if the patients are properly questioned (for our purpose, that is) and guided to give an account of what they experienced and to analyze their ideas which are no longer regulated by their free will, the prime source of the mental disturbances will surface later. One of the patients declared she believed she was becoming *stupid;* another was convinced that *everyone was drunk;* etc.

Generally, when describing a fact, an individual concentrates on the more salient aspects or even on the facets that preconceived ideas show in sharpest relief, to the exclusion of the others. For this reason, in the descriptions of authors who have reported cases of hallucinations, we rarely find any mention of the primary fact which, although essential from the dual point of view of treatment and etiology, easily escapes notice because of its poorly defined, ephemeral characteristics.

In studying the physiological origin of the hallucinatory phenomenon, we find scant support from our predecessors. Happily we have sufficient data of our own to demonstrate that, in cases where we can obtain clear precise reports at the start of the illness, then the original lesion has invariably shown the characteristics that we have attempted to make known.

Mrs. . . believes that she is guilty of a series of crimes that have rendered her odious in the eyes of God. She is damned and, because of her, all the creatures of God are going to be annihilated. In November 1844, a hypomanic excitement occurs. Her face is animated and flushed; her eyes glow with an unusual sparkle; her lips are dry; and her pulse is weak and fast. . . . Mrs. . . has never been so tormented; her anguish has never been so great. She no longer sleeps. She has suicidal ideas, and she attempts to carry them out. She cannot understand how a monster such as she is permitted to live. . . . Delusions, hallucinations proliferate under the influence of her manic excitement. In the morning when the shutters of her bedroom are opened and the light enters, Mrs. . . declares that it is a ray of fire from hell and that demons are going to appear and take possession of her body.

At night she hears the voice of her mother, who calls to her, warning that there are two demons waiting at the door of her bedroom to take her to hell. Her mother adds, "Every time you feel warmth going to your brain, you must be prepared to die. Your last hour will have come."

I asked her if she actually felt this heat. "Whenever my mother or my son talks to me, this sign warns me of their coming."

A young woman has a miscarriage. A metroperitonitis follows, accompanied by a general delirium during which appear several delusions and at times illusions and hallucinations. After some time, the physical conditions gradually disappear. The disturbance of the mental faculties persists, less intense and in a modified form. The incoherence of thoughts ceases, but delusions and hallucinations remain. These mental anomalies are intermittent and irregular and assume strange, unusual forms. The slightest emotion, a simple observation, gently made, suffice to cause them. Mrs. . . suddenly passes with no transition whatsoever from the state of health to a state of illness, exactly as one goes from sleeping to waking. Mrs. . . feels dizzy; her thoughts are muddled and scattered. Gradually she loses her self-awareness and is carried to an imaginary world. There is only one way of explaining the state that creates these features; Mrs. . . is asleep with her eyes open. In fact, her eyes stare vacantly, she is motionless, no intellectual light flickers. The movements of her body are uncertain, rapid, and confused. Her hands move about, touching at random whatever objects are within reach. It is a kind of tremor similar to that of a fever. Mrs. . . speaks to herself, murmuring words that are usually unintelligible.

These incidents (which Mrs. . . calls her *dizzy spells!*) vary in length. Often they are so swift that the patient is the only one to notice them. When they last longer, there is only one way to stop them, that is to touch the patient, which wakes her immediately, as if she had received an electric shock. Touch seems to be the only sense capable of receiving external impressions. Vision, hearing, and smell remain numb.

Until now the incidents I have described offer, as you see, a marked resemblance to those that are peculiar to somnambulism or rather to ecstacy, but they are far from being the only characteristics of the illness of Mrs. . . . You could say that they are only the canvas on which other mental disturbances are painted. Rarely does one see the state of waking and the state of sleep at the same time more distinct and more confused. Here are several examples:

Mrs. . . (she gave us these details herself) was running along Saint-Denis Street alone and in that mixed state we are talking about. Although completely absorbed in her innermost feelings, she nevertheless was aware enough of external objects to avoid colliding either with carriages or with the individuals who happened to be in her way.

When she *woke up* Mrs. . . realized she had walked much farther than she should have, and she retraced her steps.

Another time, in the company of her husband and me in a room with a piano, she felt like playing some music. After trying several tunes, we saw her carefully bending slightly to the right and listening. Then, without ceasing to play the piano, she entered into a conversation with an imaginary person, a broken conversation, intermingled with harmonic outbursts.

Usually Mrs. . . failed to recognize people around her, even her husband, whom she adored. She feared all kinds of dangers for him: they were going to abduct him; they were going to murder him. She was convinced that she had had a baby and that this baby had been taken from her. One of her most frequent hallucinations consisted in seeing a man with a sinister face holding this baby, murdered and bloody. When her husband was away, voices kept repeating to her that he was lost to her, that she would never see him again or that he was unfaithful to her.

This interesting patient was fully aware of her condition. We have at this moment in our establishment at Ivry a young person whose illness has several points in common with the preceding case, but who more closely approaches a case of ordinary madness (partial delirium with hallucinations) .

Miss. . . has auditory illusions and hallucinations and general delusions most often involving extravagant beliefs. Her behavior, without being irreproachable, only imperfectly reveals the bizarre thoughts that dominate her. Miss. . . is very much aware of the nature of her ideas and of her false sensations, at least in her lucid moments. At times she can account for them with remarkable lucidity.

There is a strange noise in her head; she hears the voices of various people she knows or, often, the voices are entirely unknown to her. Her mind and her body are affected: bumps grow on her body; she squints; she imagines that she has a monstrous face, all bloated; she complains that one of the women around her "has taken possession of her being, has entered her body and speaks with her mouth, often using indecent language, shouting like a madwoman." (Miss. . . sometimes experiences a sort of brief manic excitement.) She is even convinced that a lady who occupies a neighboring room pulls her feet *"during her sleep"* and imitates the voices of people of her acquaintance to frighten her.

One day when Miss. . . was in an almost lucid moment, I asked her several questions. After reminding her of her extravagant statements of the past few days, I said "You realize now, as you should, that these are delusions?"

"Perfectly, but I do not feel any less dominated by them. I have a strong tendency to believe them, but more by *instinct* than by reason."

"Try to remember. When you experience these illusions, these bizarre sensations that you have sometimes talked about, is your mind in this usual state, in its customary calm, in the state it is in now, for example? In other words, do you feel anything out of the ordinary?"

"Oh, definitely. I feel indeed as if I were losing my head. I feel as if I were about to faint. I do not know where I am. I am frightened, and I feel my heart pounding. I feel expanding gases in my brain. I believe that is why I feel that my face is hideous. Something like this also occurs in my limbs. . . . Then a host of ideas I cannot get rid of comes to my mind, and I have to heed them in spite of myself. It appears evident to me that someone is forcing me to think and to speak in spite of myself. All this is most peculiar, and I suffer a great deal."

I shall make only one remark here, and you can appreciate its importance. Had Miss. . . taken hashish she would not have described what she felt differently. Miss. . . affirms that it is mainly when she is about to fall asleep, and sometimes also at the moment of waking, that she hears the voices. One day, while she was taking a bath, I entered her room. She had just fallen asleep. I sat beside her, as silently as I could. A few minutes later Miss. . . opened her eyes and looked about without seeming to notice me. Evidently she was still under the influence of some dream, because she murmured words that I could not understand. Finally she saw me. "This time," she said, "they were so loud that you heard them as well as I did."

"What are you talking about? You were talking so softly that I could not hear you."

"I was not speaking, the voices were."

"I tell you I heard nothing. What about you? Do you still hear them?"

"No I don't hear them."

"Listen closely." She closed her eyes and seemed to be listening attentively. "Now I hear them; It is Mr. d'H. . . who is angry. Don't you hear him?

"Mr. d'H. . . is not here; how can I hear him?"

"I know perfectly well he is not here; his voice is in my head, but it seems to me that the sound it makes is coming out of my right ear and that you should be able to hear it as well as I do."

The fusion of the state of waking and the dream state could not be more evident, and the hallucinatory phenomenon appears stark naked, as it were.

Now let us listen to an hallucinatory monomaniac who came to Bicêtre voluntarily seeking a cure for the illness that had beset him for several years. A former teacher, his education helped him recognize the state he was in, a state that he described as follows (I copy verbatim a part of the manuscript he gave me) :

> 1. Visual hallucination—When I am having a seizure I see men before me who make horrible faces or threatening gestures. I see them everywhere I am, alone or with people. I see them clearly as I would in a normal state. They frighten me because I cannot help believing in their existence. When the seizure ends, I sometimes have the courage to go to the place I see them. Then the vision disappears, and I recognize my error. If I am confined to my room, I see people everywhere, on chairs, in corners, in my bed. I see all kinds of faces in the mirrors, especially by candlelight. If I wish to read or write, I can only do so with extreme difficulty, because my vision is blurred and my hand, like all my other limbs, is shaking with a nervous tremor. I see someone beside me (the vision is always at my right). I hear his breathing. Often, trembling with fright, I stay two full hours without daring to move. Sometimes, unable to stand it any longer, I extend my arm, as if to touch the phantom, which disappears at once.
>
> For seven or eight consecutive nights I do not have a moment's sleep. When the attack is on the wane, I get a little sleep, almost always disturbed by a distressing nightmare, from which I awaken in an extraordinary manner. I feel as if a spring snapped in my head, with a violent sound. I can only compare this sound to a pistol shot; nevertheless I feel better.

The next night I sleep better, but I am besieged by extremely painful dreams that affect me as though they were real. I seldom awaken without sobbing or shaking with laughter. Finally, my sleep is undisturbed. The seizure is over.

2. Auditory hallucinations—These are more frequent than visual ones. They occur mainly during the night. They consist of insults and heckling: they mock me for the miserable way I dress; they compare what I was, what I might have been, with the position I am actually in. I do not always hear unpleasant words: they console me, they sympathize with me, they try to relieve my despair. Above all these voices I hear a serious, imposing one that never ceases to predict, throughout my seizure, that some day I will be in my proper place in society, that I will become very rich and powerful.

This voice causes such an impression on me, that even in my rational state, at my healthiest, I cannot help believing in all these riches and this power which are promised to me.

The voices also often respond to my thoughts. It is not rare for me to hold a conversation, with myself speaking aloud to them, responding to or questioning what I hear.

When I am in the street, I believe I am the object of any passerby's attention. If I see two or three people chatting together, they are talking about me. They are planning to harm me, etc. I am afraid of being assaulted, murdered.

I had just glanced through the manuscript I transcribed. "From what I have just read," I said to R. . . , "it seems that you understand the state you are in."

"Perfectly; it results from my overexcited imagination."

"You say that you see and hear as distinctly as if the objects were real; however, between the sensory impressions, whether of vision or of hearing, and that mental act which consists in imagining, seeing or hearing, there is, you will agree, a fundamental difference. They are two psychological facts that you cannot confuse."

"Neither do I confuse them, at least, in my normal state. But as a result of my illness, and the disorder that has occurred in my mind, my imagination acquired the power to portray imaginary objects as if they really existed. *I see and I hear as we see and hear in dreams.* It also happens sometimes that I stretch out my hand to grasp objects, but they disappear all at once, just as in dreams when you are awakened abruptly. It seems to me that I dream while I am wide awake. That is the best possible way I can explain what I experience. Moreover, this vividness of imagination, which seems to surprise you so, is not surprising to me, since I am accustomed to it. Thus, I can summon a host of hallucinations at will. In the silence of the night, with my eyes closed and my head in my hands, I concentrate all my powers of imagination on the object I wish to summon. At first that object does not appear to me as distinctly as I wish. But at the end I see it as clearly, as plainly as real objects in broad daylight. Thus, by my will I summon a person I know, however slightly, a landscape I have seen or not, an army arrayed in battle formation."

"Doesn't anything happen to you when you have your visions? Is your head in its normal condition?"

"Certainly not. I have hot flashes. My brain is in turmoil. Look at what I say in my manuscript: 'In addition to the exaggeration of the *representative imagination,* I have an overabundance of thoughts that crowd each other in my brain. This proceeds, I feel, from the exaggeration of my *thinking imagination.*' From time to time, almost every month, that is how my attacks begin. I feel like talking, singing, saying any number of things that go through my head. But I feel that would be ridiculous, and I restrain myself. But what I cannot completely suppress are the visions, which torment me terribly."

"You are saying that your visions are completely involuntary?"

"Without question."

"But when you are not under the influence of this excitement, you don't have any visions?"

"No, unless, as I told you, I try to."

"Try now."

R. . . goes and sits near his bed, hides his head under his pillow, and then, after a few minutes, "It is impossible for me to do it today. I can only do it a few days from now when my attack will be near."

"But then the *boiling* in your brain will return?"

"It is possible. However, I do not notice it immediately."

B. . . , upon his admission to Bicêtre, was originally placed in Dr.

Voisin's ward. I did not see him during the first days after his arrival. I was told that he was in a state of mild manic excitement complicated by delusions and hallucinations.

When he entered my ward, the excitement had subsided. The delusions and hallucinations persisted. B. . . is convinced that he is in the power of a being whom he cannot define otherwise than by saying that she is a *sovereign*.

This *sovereign* exerts absolute power over him. Not only is she the prime cause of everything that happens to him, but she controls his slightest actions, even his most intimate thoughts. B. . . is nothing by himself. He is nothing except for his *sovereign*. When she visits him, mostly at night, he hears her talk. He distinctly feels her presence in his body, recognizes her, he says, by certain pains, certain sensations, now in one place, now in another. He has never seen her. The word *sovereign* is constantly in his mouth. His fellow patients in the hospital have nicknamed him "The Sovereign."

From the beginning of December 1843, until February 7, 1844, B. . . seemed to abandon his false convictions and we considered him cured. He was the first to make fun of his belief in the *sovereign*. He pretended the idea came to him in dreams and that he knew neither why nor how he had been so naive as to believe it.

On February 7, B. . . had a relapse. In fact, although he sits calmly at the foot of his bed, one can see at a glance that changes have taken place in his mind. His face is more animated than usual. His eyes are bright and watery. His nose, in particular, has become that crimson red peculiar to drunks. His pulse is normal, his bowel movements and his breathing are regular. However, his tongue is whitish and a little caked.

I have hardly spoken to B. . . when he begins to complain volubly about the orderlies, other patients, everybody. His talk is often incoherent; his lips and the muscles of a portion of his face are shaking with a slight convulsive motion. Manic excitement is evident. However, after a mild admonition, B. . . becomes quiet, listens to what is said to him, responds quite appropriately to my questions.

"There you are back to your past extravagances, my poor B. . . Have you received another visit from the *sovereign?*"

"Dr. Moreau, they are not really extravagances. It is true that I have not felt anything for a long time, but she did return tonight. *I had fallen asleep, and she woke me.* She forced me to speak, to say many things that I did not understand. She even made me whistle and sing."

"Everything you are saying here is absurd. You were dreaming, and that is all. How can you believe that your so-called *sovereign* forces you to speak, to sing in spite of yourself? That is impossible."

"Dr. Moreau, she makes me speak by moving my tongue."

"Haven't you forgotten that I silenced her, that I myself chased her from your body by threatening to make an opening in your side with a lancet and tear her out?"

"Dr. Moreau, the *sovereign* has told me that it is all the same to her and that this operation will not make her go away."

"Where is she right now?"

"Dr. Moreau, she is in my head."

"Is she talking to you? Listen carefully." B. . . smiles as he looks at me. He says he definitely feels she is in his head, but she does not wish to speak.

It is evident to everyone, I believe, that the general disturbance of the faculties, the dissociation of ideas, preceded the delusions and hallucinations. It is no less evident in our opinion that the delusions derive from the disturbance. In fact, it is because B. . . feels irresistibly compelled to talk, to sing, to do things he would rather not do that he believes he is under the influence of an invisible and mysterious being, thence his delusion of the *sovereign.*

Moreover, already convinced that he is being forced to speak against his will, he believes without any trouble that the mysterious being in him speaks on her own behalf and, from then on, he attributes his own thoughts to her. He talks aloud in his mind and takes his spoken thoughts for the words of someone other than himself.

Are these not essentially the phenomena of the dream? And is not B. . .'s madness, which first appeared during sleep, none other than a dream continued into the waking state?

I shall report a final observation in which the primary fact and its immediate result, the dream state, are no less obvious than in the preceding case. This observation is still extremely curious because of the perfect resemblance between the symptoms of the disease and those that ordinarily occur under the influence of hashish.

Eight or nine years ago, M. . . felt a state of excitement in his genital organs that manifested itself by heat and frequent erections.

Rarely, at most once or twice every five or six weeks, did his erections involve nocturnal emissions. M. . . , however, was not one to indulge in venereal pleasures, for which he had never had a pronounced penchant. In the course of a year, he had relations with a woman at most about 20 times. As far as he could recall he had never indulged in solitary pleasures.

Without being very concerned about his condition, M. . . had nevertheless sought the advice of physicians several times. He believed that the incidents he complained about and, above all (this is worthy of note), the small size of his organ might cause him to be impotent.

His general health had always been good. However, M. . . believed that he had heard his mother say he had had convulsions in his infancy, caused by intestinal worms.

About two months ago, M. . . noticed that his erections were less frequent. He felt an unaccountable sensation of warmth in the epigastric region.

Finally, eight or ten days ago, in a drawing room where music was being played, M. . . was affected in an extraordinary manner. Music had never had such an effect on him. He speaks: "All the fibers of my being were shaking; I withdrew to a corner of the room, covering my face with my two hands in order to enjoy in mental repose all the emotions that were overcoming me. After I was home and about to go to bed, I felt a highly unusual feeling, of well-being, of inexplicable happiness. This was more physical than mental. I was convinced that it was a result of the music I had just heard. Suddenly it seemed to me that my brain was expanding and dilating. A moment later all my body seemed alternately to expand and shrink in all directions. I ceased, literally, to be myself. I have but a vague recollection of what has happened since. However, I recall having ridden in a carriage with three people of my acquaintance. These people talked a lot, screamed, and everything they said concerned me, at least I thought it did. Several times I thought they wanted to suffocate me in my overcoat or use my tie to strangle me. I thought of jumping out of the window of the carriage, but I was not able to. When I was alone in my room or in my bed (I must have slept for five or six days) I heard voices that insulted and mocked me, talking about obscene subjects."

The manner in which M. . . accounted for his past state indicated, as you can see, that a great improvement had occurred in his condition.

Recovery was far from complete, however, and there were still enough serious symptoms to make us fear imminent dementia, perhaps general paralysis.

M. . . said that he was followed by a strong odor of sperm, which emanated from the surface of his body, mainly through his fingers and his hair.[1]

When talking with someone who could command his attention he was able to control himself, but his memory was extremely sluggish. "I believe that such a thing happened to me. It is possible that it did. It seems to me that . . ." Such are the expressions he inserted in each phrase. He reported a dream of which he had only a confused memory. This expression recurred every few moments. "In my dream I saw . . . My dream told me . . ."

"Are you still dreaming?" I asked him.

"Not now, while we are chatting, but when I am alone."

"And a moment ago when you were in the billiard room with all these gentlemen, were you dreaming?"

"I do not know. It is quite possible, because it seemed to me that these gentlemen, whom I do not know and who do not know me, were talking about me, were perfectly aware of what had just happened to me, and were discussing it."

"But that is impossible; the conversations you are talking about took place in your head and nowhere else."

"That is probably true; thus I was dreaming, and yet this is quite extraordinary, because in short I was not sleeping anymore than I am sleeping now."

In the middle of my conversation with M. . . I was distracted for half a minute by another patient who wanted to talk to me. When I returned to him, he was already different. He started to mumble several meaningless words; then he told me he had never been afraid of death but that after all it was good to take precautions, that he could die at any moment and that he wished to see a priest.

---

[1] Like all delusions, this one has its source in a *fixed idea*. Here is that idea which I neglected to discuss earlier. M. . . had heard it said that an excess of continence had made some people mad, just like the excessive use of mercury that is ordinarily used to treat venereal disease. They had also told him that sperm and mercury, after having circulated for a long time in the veins, finally exited through the pores.

Since he became ill he has not felt the slightest excitement in his genital organs. They are presently in a state of complete flaccidity at this writing.

It would be easy for me to add to the observations just reported, but it would lengthen this work needlessly. They suffice to arouse everyone's attention to see clearly the etiological law or the law of generation of delirium in general, a law that we have found to be applicable to hallucinations, as well as to all the other partial lesions of the mind.

Without asking for support from the observations of our predecessors, a support that we cannot find since the observations are necessarily incomplete from our point of interest, it would still be wrong for us to regard them as completely sterile. With a little attention, we rarely fail to discover in them unquestionable signs of the primordial fact. However, unrecognized in its simplest form, imperceptible to the observer, if the patient himself is not in a condition to report it, this phenomenon will appear to us only with its more obvious characteristics: simple excitement or manic agitation.

If you will direct your attention, for example, to the article *Hallucinations* written by one of our best-known scholars, you will see that all or almost all the cases selected "show hallucinations as isolated as possible from the other symptoms of madness"—as mentioned at the outset a general disturbance of excitement and/or of manic excitement or at least some of the signs we know to be specific to the primary fact.

I will cite only those cases related to what I have just said.

First case. M.N. is bilious-sanguine in temperament, with a short neck and a ruddy complexion. He believes he has been accused of high treason and dishonored. He cuts his throat with a razor. When he comes to, he hears voices that accuse him.

The predisposition of the patient to cerebral congestions, the acute delirium, the irresistible impulse that led him to cut his throat, for example, the appearance of hallucinations immediately after a hemorrhage and a fainting spell, are certain signs of the primordial fact in the case in question. Although few in number, they have a certain value, because it is clear that the observer had no intention of pointing out this psychological change, which he did not even suspect. This remark, moreover, applies to all the cases that follow.

Second case. M.P. has had at various times three seizures of delirium (the nature of which is not specified). The fourth seizure is complicated by religious concerns. He takes a trip to Rome. Hardly has he set foot on the soil of Italy when, overcome with fatigue, he sits on a rock, and feels something extraordinary: God appears to him, The following comment is made regarding this *extraordinary feeling* of M.P. at the moment of having the visions: this is, in general, the way patients express themselves when they want to describe that mental turmoil, that nervous commotion, sometimes as swift as an electric shock, that immediately precedes the outburst of their delusions and hallucinations. This expression is used by an "hallucinator" whose case was reported earlier, and who said, in the nature of a commentary, that his brain started to boil. Many times I have heard users of hashish employ the same expression to describe their feelings at the beginning of their experience.

Third case. I am well acquainted with the patient in this case. On several occasions I witnessed attacks of agitation which, ordinarily, signaled a recrudescence of his delirious thoughts and his hallucinations. M.H., I remember perfectly, became as impatient and intolerant of any contradiction at these times as he was calm and docile at all other times.

Fourth case. Mrs S. . . manifests some oddities of character and a few unimportant eccentricities for a period of ten years. She is deeply affected by the death of her oldest daughter and becomes excessively religious. After taking part in the memorial service for her daughter, she becomes sad, morose, and suffers from insomnia and loss of appetite. Several days later, lamentations, convulsions and loquacity occur. Mrs. S. . . talks and screams endlessly of God, who informs her of great events. Heaven is opened to her; she sees her daughter.

Fifth case. At thirty, Mrs. R. . . , a wet nurse, gets into a quarrel and becomes angry. Her milk stops. She has a *mild delirium* for eighteen months. After that she is in good health. At forty, she gets into a quarrel. In the evening there is agitation, delirium, violence, loquacity, screams, songs, dances, and acute mania that lasts five months. She sees Jesus Christ, who has a beautiful face and a pretty mouth. His voice is soft, as are his words. He takes her by the arm and leads her to the chapel at the end of the garden.

We will note some of the delirious symptoms of Mrs. R. . . . because of their similarity to the dream state. At Salpetrière, Jesus Christ visits Mrs. R. . . every evening. He has promised that there will be an abundant crop; he will give her an income; he has sent several letters to her (she has the letters, but she refuses to show them to anyone). He sends the sweetest fragrances of jasmine and orange into her room. On the walls he has painted landscapes and vistas. He lights the room every night with the brightest stars. She alone is allowed to see or hear these beautiful things.

Sixth case. Miss C. . . has romantic sorrows at sixteen; she is depressed, refuses food, has cephalalgia, convulsions, and faints at the slightest offense. At eighteen, Miss C. . . loses her parents; the depression returns with a deat'ı wish; pronounced delirium occurs for five to seven hours every day. There is intermittent fever with delirium during the attack. The patient sees her dead parents at her side (the first hallucination occurs during feverish delirium). Later, in church, the Virgin appears to her, seated near God, comforts her, and assures her of her protection. The same apparition occurs every day during the delirium and the intermittent fever, which lasts more than a year. At twenty-three, there are new sorrows and new depression. After fifteen days of abstinence, she returns to the church, and there, in a state that she cannot explain, despite the tumult of her emotions and her thoughts, God appears to her. From twenty-five to twenty-nine, Miss C. . . . lives in Paris; she becomes a libertine with a passionate temperament and a flaming imagination; she becomes pregnant twice. She becomes deeply discouraged and miserable. She develops fever and goes for several days without eating. Then she sees God as she did the first time, one morning at eight. She is heavenly happy. Miss C. . . has these visions for three weeks. Finally an attack of intense mania strikes and lasts several months, during which she has numerous visions.

It is necessary to note that the hallucinatory state, throughout the course of Miss C. . .'s illness, is closely linked to a primary excitement, febrile or otherwise. Grief, misery, and despair can very well generate depression and aggravate illness to the point of suicide. Then, in order to increase, the hallucinations wait for the excitement to fertilize them, in a manner of speaking.

Seventh case. M.D., a doctor of medicine, after a sharp dispute that took place during a consultation, suddenly feels agitated and delirious, with incoherent ideas and hallucinations. Upon his arrival at Charenton, the agitation is considerable. M.D. has auditory and visual hallucinations.

I will limit my citations to these. The fame of the writer who supplied them can release us from borrowing any more, which is so easily done with authors whose cases have been studied with precision.

II. RESUMÉ OF THE PRECEDING CHAPTERS

From what I have just said concerning hallucinations, their origin, the conditions necessary for their development, etc., I propose the following theory as to their psychological nature.

Mental illness constitutes a way of life apart, an inner life whose elements and whose materials have been drawn from positive real life, of which it is only a reflection and an inner echo.

The dream state is its most complete expression; one could say that it is the normal, physiological standard. In some respects, the man in a dream state feels to the utmost degree all the symptoms of madness: delusions, incoherence of thoughts, false judgments, hallucinations of all the senses, panics, outbursts of emotion, irresistible impulses, and so forth. In this state, our self-awareness, the awareness of our *real* individuality, of our relationship with the outer world, our spontaneity, and the freedom of our mental activity, are all suspended or, if you will, operate under conditions essentially different from the waking state. Only one faculty persists and acquires a limitless energy. From the underling that it was in the normal or waking state, imagination becomes sovereign, absorbing, as it were, and encompassing all cerebral activity. *The jester of the house* has become its master.

From this general data we may conclude that strictly speaking, *hallucinations* do not exist; we only experience an *hallucinatory state*.

One must see in hallucinations a very complex psychological phenomenon that is only one facet of the mind leading an intracerebral life.

The hallucinatory state includes all that, in the exercise of the mental faculties, is related to the senses, to the general internal and external sensibility. In this state, identical (from the psychic point of view) to the dream state, the spirit, a captive of the inner life, variously affected in its auditory, visual, and tactile powers, carries into real or external life the products or creations of its imagination and is convinced that it has heard, seen, and touched, as in an ordinary state, whereas in reality it only imagines it has heard, seen, or touched.

In the normal state, to imagine that one has been impressed differs essentially from actually being impressed. But things are not so when we are dreaming, for then there is hardly any difference, and the dreamer is actually as affected as the man who is awake.

What is true of dreaming is equally true of an hallucinatory state of madness, where sensations are as vivid, I almost said as *real,* as in a sane state.

Like the dreamer, the "hallucinator" will not only hear sounds that have reached his ears at other times, but he will hear consistent discourses. In the normal state, thinking is internal speech; in the case of the hallucinator, it is speaking aloud, because the mind cannot speak its thoughts without hearing them, by virtue of the peculiar state it is in, a state in which all creations of the imagination necessarily take a perceptible form.[2] The hallucination, or rather the error of the "hallucinator," thus relates to his private thoughts, principally those that preoccupy him most, those upon which his attention is focused.

The hallucinator will think, judge, compare, and reason instead of and in the place of imaginary persons whose words he hears. In other words, he will attribute to these fictitious people, created by his imagination, his private thoughts, which reach his ear as if they really came from someone else.

Tartini composed his famous sonnet by the mediation of the devil. Saint Cedily performed on the harpsichord the sublime harmony that a troop of celestial spirits created in the heavens. Scores of monomaniacal hallucinators wrote at the dictation of inner voices.

A patient at Bicêtre has been pursued for more than three years by

---

[2] "All our ideas," says Bonnet,[i] "are represented by signs. . . . These signs affect the brain through vision or through hearing, or through both senses at once."

So when we think, we speak mentally. No thought arises in us other than by written or spoken sign that represents it. If we think carefully about this, we will easily realize that when we think, we hear in a sense the sounds of the words that translate our thoughts. We hear them in a certain manner, in our imagination, it is true, but *we sense that they are not far from reality.*

[i] See Appendix.

a voice whose speech changes little and who never ceases to call his name—James. Frequently, when I pass by him, I suddenly ask: "Do you hear the voice?"

"Always."

"Now, at this very moment?"

"Oh, no."

"Well, listen." B. . . concentrates, his eyes half closed or staring vacantly. His lips move imperceptibly, as if he were talking to himself or pondering something, speaking in a low voice. Then he reports what the voice has said to him.

"But you are the one who said that, and you believe it was someone else."

"Oh, no, it isn't me, it is that voice." I take his lips between the thumb and the index finger of each hand; then I tell him to listen again. I very distinctly feel the movement of his lips, which cannot be stopped even by a strong pressure. The response is always the same.

It is not enough that B. . . hears his thoughts and speaks them internally. He must also go through all the motions of tongue and lips to articulate the sounds. One can truly say that nature is caught in the act! It is evident that in him the phenomenon of auditory hallucination is a spoken thought, a thought which he hears as though it were clothed, if I may use the expression, in the sensory sign of the articulated sound.

A young man of about thirty, of lymphatic-sanguine temperament, eminently predisposed to cerebral congestion, arrived at Bicêtre in a state of complete stupor, which lasted only eight to ten days. Shortly thereafter, without caring to explain why, he refused to eat and remained stubbornly silent when we spoke to him. However, at night he spoke to himself and sometimes laughed aloud.

When his condition had improved, we quickly realized that he was the victim of numerous auditory hallucinations. First he was threatened, then he was menaced and ridiculed and told many nonsensical things that he did not understand at all. "Besides," C. . . told me once, "Why question me? You know all this as well as I do."

"How could I know it if you didn't tell me? I am not a mind reader."

"Bah! Don't you hear everything that is said in me? Don't you hear everything I think?"

"I hear you when you speak. But only your voice and not your thoughts. What about you? Do you hear what I think?"

"I hear you when you speak. But only your voice and not your thoughts. What about you? Do you hear what I think?"

"Oh, your case is different. Your thoughts do not come out of your ear the way mine do."

"You are jesting. Do you speak through your ear?"

"Definitely. It seems to me that I hear a voice coming out of here [he points to his left ear], and it says exactly what I am thinking. Come on, come closer and listen well."

"I don't hear anything."

"Put your ear next to mine."

"I still don't hear anything."

"How can you not have heard it? The voice said quite distinctly: 'Good day, Mr. Moreau. How are you?' "

"Does the voice come out of both ears indiscriminately?"

"Yes, sometimes out of one, sometimes out of the other."

"And out of both at once?"

"Oh no, never."

"Do they still insult and threaten you?"

"Certainly, but less often."

"Is it the same voice as the one that comes out of your ears?"

"No, but they are trying to imitate it. I will not be fooled by them."

"Fooled by whom?"

"Why, by those who speak to me."

C. . . finally recovered, and he left the hospital. He could never tell me clearly what he had felt during his illness. His memory failed him. He could not explain what had happened to him. "I do not understand how I could have believed such things. I must have been very sick. I lost my head. I was afraid of dying of a stroke, and the voice said that would eventually happen." There his explanations stopped. Moreover, C. . . was not very intelligent and had never been anything but a poor laborer.

Chapter 6

OTHER AUTHORS WHOSE OPINIONS CAN BE RELATED TO THOSE PRESENTED HERE

When a scientific point has been the object of a particular study and when new and unexpected insights have demonstrated its importance, one wonders whether someone may not have been concerned with it before or at least if some thoughts scattered here and there in the works of the great scientists are of such nature as to confirm the new findings that have been made.

We believe that the *primary fact,* whose characteristics I have sufficiently outlined in the course of this work, that this primitive, necessary source of the fundamental components of delirium has completely eluded the observation of our predecessors.

As for the psychological nature of delirium, everyone has conceded a certain similarity or resemblance among its phenomena and those that are peculiar to dreaming. There is never any mention of their *identity.* Lacking the tool of self-observation or awareness, scientists have retreated before the apparent impossibility of merging dreaming with the waking state, of coupling the phenomena peculiar to both of these states.

I. PINEL

When Pinel undertook to systematize the study of mental illnesses and devised that great and brilliant classification that has been adopted by all his followers, he had to observe from too distant, from too general a point of view so as not to neglect the symptomatological details that, although of utmost importance, are apt to be easily overlooked.

Pinel wanted to restrict his study of madness to its distinctive characteristics as manifested by external signs. "If one wishes," he says, "to interpret objective phenomena, one yields to another temptation, that of mixing metaphysical discussions and ideological ramblings with a science of facts."

These ideas could seem exaggerated if they did not come from a man such as Pinel. He is concerned, after all, with perturbed and perverted mental functions. A superficial examination cannot suffice. Only by way of analysis can one hope to penetrate these diverse disturbances and recognize partial or general injuries to the faculties. This is still observation, but it is psychological observation and, in mental medicine, it cannot be separated from that which deals with purely organic phenomena.

However, if the vantage point from which Pinel applied the brilliant flashes of his genius to the chaos of mental illness caused him to neglect details, one still finds in his immortal work many passages that we have a right to invoke in support of our thesis.

Thus, to cite a few examples, if he wishes to give an idea of the disturbances that characterize manic excitement which, as we know, is the most complete expression of the *primary fact,* the terms he uses are the transparent envelope of ideas relative to the imaginary or intra-cerebral life similar to the state of dreaming. "The inner feeling of his private existence is entirely destroyed," he says of the manic. "Incapable of reflecting on his situation, he ignores his relationships with external objects. One sees in him, his gestures and his words, another order of thought than in impressions on the sensory which would arise from organs. . . . A young man," he adds several lines later, "in this condition (mania) because of excessive studying, appeared to retain all his sagacity and utilized it most willingly to go into the source of his illusions. Former ideas revived, therefore, with extreme vividness, *to the point of rendering present impressions very obscure; he seemed to live in a world different from that of other men;* and he added that it would be impossible for him to be understood while he remained subject to this because of illness."

Had this young man been under the influence of hashish, he would not express himself differently. Do his words not remind us of the language that Davy, the opium-eater, previously used to describe the sensations produced by the sedative he had taken?

Pinel cites the words of the young manic as the true expression of what he experienced during his seizure. And we cannot better characterize the real condition of the psychotic, self-observation has shown us, than by repeating with him "that he seems to live in a different world from other people." Finally, the similarity between the state of mania and the dream state impressed Pinel so vividly, in the case of a certain patient, that he closes his observation by saying that "at the end of her attack of mania, which lasted *twenty-seven years*, she seemed to come out of a deep *dream.*"

The curious phenomenon of hallucinations seems to have attracted Pinel only by accident, and merely as one of the external signs of manic delirium. However, what he says about it leaves no doubt that he traces the source back to the imagination, that is, to the errors or aberrations of that faculty, which he considers to be "the complement of all the others, since it seems to control at will *prior perceptions, memory, judgment, and feelings and create systematic pictures with them.*" [1]

Viewing imagination in this manner, Pinel was quite close to understanding the hallucinatory state in all its reality. Obviously, if his dislike for ideological discussions had not interfered, he would have seen quickly that injuries to this faculty extend far beyond previously received perceptions and can also injure judgment, that is, thought and the entire intellectual act, and that the hallucinatory state is only one isolated case of this inner mental life of which the imagination is the source.

Among the few examples of hallucinations that Pinel cites, there is one that supports marvelously this interpretation of the hallucinatory state. "Nothing is more common, in the hospital," he writes, "than the nocturnal and diurnal visions experienced by certain women with religious depressions. One of them believed that during the night she saw the Virgin Mary come down into her room in the form of a tongue of fire. She requested that they build an altar in order to receive the sovereign of the heavens in the proper manner when she came to talk to her and to console her in her sorrows."

Evidently we are not concerned here only with sensory impressions. The entire intellectual act is involved and takes part in the scene. There is an exchange of thinking and reasoning between the "hallucinator" and an imaginary being. These thoughts relate to the hallucinator's mental condition. She is afflicted, and the Virgin comes to console her.

---

[1] *Traité Medico-philosophique*, 2nd Edition, p. 107.

Here then, in this briefly noted case, do we not find a delirious imagination willingly providing perceptions, judgments, and feelings? Is dreaming any different?

II. Esquirol

Pinel, in his *Traité philosophique,* erected the everlasting monument of the classification of mental illness. But this beautiful edifice, resting on the solid foundation of observation, whose architectural lines have at once such grandeur and such simplicity, was far from being complete in all aspects. A multitude of details was omitted. Important, necessary works were still to be done and demanded a new architect whose genius could grasp Pinel's, replace him in many instances, and complete his work.

This task fell on Etienne Esquirol. Taking the same position as his teacher, adopting, save for a few reservations, the same major divisions, endowed with a more searching genius, perhaps, and delighting in details, Esquirol was not always strictly faithful to the steps he laid out at the beginning of his book. Happily he failed to keep the resolution he said he had made (following the example of his illustrious predecessor) never to deviate from a simple and rigorous observation of the distinctive characteristics of the illnesses and their objective signs. He dared to make frequent and rewarding excursions into the domain of psychology.

Some observers have not always resisted the temptation of interpreting the phenomena gathered by Pinel, who never attempted to raise the veil that hides their psychological nature. Let it be said that Esquirol was in the most favorable circumstances to judge and probe this side of man's pathology. At the beginning of his career, he founded an establishment for the treatment of the mentally ill. In this establishment he treated intelligent and educated patients from the top levels of society. They provided a rich harvest of psychological details, of knowledge, of personal observations unavailable among the numerous psychotics that ordinarily fill the hospitals. All physicians who treat psychotics know that there is infinitely more to learn from patients whose education has been extensive than from those whose intelligence was neglected. I am not afraid to assert that the study and understanding of mental illness can only be accomplished thanks to that source.

We are concerned here with a disturbance of the intellectual functions. The exercise of these functions differs greatly from one person to another. Only a portion of the disturbances of the mind are detectable by objective observation. Their mechanism will remain unknown to us as long as the patients themselves have not confided what happens in the depths of their soul; the only patients who can do this are those whose education allows them to realize the play of mental faculties and to synthesize their actions.

Esquirol knew how to take advantage of his position, and almost all his psychological studies of mental illness were based upon patients in his establishment. I will quickly summarize his main conclusions, in order to see to what extent they confirm our own.

A supporter of the philosophical doctrines of the celebrated Laromiguière, Professor at the Collège de France and his friend, Esquirol wanted to apply these doctrines to disturbances of the mental faculties. Assigning to *attention* a supreme role, he admitted that this faculty was essentially injured in a psychosis and that "all injuries to the judgment can be traced back to that of attention."

In a mania, attention is flitting and distracted by numerous fugitive impressions; it is incapable of focusing on a single idea. The weakening of the organs produces a similar result in the *demented*. Finally, the exclusive concentration on one or several ideas in *partial delirium* is the cause of delusions or fixed ideas.

I shall not repeat what I have said of the manic state. I have shown that it could be regarded as typical of the primordial change.

It is amazing that Esquirol, who described this state so admirably, did not notice its existence in delirious convictions (partial delirium), delusions, and hallucinations, in brief, in the main phenomena of delirium.

According to him, if attention is impaired in the monomaniac, it is in a manner diametrically opposite to that which takes place in manic delirium. But fixations and concentration of attention are phenomena that relate to a basic impairment that never varies and is none other than mental excitement. Of these two classes of symptoms or psychological injuries, Esquirol recognized only the first, which eventually prevailed in the monomaniacs. The second class completely escaped him. He therefore stated that he definitely regarded the various kinds of insanity as "too distinct to ever be confused."

As for the psychic identity between madness and dreaming, Esquirol frequently alluded to the numerous *similarities* that he observed between these two states, and often referred to one to explain the other, such that we have almost the right to claim his doubts and suspicions as positive affirmations in our favor. Thus he is content to repeat the words of the manic depressives who say that they "are without reason because they perceive poorly," that they are separated by an abyss from the external world. "I hear," said a patient, "I see, but I do not hear or see the way I used to; objects do not come to me; they do not identify with my being; a dense cloud, a veil changes the color and appearance of things. The most polished surfaces seem to be bristling with asperities."

Esquirol says elsewhere:

> In hallucinations there is neither sensation nor perception any more than in dreams and sleepwalking, since external objects do not impinge on the senses . . . The individual who is delirious, *who dreams,* cannot control his attention, cannot direct it, nor distract it from these fantastic objects. He surrenders to his hallucinations, to his dreams . . . *He dreams while wide awake.* In the dreamer, thoughts of waking life continue during sleep, while he who is delirious completes his dream, as it were, although wide awake. Dreams, like hallucinations, always recreate old sensations and ideas. As in a dream, the sequence of images is sometimes regular. More often the images and the ideas occur in the greatest confusion and provide the strangest associations. As in a dream, those who hallucinate sometimes are aware that they are delirious, without being able to release their mind. . . . One observes in the "hallucinator" a kind of apartness, as rational men who are absorbed in some profound meditation.

If you recall what we said about *illusions* provoked by hashish, you will understand that we do not share the opinion of Esquirol, who thinks that "in illusions, the sensibility of the nervous extremities is altered, exaggerated, weakened, or perverted." In our opinion, there is no disturbance except of judgment, and this disorder is caused by the exercise of sensibility or the action of special senses.

I will not make an exception for the curious case so inexplicable in appearance reported by Reil and Esquirol.[2]

> I treated a young soldier related to the Bonaparte family. After much intemperance and many misfortunes, he became *manic* and was put in my care. He saw all the people who surrounded him as members of the Imperial family. He became irritated and lost his temper as soon as he saw the servants doing some menial thing. He prostrated himself at the feet of one of them, whom he took for the emperor. He asked for mercy and protection. I decided one day to blindfold him with a handkerchief. Immediately he was calm and tranquil and talked rationally about his delusions. I repeated the experiment several times, with the same success. On one occasion I kept him blindfolded for 12 hours. He was rational during the whole time, but as soon as he could see, the delirium began again.

It does not matter whether the senses are erratic. There is no error, mistake, or *illusion,* except through the confusion of the judgment that is no longer in a condition to judge, to appreciate the products of the senses. One does not have an illusion (in the pathological sense of the word), because an affliction of the eyes or ears distorts images and sounds, but one truly has an illusion when, as a result of some mental disturbance, he makes an erroneous judgment.

Manic excitement is not always delirium; that is, it implies neither incoherence of ideas nor delirious convictions. Assuredly there is some intellectual modification; one can even regard it as a true period of incubation, but this is still not the declared illness—it is not delirium.

However, lest one forget, under the impact of this incubation, of this

---

[2] A psychotic lady had seizures of *agitation* and even of fury. This lady's chambermaid wanted to comfort her one day, and passed her hands over her eyes. The patient came to immediately and was perfectly calm, saying that she no longer saw anything (Reil).

morbid influence whose symptoms are not yet those of madness, the mind can suddenly fall into the most total confusion caused by the most trifling and insignificant incident.

That is the case we are concerned with. Here the action of the senses or of one of the special senses is the cause of delirium. It is the spark that sets fire to the powder. There is a reaction of the effect upon the cause and, consequently, an increase of the intensity of the cause. Manic excitement is the cause of the illusion, and the illusion, reacting on the judgment, carries this simple excitement to a raging delirium.

This is what happens in the mental change produced by hashish. So long as the senses are unaffected, the disturbance of judgment is limited to the excessive rapidity of concepts. If an impression triggers an illusion into this explosive situation, the illusion would become the point of departure of exaggerated thoughts, false conviction, foolish joys, or exaggerated fears. I found myself in this situation when the candle which lit my bedroom dimmed and had the appearance of funeral tapers, I thought for a moment that I had died and that people were making preparations for my funeral. They removed the candles and the vision disappeared and with it the terror that had begun to take possession of me.

I will make one more remark concerning illusions among which were included several pathological facts that, I feel, are irrelevant to them.

If self-observation does not fool us, illusion does not differ from hallucination except insofar as it is provoked by a sensory impression. Imagination replaces the sensation caused by the sense of vision or hearing by another purely subjective sensation, born in the *common sensorium* on the occasion of the real, normal sensation.

This is true of the two senses that I have just named, intellectual senses par excellence, because they provide the intellect with the most extended, complex notions. But I would not venture to state that the same is true with the sense of taste, touch, or smell.

These senses are frequently changed in psychotics, particularly at the onset of the illness. This change can give way to extravagant thoughts and convictions. The bad taste caused by a coated tongue can cause a patient to believe that his food has been poisoned. He can also mistake bad odors diffused in the air for poisonous gas. These are ideas, unfounded convictions, caused by a sensory impression. But I see no *illusion* there. There was nothing unusual about the sensory act; it could not be other than it was by virtue of organic laws. Only the intellect is faulty; it has made an illogical conclusion.

These reflections are properly applied to the morbid phenomena included by authors, followers of Esquirol, among the *internal illusions*.

A general, suffering from a toothache, accused the sun of causing it and threatened to wipe it out with his division. When he felt pains in his knees, he believed that a thief was ensconced there, and he hit them with his fist shouting, "You rascal, won't you get out!"

Consumed by a horrible cancer of the stomach, an unfortunate woman was convinced that she had dogs in her abdomen and that she heard them barking.

A young lady, whom I knew well at Charenton, was tormented by strong erotic urges and imagined that men, even monkeys, came to sleep with her every night and exhausted her with their passions. All I can see here are false judgments based on positive, true internal sensations that are so completely independent from the errors of judgment that it is not rare to see these errors change character, as happens among hypochondriacs, principally, who adopt in turn the most opposing convictions.

As I noted above, however, there are cases where internal sensibility undergoes such a change that one can say that it is *illusioned* (sic), that there is a true illusion.

There are true *illusions* of general sensibility, the only ones worthy of this designation, because this word undoubtedly is intended to designate an illness, an injury, and this injury could not exist other than in the very function to which it is applied.

Certain patients suffer from strange changes in their general sensibility. I have spoken to a young woman presently in our establishment at Ivry, who was certain that her head and her face were horribly inflated, that her back was twisted, and that she was completely distorted.

A young man who was at times well aware of his illness, told me the other day that he felt a very strange sensation: it seemed to him that his brain was slipping into his feet.

Judging others by what I have felt myself, I do not doubt that the feelings were in fact as the patient described them. The sensibility is actually injured; that is, in these particular cases, the impression that reaches the common *sensorium* is essentially false considering what really takes place in the organs. It causes an irresistible error, a fallacy as to the real condition of the organs from which it emanates. No mental power, judgment, or reflection can correct this error.

III. Leuret [i]

In his *Fragments Psychologiques,* Doctor Leuret takes issue with the opinion of those authors who have attributed the phenomenon of hallucinations either to memory or to imagination. In the manner of his teacher Esquirol, he makes it a purely cerebral phenomenon, a true sensation produced without the presence of an external agent affecting one or another of the senses or all of them at the same time. In hallucinations, there is, to quote Leuret, "a new element occurring in the mind of the hallucinator, an element foreign to the minds of other men."

This point of view is the same as Esquirol's. I review it here only because of the conclusions that the author feels he has the right to make and that we cannot accept.

According to Leuret, hallucinations cannot constitute a psychosis by themselves because they are found in people who appreciate them and judge them rationally. One must agree with this point. But Leuret adds: "Place these same phenomena (hallucinations) in the head of a crude, ignorant man, and try to dissuade him. He will sooner believe what he has seen and heard than what you say to him; he is crazy." So madness depends solely on the mental condition in which a person finds himself. The same phenomenon, the hallucination, which brings madness to a simple, ignorant man will not touch the sanity of an educated person.

It is obvious where such a theory can lead—to the assertion that the clearest case of madness could be in reality a mere error, a relatively false judgment, but accurate in itself, originating in some cases from faulty information.

This takes us back to the theory of postulated mental madness: madness without organic lesion that can be treated by the same mental means used to correct errors of sane men.

We cannot share Leuret's opinion. When any person believes that hallucinations are assailing him, we have a fact of mental pathology

---

[i] See Appendix.

whose origin must be found elsewhere than in his ignorance or in his incapacity to appreciate a phenomenon with ignorance or in his incapacity to appreciate a phenomenon with which his mind has been unacquainted until now. Because the man of whom Leuret speaks "will give more credence to what he senses than to the words of others," he will not be mad, at least not in the ordinary sense of the word. Indeed, having kept his judgment and his free will, might he not believe those who, with the authority of science and education, will tell him that the noise, the voices he has heard are pathological phenomena, similar to those of dreams or delirium? At least you cannot deny that one can hope to inculcate in him the sane ideas you owe to your education, therefore this man is not mad; because *madness* means an irresistible urge, a compulsion to have certain thoughts. A madman believes because he believes, just as he is afraid because he is afraid; there is no other reason for acts of madness except their very fact. With a higher degree of excitement, Leuret cannot deny that he himself would have believed the hallucinations that he had one day, despite his knowledge of chemistry. He would not have given credence to what anyone told him to calm him.

In the second place, what does it matter if the scientist, whose history Leuret gives, appreciates the false sensations he is experiencing? Are there not educated men in our mental institutions who are completely, incurably fooled by their hallucinations? Nevertheless their education should suffice a hundred times over to tell them their eyes are wrong, to put them in a condition to judge sanely the sensations whose falsity is repeatedly pointed out to them.

By contrast do we not see every day in our hospitals the simplest men, completely aware of their hallucinations, although these strange phenomena are extremely complicated and appear in the guise of the most specious, contrived truth in order to convince them?

It often happens that "hallucinators," in the course of their illnesses, are in turn capable and incapable of realizing the falsity of their sensations. Leuret must certainly have heard hallucinators declare: "Now, in this moment of calm, I hear the voices clearly, but they don't bother me. I take them for what they are and what they are worth, but perhaps tomorrow, perhaps tonight, I will not be able to do this. I will be carried away by them and believe what they say to me. Then I will not know what is happening in me, nor what I feel."

If the theory we are disproving were true, nothing would be easier than to cure an hallucinator. Provided the patient is not an idiot, with a host of convincing arguments, you would soon make him feel that the sensations to which he was giving credence were nothing but morbid phenomena. You would say to him: "I do not question that you hear, that you see what you say you hear and see, but, on the other hand, grant me that this is happening in an unusual manner, that it is something other than an ordinary sensation. Wait patiently for this mental disturbance, this mental neuralgia to dissipate, but do not be knowingly fooled, and above all do not allow it to determine your actions."

Can anyone cite a single case of hallucinations cured by reasoning? If you fail to find one in a person without education, in a less cultured mind, do you at least succeed when you address yourself to educated men, versed in matters psychological, to philosophers, for example, or to physicians? Not at all, and for the very reason that has made them believe in their imaginary sensations as an ignorant, unenlightened man would.

Moreover, this is in no way extraordinary. False sensations are like fixed ideas and false convictions. Do we not find these ideas, these wildest of convictions, in people whose mental faculties are otherwise quite distinguished? For example, this man of superior intelligence whose reason is, nevertheless, faulty in this one instance: he believes himself to be ruler of the world and that he owns all the riches of the earth. If, as Leuret says, he is simply making an error, why does he not use his reason, which he otherwise uses so efficiently, to correct this error? Why do certain patients reply to those who try to reason with them: "What you say is very sensible, I know, but I cannot believe you. I still believe my ideas."

According to Leuret's hypothesis, there could be no partial delirium. Monomania would be an idle fancy because the majority of those it afflicts have a hundred times more intelligence and judgment than they need to correct their fixed ideas if they were merely errors of judgment.

Thus, there is something other than what Leuret sees in the "hallucinator." There is more than a new factor in the mind, a factor that would be correctly or incorrectly understood, according to the intellectual status of each individual. In addition to the new phenomenon, there is another basic morbid psychocerebral factor that is the necessary origin of this same phenomenon and also of the uncritical credence given to it against which all reasoning runs afoul, because this factor resides outside of free will, reason, and common sense. It is this same fact which is dimly felt by the individual who, at the onset of an attack of mania, notices that he is uttering disconnected words and disjointed phrases, and who, feeling acute terror, fearing that he will be poisoned or assassinated, senses deep inside that his fears are absurd and fanciful. It is the same fact that modifies all the conditions of judgment and tears the individual from himself as he loses touch with his surroundings. Is it necessary to name this phenomenon the *primary fact?*

IV. LELUT [ii]

Lelut says of the depressive: "His feelings, his thoughts, are transformed into real external sensations, as distinct, almost as physical, as the objects themselves. These thoughts seem to materialize and to become a visual image, a sound, a smell, a taste, a touch; these latter phenomena are *hallucinations.*"

In this statement Lelut was certainly not referring to dreams, and yet what he says relates to the dream state; otherwise his words are devoid of both literal and metaphorical meaning. Nevertheless, while misunderstanding the real nature of the hallucinatory state, Lelut defined it much more accurately than those who preceded him. He came as close to the truth as he could, without the help of self-observation.

Lelut called attention to a feature previously unnoticed, of the phenomenon of hallucinations, but the language used proved that the psychic nature of the phenomenon was misunderstood. There is no transformation of thought except in dreaming, when a transformation of the collective intellectual functions occurs. In any other sense, the word "transformation" is wrong. Actually, how can we assume that the voices which the "hallucinator" hears are his transformed thoughts, composed of sounds heard only by him about things *he was not thinking of,* seeming to express the thoughts of people unknown to him? Mr. X. . . , for example, whom I discussed earlier, wondered whether his enemies would sue him, and a voice spoke these very words to him: "There *will be* a lawsuit." Lelut tells a patient that "he is looking for a way to free him from the unwanted persons who torment him." The

---

[ii] See Appendix.

patient trusts him, but what do the voices tell him, nevertheless? "That in spite of all his efforts, he will not succeed, that he must pledge allegiance to the devil."

Obviously, in these two cases, the hallucination reflects the habitual preoccupations of the patients. It expresses but it does not convey their thought as literally as the word "transformation" would imply. They doubt, and the voices speak. A manic depressive believes he is the butt of persecutions; he is threatened, hurt, and accused of sins, of crimes he has not committed, and has never even considered. He is driven to despair, to suicide, to murder. These threats, these reproaches, these homicidal urges are not vague, transitory thoughts that function in an inattentive mind. On the contrary, they are quite precise and distinct, and clearly formulated: *"You* will be hanged, *you* are a scoundrel, *kill* yourself, kill him, or he will kill *you."*

There is undeniably something else here besides transformed thought or a thought spoken aloud, if not the sensory signs, the auditory perceptions, would have to be precisely *copied,* word for word, phrase for phrase, from this very thought.

Baillarger, in a memoir entitled *Fragments pour servir à l'histoire des hallucinations* adopted Lelut's opinion and supported it with further observations.

There are rare cases in which the auditory hallucination seems to reproduce the thought exactly. But we must not lose sight of the fact that this thought, transformed into a sensation, is foreign to the personality of the individual, independent of his consciousness. He then attributes it to another person. Therefore, there is not only a transformation, but a veritable *alienation* of the thought.

In all necessity we have to connect this transformed thought that has no awareness of itself, does not recognize itself because of the new psychocerebral conditions in which it has developed, to another mental life, a subjective life, of memories, of imagination, of dreams, in brief, a life of madness!

We have already said this: the hallucinatory state is not, as has been said, just an abnormal condition of the *perceptual* faculty. It includes an intelligence which understands, judges, expresses, fears, desires, hopes, despairs, no longer conscious of its own acts, divided, in a sense, so that one part of it can exchange thoughts in conversation with the other part.

Accept the psychological identity between madness and dreaming and you see how easily the hallucinatory state, envisaged in all its forms, all its aspects, in its minutest details, can be explained and understood. How accurate once again is this common expression: "He is crazy; he has *visions;* he mistakes *his dreams* for reality!" Dreams present all the phenomena of the hallucinatory state.

In dreams, we usually hear conversations between imaginary people, we chat with them, most often about subjects that have preoccupied us during the day, or about neutral subjects related to one another by the normal laws of association of ideas, laws based on affinities of time and place. As in delirium, whether we are aware or not of the state we are in, the presence of our interlocutors is a real, positive, indeed, concrete fact. Their thoughts, and not ours, are expressed, because their words are those of people entirely distinct from us.

Thus it can be said that the theory based on the most advanced objective observation yet to be formulated, confirms the fact revealed to us by self-observation: all the explanations of the phenomena of hallucinations collapse if they are not based on the identity of this phenomenon with dreaming.

V. BAILLARGER

Just as certain ideas, before becoming fixations, had preexisted in the brains of people who were subsequently afflicted with delirium, just as certain morbid impulses are the same or almost the same as those that are experienced in a state of sanity, so "a strong past sensation can recur spontaneously and always in the same form, thereby creating an isolated hallucination of a particular kind." After having been produced by a real, external cause, the sensation recurs spontaneously, that is, independently of the original cause. The sensory fact has been transformed into a purely cerebral fact. This proposition has been developed by Baillarger in a memoir we have had occasion to mention and which is supported by some interesting cases.

We propose to examine these facts in the light of our opinion on the immediate and basic cause of hallucinations in general.

We have said that prior to all phenomena of mental illness there existed a psychocerebral modification which generated all of them and without which they could not develop. That modification is found (we could easily demonstrate this) even though the hallucinatory phenomenon, reduced to its simplest expression, "is merely the sensation repeated and spontaneously reproduced."

There could be no hallucination, that is, the transformation of an external impression into an intracerebral sensation, only because that impression was vivid and striking, like those in the cases related by Baillarger. The vividness of the impression had the immediate result of triggering the primary fact, which in turn, effect becoming cause, transformed the impression received by the senses into a subjective sensation.

Indeed, let us study those sensations that become hallucinations. Let us analyze them: we notice, first of all, that they owe their energy to vivid, disturbing passions, to violent emotions. Terror has always played a role in the cases we are alluding to. Besides, it can be said as a general rule that from the mental point of view auditory and visual sensations are unimportant in themselves. They do not move; they do not affect one except by virtue of the ideas they connect and the passions they arouse.

We have sufficiently established in the preceding pages that the immediate result of sudden, instantaneous emotions was, in many cases, a disturbance, a more or less permanent mental shock, a state of stupor whose rapid passage was hardly registered, and finally absolute dissociation and incoherence of ideas.

The practical confirmation of our thesis will be sought in the cases contained in the memoir of our colleague, where we shall consistently find the primary fact, be it isolated or be it dependent on vivid emotions caused by a sensory impression.

The patient who was the subject of the first observation had already had *four episodes of mental illness.* She had been an alcoholic for several years, finally remaining in a stupor for several days, during which she had hallucinations.[3]

These antecedents establish a sad predisposition to hallucinations that, as we know, are most frequently only an incident, an epiphenome-

---

[3] While crossing a street of suburban Saint-Antoine, she was struck on the head by a flowerpot that fell from a window ledge. After being in a coma for several days, she imagined at times that she was injured again in the same manner. "The pain wrenched a cry from her, and hardly had she been struck when she very distinctly heard the sound of the pot smashed to pieces on the ground."

non of the mental disturbance. Thus there existed, independent of the shock to the brain produced by the fall of the flowerpot, and long before the symptoms were manifested, a latent, basic cause. The accident was only an incidental cause.

The second observation is of great value for the subject which concerns us. "In one of the riots that raged in Paris in 1831, a laborer's wife, who was eight months pregnant, saw her husband mortally wounded by a bullet. A month later she gave birth without complication. But ten days after, delirium struck. At the onset, the patient heard the sound of a cannon, the clatter of the firing squad, the whistle of bullets. She fled to the country."

At what point do hallucinations appear? Is it when the woman in question sees her husband fall, when she is stupefied by the sound of the cannon and the whistle of the bullets that killed her husband before her very eyes? At that terrible moment, the sensations are at the peak of their intensity. It is not then, however, that they are changed into hallucinations. It is 40 days later, when the vividness of the sensations has had time to pale considerably.

But also at that time there occurred a psychocerebral change that we know to be eminently favorable to the development of hallucinations. We have heard about the delirium caused by labor pains, a mental state that, as we have already said, is the most complete and absolute expression of the primary fact.

We think that it would be superfluous to analyze in the same detail the other cases included in the memoir of our colleague at Salpetrière. Suffice to note that they present practically all the psychological circumstances which, as we have proven so many times, develop the basic, necessary cause of the fundamental phenomena of delirium, such as a profound shock, terror, or simply the peculiar mental change which constitutes the intermediary state between waking and sleeping.

Chapter 7

USE OF HASHISH IN THERAPY

I. GENERAL CONSIDERATIONS

As I conclude this work, I cannot avoid a few remarks on the therapeutic consequences derived from the physiological insights that have been revealed and on the resources that extract of Indian hemp can offer as a medication.

I have continually ascertained that there is no disturbance of the mental faculties that does not owe its origin to a primary modification essentially identical in all cases. This is a fact of mental pathology that should always be kept in mind during the treatment of madness.

It matters little how deep the disturbances of the mind are or how many faculties are affected in the infinitely varied forms of mania, monomania, and so forth. We already know that these differences relate exclusively to the external signs of the illness and have no connection at all with its seriousness. We know also that prior to these disturbances, and as a point of departure, there exists a psychocerebral modification, a dynamic injury to the mind that varies only in intensity.

The same must be said of the different causes of madness which cannot perturb the mind or cause a functional lesion, however slight, without upsetting the entire mental economy, either suddenly, in the manner of an electric shock, or gradually.

A most relevant question concerns the nature of the primary lesion. Whatever the cause of this lesion might be, one cannot overlook its purely organic qualities. If one observes closely the symptoms I have cited, according to the clearest and most precise data of self-observation, one will see in that slow or rapid dissociation of ideas, in that dissolution of thought, phenomena that are linked essentially to some organic disturbance. Any individual can see and observe for himself. With a little extract of Indian hemp, he can summon a most interesting spectacle. He witnesses the rapid dissolution of his capacity to think; he feels his thoughts, his mental activity, carried away by the same whirlwind which agitates the cerebral molecules affected by the toxic action of hashish. I doubt that anyone who attempts this experiment and who thus temporarily becomes psychotic will ever be of the opinion that the body is of little importance in mental disturbance. Instinctively, through deep insight, the mind tends to identify with the organs in order to materialize.

If, going beyond the natural limits of self-observation, we try to find out what type of organic lesion might cause the primary fact of dissociation of ideas, everything leads us to believe that it results from some disturbance, some change in the circulation.[1]

We have here, at least, the most immediately measurable pathological phenomenon, as indicated by the symptoms that strike at the onset of delirium. When the *excitement* is felt, when the individual hears in his head that bubbling sound which coincides with mental disturbances,

---

[1] One cannot question the extreme importance of the role that the circulation of blood plays in the production of nervous disorders of all kinds. "No organ," says Rochous in *Du ramollissement du cerveau et de sa curabilité* (The Softening of the Brain and Its Curability), ". . . with the exception of the lungs, is irrigated by as much blood as the brain; but none retains so little blood in its tissues or is as truly bloodless as it is. And those Ancients who glimpsed this important peculiarity followed the example of the author of the book on glands, and classified the brain among the organs with moist parenchyma. Obviously, its active, abundant circulation has as its goal the production of the *excitement* without which the functioning of the nervous system would instantly cease. Everything has been marvelously arranged to assure this function. The blood vessels, more numerous if the animal belongs to a more advanced evolutionary class [Guillot in *Exposition anat. de l'organ du centre nerveux* (Anatomical Exposition of the Organization of the Central Nervous System)], already divided into capillaries in the meninges, and before entering the encephalon, distribute themselves in a very regular fashion. A portion of those that irrigate the cortex cross others that come from the medullary substance in order to establish opposite currents, as Guillot has so clearly seen. [Guillot does not confine himself to this remark; elsewhere he has verified that in idiots the blood vessels of the brain are much less numerous than in other humans.] Thus circulation functions in the encephalon with a regularity shown by no other organ."

he cannot help but relate all these phenomena to a circulatory failure. Besides, we should not forget that in all the circumstances where the primary fact appeared, we found almost certain signs of a disturbance originating in the bloodstream following congestive ruptures, falls or blows on the head, hemorrhages, the interruption of periodical blood-letting, the action of certain nervous stimulants such as alcohol, Indian hemp, opium, and in general of all narcotics, or even mental causes, an influence which, as we know, reveals itself so decidedly in the acceleration or the slowing of the heartbeat, chills, hot flashes, dizziness, fainting, and so forth.

People have often discussed a question that we feel is quite easy to answer, one that they have nevertheless succeeded in confusing so much that until now it was regarded as insoluble. Until now it had not been examined from the only point of view from which it can be seen in its true light: that of subjective observation.

Does psychosis, like all other illnesses, depend upon organic lesions, or is it rather a purely functional disturbance of the intellect? The partisans of the physical lesion theory, completely unable to show these lesions, as, for example, with tuberculous deposits in pulmonary consumption or the swelling of the glands of Peyer and Brunner in chronic fevers, blame the imperfections on our methods of investigation and resort to reason to establish the existence of these lesions. No functional disturbance can exist without a lesion in the organs in charge of those functions. That is unquestionable; but what do those people say who recognize only functional disturbances? So long as we have not been shown an organic lesion, we must at least be permitted to remain in doubt. Furthermore, we should take into consideration that in many cases madness is simply a way of viewing the world that differs from the accepted one, a few eccentric, isolated ideas that have no bearing whatsoever on the collective mental faculties. When one sees certain delirium disappear as if by magic under the influence of a strong emotion, then it becomes impossible to look for organic alterations. Only the mind can be accountable for the disturbances of the mind. Has it ever occurred to inquire what lesion of the brain, what arrangement of cerebral molecules, are responsible for false beliefs, erroneous ideas which we are all subject to, whether we are educated or ignorant?

Both sides, as you can see, present excellent arguments to support their opinions. Approached in this manner, the problem will necessarily remain unsolved. It must be tackled from another angle, the one illuminated by subjective observation.

Yes, changes (I dare not use the term "lesions") undeniably exist in the organ in charge of our intellectual function, but these changes are not what one would generally wish them to be. In the form usually ascribed to them, they always escape the search of investigators. It is not in abnormal arrangements of various parts of the brain, of fixed molecular arrangements in which the texture of the organ would be changed, that we must search, but in an alteration of sensitivity, that is, in the irregular, increased, decreased, or distorted action of its unique characteristics upon which depends the performance of mental functions. We discussed above what part the circulation seemed to play in the anomalies. This is the only change, the only disturbance, that can be accepted.

One sees from this that we too concede a functional lesion, not independent of the organs as believed by the partisans of some unknown mental *dynamism,* but linked essentially to a completely organic and molecular change,[1] however imperceptible its nature, imperceptible as the changes that take place in the intimate texture of a rope to which one applies vibrating motions of variable intensity.

The existence of this organic change is revealed to us with nearly complete certainty by subjective observation; but how are we to discover its traces when life is gone from the organs, supposing that this change can leave traces? Take apart, piece by piece, the harpsichord that formerly sounded so discordant in inexperienced hands, and you will look in vain for the cause of the disharmony that offended your ears. By the same token, in your quest to account for delirium you would look vainly at the inner texture of the organ whose functions had been disturbed for some time by some cause.

Now if we seek the most effective means to combat this change in the organs upon which we base all mental disturbances, this change itself being only an effect, it would be logical first to investigate various causes.

---

[1] The extraordinary insight of Moreau linking mental illness to molecular changes in neurons or synapses is supported by modern molecular biology. However, the nature of these changes which might be linked to configurational, steric alterations in receptor molecules, has not yet been established.

Unfortunately, if a small number of these causes are known to us, we are completely ignorant about the greater number, those, for example, which hide and develop in the secret depths of our tissues,[ii] which flow from one organism to another, so to speak, and are transmitted by heredity.[2]

Since we are unable to do better, it is convenient to direct our therapeutic efforts toward the primary change, without further concerning ourselves with the causes that produce it. We are not prepared, incidentally, to deal here with a question of general therapy, the development of which would require an entire volume. I intend to deal with it in a later work.

At this time I wish to discuss only the substance, hashish, whose physiological action has been the principal subject of this work.

II. THERAPEUTIC ATTEMPTS—OBSERVATIONS

If you will recall the details reported regarding the influence of Indian hemp on the cerebral functions, you might be surprised that such an active substance, in use in the Orient for centuries, has remained almost unknown in Europe and that no one has ever dreamed of utilizing it for therapeutic purposes.[3]

---

[2] In our opinion, the mental causes that appear so frequently in the development of madness have, most of the time, only *occasional* value. I mean that they do not contain in themselves the power necessary to generate the disease. There is almost always a latent organic predisposition. Also, one sees the most insignificant mental causes, truly without any real effectiveness, cause the explosion of the most violent disturbances. Perhaps this explains why, when we see mental causes giving rise so easily to mental disturbances, methods of the same nature are so completely powerless to cure, except in some circumstances where we still find the confirmation of what we are postulating. If the mental influence seemed almost undeniable in these cases, it is because (a) there already existed a cerebral change that predisposed toward a cure, as I demonstrated above in the case of Mr. X. . . , a change that has almost never been noticed, but that can easily be established, or (b) (and this rarely occurs) these methods could be assimilated, by their mode of action, by physical agents; such are vivid emotions, or violent shocks. . . .

[3] Let me hasten to point out an exception, Dr. Aubert-Roche, who was the first in this country to call attention to hashish, whose effects he studied during his long stay among the Arabs. "I wish to mention [see his book *De la peste ou typhus*

[ii] This is the first hint ever made at the possible contribution of enzymatic changes in the genesis of mental illness.

Many substances deserve less than this one to be placed in the immense collections that comprise our pharmacological arsenal! Whatever the effects of hashish may be, at least it should be in the hands of all the people in the healing arts who, in a number of cases, could utilize the powerful action of this medication.

As for me, as soon as I was able to appreciate its effects not from the

---

d'Orient, 1840] this substance which can become very useful in medicine. I believe it is not a medicine to neglect. Those who experiment with it will quickly recognize its therapeutic value, in the plague or other illnesses." In the book from which we have taken this passage, Aubert-Roche reports the results he obtained from using hashish against the plague. In eleven serious cases of plague, seven were cured! These results are certainly of a nature to inspire a certain confidence, and we hope they will signal new experiments which must be more numerous to be conclusive.

I believe I recall reading in a copy of La Gazette Médicale that an English physician in India used hashish to treat several cases of convulsions and achieved rather interesting results.[iii] However, we must remain in doubt concerning the nature of these results, because we know that in India extract of hemp is always mixed with other substances, usually aphrodisiacs, which are liable to modify its effects.

I do not assume that hashish, whose action on the cerebral functions can be carried to the most extreme excitement, can otherwise be considered to exert a very strong toxic influence.

In 1841, I gave some pigeons and two rabbits, aged three and seven months, a very strong dose of pure extract, without observing any results other than a light excitement followed by an apparent somnolence of short duration. It would be interesting to repeat these experiments, but on animals higher on the evolutionary scale such as cats, dogs, and especially monkeys.[iv]

[iii] Moreau is referring to the studies of O'Shaugnessy (see Appendix, Cannabis in England).

[iv] Moreau's observations on the very low acute somatic toxicity of cannabis extracts were confirmed by many other authors.

At the same time, wishing to know if our European hemp possessed at least some of the properties of Indian hemp, I sent for some from around Tours, and I gathered some from the fields around Bicêtre. Mr. Cloes, a pharmacy student in the hospital, prepared some extract very carefully. He and I took doses ranging from one to thirty or forty grams without feeling any noticeable effect whatever. He also made a greasy extract, which I prepared exactly in the manner of the Arabs.[v]

[v] Moreau thus confirmed the existence of two main variants of Cannabis: the hemp type grown in France and Europe for its fiber and the drug type grown in the Orient for its intoxicating properties.

reports of those who had used it but by myself, I thought of the advantages that could be derived from it, first of all in the study of madness and perhaps also in the treatment of this illness.

One of the effects of hashish that struck me most forcibly and which generally gets the most attention is that manic excitement always accompanied by a feeling of gaiety and joy inconceivable to those who have not experienced it. I saw in it a means of effectively combatting the fixed ideas of depressives, of disrupting the chain of their ideas, of unfocusing their attention on such and such a subject. It was perhaps no less appropriate to arouse the drowsy intelligence of mute [vi] (*stupides*) psychotics or even to return a little energy and resiliency to the demented.

Were my conjectures mistaken? I am led to believe so, without, however, considering the matter closed. I administered hashish, either in the form of *dawamesc* or extract of butter, in gradually larger doses to the demented, depressives, and mute psychotics. In the demented, the results (I am speaking here only of the physiological action) were almost nil, despite an increase in the dosage; it was the same with the mutes. Two depressives felt a rather strong *excitement* after five or six hours, with all the characteristics of gaiety and garrulousness that we know. One of them in particular, who for more than nine months had not pronounced more than ten words a day, tormented as he constantly was by imaginary terrors and fixed ideas, could not stop talking, laughing, and doing silly things for an entire evening. Something worthy of note is that I rarely found any relationship between his words and the thoughts that usually preoccupied him. Be that as it may, when the *excitement* passed, he soon regressed to his previous state.

Virey (*Bulletin de Pharmacie,* 1803) reports the following case: "The botanist Guillandin brought back a root from Egypt and gave it to Bernadin Petrella, a professor of logic at Pavie. The professor, having a young student who was deeply depressed, had him take a little of this root in some wine. In less than a quarter-hour, the student felt such a wild happiness that he rushed out, drunk with elation, and began to run in the street."

Must we conclude from what has just been said that there is nothing

---

[vi] See Appendix.

to expect from hashish in the treatment of depression? Certainly not. These therapeutic attempts are quite imperfect. With such limited results, we cannot judge the action of any medication. Possessing only a small amount of hashish, I had to use it sparingly. Many depressives, particularly the demented, seem to resist its action to the extent that very strong doses never suffice to excite them.[vii] I cannot tell if, through repeated attempts they might eventually overcome the rigidity of their ideas, or if, by occasionally coming out of their reveries, they might finally manage to break the chain of their thoughts.

Be that as it may, having failed on that score, I directed my attention to a mode of medication for which I confess a decided preference, because it seems to address itself directly to the most immediate morbid causes without prejudging their nature. I am speaking of the method called *substitutive*. We thought we would direct our efforts against *manic excitement*, a form of delirium which is strikingly similar to the effects of hashish. By the nature of these effects, hashish seemed to satisfy all the requirements of the substitutive medication.

Still other motives pushed us in this direction:

1. It is an axiom of mental medicine that, as long as delirium (short of dementia) keeps some acuteness, one should not give up hope of a cure.
2. Pinel, and with him all psychiatrists, have gauged a mental illness by its attacks of agitation, precisely in cases where the length of the illness, the prostration, and the apparent weakening of the mental forces remove all hope of cure.
3. Cures usually coincide with the change of seasons, and it is not rare to see these cures preceded by a recurrence of *excitement*.
4. Muteness, especially, appears to end in this manner.
5. I have noted several times that, when *excitement* occurs in paralytic psychotics, they are often more rational.

[vii] These observations of Moreau which indicate the lack of effectiveness of *Cannabis* in the treatment of depression were confirmed by recent investigators who used synthetic derivatives of *Cannabis* (pyrahexyl) [L. J. Thompson and R. C. Proctor (1953) : Pyrahexyl in treatment of alcohol and drug withdrawal conditions, *N. Carolina Med. J.*, 14:520–523].

From these various considerations, we draw a principle that we could formulate as follows. In cases of chronic delirium, keep the initial acuteness, or rather recall this acuteness, and revive it when it threatens to dim. Indian hemp extract is, among all known drugs, most eminently appropriate to fulfill this requirement.

Delirium in its general form offers the most hope of cure. Among psychotics who undergo no treatment, manics are sometimes cured; delusionals rarely are. So I have had to be cautious not to deceive myself and exercise the greatest care to distinguish clearly the specific effects of the remedy, the influence of the medication (if any), from the natural course of the illness. How many "cures" owe their existence to this common error? You will see from the following details that I have purposely selected cases which, if not incurable, at least offered, in view of their histories, the duration of their illness, and their stubborn resistance to all treatment, only a slim hope of cure. Nevertheless, I am making an exception for the first two. The patients were in excellent condition, but the promptness with which the cure appeared to follow the action of the remedy made it impossible to ignore them.

Unfortunately, I have only a few cases to present, and I am not ready to assert that these cases can justify any opinion concerning the effectiveness of extract of Indian hemp upon a specific mental illness. I believe I know as well as anyone the cogent reasons for not drawing precise conclusions. I report them here only to call attention to the prophylactic action of a substance that could offer valuable therapeutic resources.

To avoid lengthiness, I will list only the main symptoms, those that most clearly characterize the delirium and are the most valuable for the prognosis.

D. . . (Eleonore-Louis), born in Paris, age twenty-two, was a grocer's helper. He was admitted to Bicêtre on December 23, 1840. After nearly six months, this young man was in a state of manic excitement that finally required his isolation. According to his parents, this state whose actual onset seemed to us to go much farther back in time, was provoked by romantic difficulties. D. . . fell in love with his employer's wife, although she was almost twice his age and not at all attractive. Quick-tempered, unpredictable, overly irritable, he displayed a remarkable aptitude for learning in his youth. When he was born, his mother had become acutely disturbed for more than two months.

At the time of his arrival at the hospital, D. . . presented the picture of a frank, uncomplicated manic excitement. There was no incoherence in his thinking; he showed a great mobility of ideas and was overtalkative and overactive. He talked without stopping, passing quickly from one subject to the next, but still with a certain consistency and often sensibly. His confinement, the reasons for it, the mistake regarding his confinement among the mentally ill, seemed to preoccupy him most. Highly susceptible, a word or an ambiguous gesture irritated and angered him. He liked to tease the other patients, to be unpleasant with them. He was especially sarcastic and insulting to the help. He was disobedient and refused to work as his fellow patients did. For the slightest reason he would break into laughter or tears.

He seemed to be in excellent physical health. "It is very strange," he told me one day. "I am supposed to be sick, and I have never felt better and I am gaining weight. I am supposed to be crazy, and I have never been more lucid of mind and spirit. I am sometimes tempted to think that I am a genius!"

On May 29, D. . . swallowed approximately sixteen grams of *dawamesc* with a cup of black coffee. I had lunch with him in order not to lose sight of him for a single instant. D. . . had eaten nothing, and on the previous day, following my instructions he took only a light soup for dinner. The action of the hashish was rapid but not very strong. Hardly had fifteen minutes passed when D. . . was seized with uncontrollable laughter, which I nevertheless easily restrained by pretending to find it improper. D. . . apologized, explaining that he had never felt so gay and happy. He told me a host of stories upon which he elaborated with wit. I sent him back to his fellow patients, and D. . . told them that he had just lunched with the doctor, that I had treated him magnificently, that the table was set with the most exquisite, delicate food, served on gold and silver platters, that he had drunk glass after glass of champagne, and so forth.

His happy fantasies were short-lived. Within an hour, his excitement suddenly abated, and he spent the remainder of the day in a state of unusual calm. I even observed a certain tendency toward depression.

In the evening, at bedtime, he showed a slight moisture of the skin and a little stiffness. During the night he slept deeply, without dreaming.

The next day D. . . remembered everything that had happened the previous day. He was the first to laugh at the extravagant ideas that he had harbored. However, the earlier excitement tended to recur. In the evening it acquired considerable intensity, but it still did not approach its earlier level.

To my regret I could not administer more hashish to counter this recurrence of the illness. I had no more at my disposal at the moment. I tried to distract the patient and despite his resistance I forced him to work. The excitement persisted for another eighteen to twenty days, then it disappeared completely, and D. . . , restored to a completely normal state, returned to his family.

A certain hereditary predisposition, the duration and nature of the delirium that seemed to be only an exaggeration of the normal personality of the patient in this case indicated a serious condition.

When protracted, manic excitement is nearly impossible to cure, especially if it conceals itself under a specious sanity.

The hashish intoxication, after turning the thoughts of the patient in an unusual direction and causing a slight *excitement,* may be followed by calm and several hours of lucidity, during which he accurately appraises his situation.

Everything leads us to believe that if treated more energetically and in a more sustained fashion, the *excitement* would have ceased more quickly and the cure would have taken less time.

R. . . (Mathias), age twenty-two, was a day laborer, born in Moselle. He was admitted to Bicêtre on May 20, 1842. R. . . left his country (Lorraine) with hopes of finding work in Paris. He became very tired along the way. It was very hot and he was journeying on foot. When he arrived in Paris, he did not know where to go to find work. He became upset and distraught and a general delirium suddenly hit him. A cousin whom he finally met in Paris had him admitted to Bicêtre.

No previous illness, no hereditary mental illness, a gentle and cheerful personality, R. . . was a good worker, orderly and very sober. Upon his arrival at the hospital (May 20), general delirium, crying, screaming, extreme incoherence of speech, incoercible turbulence, and the predominance of certain ideas concerning customs officers and smugglers recurred often and were uttered with feelings of anger and sometimes terror.

On July 2, Dr. Voisin, in whose ward R. . . was, took advantage of a period of calm to send him to Saint Anne Farm. He returned in a worsened state of agitation on July 5. The next day I gave him eight grams of hashish (pure extract) in a cup of coffee. A half-hour later, an irrepressible laughter seized him and seemed to stem his usual flow of words. In addition, the excitement was the same, and the delirium had not undergone the slightest change; however, his face was very ruddy and his eyes were more lively and watery, as at the onset of a fever. I asked one of the patients in the room to play the flute. R. . . paid no attention, but he was convulsed with laughter upon seeing another patient, undergoing the same treatment as he was, dance, sing, and cut a thousand capers. I sent him down to the yard. R. . . strolled there for about an hour and a half, walking very fast and amusing himself by staring at the other patients and continuing to laugh loudly. I lost sight of him for twenty minutes, and when I found him he was fast asleep at the foot of a tree. In the evening, R. . . , whose laughter had completely ceased, still felt a little excited and spoke to himself, but in a whisper, without cries, without confused gestures. He appeared tired and complained of chills throughout his body. His mouth was dry and clammy. I prescribed a pot of lemonade. During the night the attendant in his room did not hear his usual uproar. R. . . assured me that he had slept at least three hours, something that he had not done in some time.

The next morning (July 7) I found him sufficiently well to send him back to Saint Anne. There his convalescence was rapid. R. . . worked diligently; he understood his condition and dreamed of his discharge. The general delirium had completely disappeared, but there was still a predisposition to illusions; thus a few days later, R. . . was convinced that he had seen his brother among the other patients. I persuaded him that this was impossible, and he recognized without difficulty that he had been the victim of an illusion. During the days that followed and until his discharge, I did not observe the slightest trace of delirium.

B. . . (Jacques), age twenty-four, was an Israelite. He was admitted to Bicêtre on August 16, 1841. I am not reporting a cure in this case, since the patient is still in the hospital. However, his case does point to the *specificity* of the action of hashish, and I must say a few words about him.

For nine or ten months, B. . . was tormented by auditory hallucinations. The occasional acute anxiety they caused was not sufficient, however, to interrupt his work. Finally, for no visible reason an acute agitation suddenly appeared and, in a few days, acquired all the intensity of a raging mania. This agitation subsided a few days after the admission of the patient to Bicêtre.

In October, B. . . was once more highly excited with auditory hallucinations. These were, moreover, always the same and limited exclusively to hearing one voice that incessantly repeated the patient's name: "Jacques, Jacques!"

On the morning of October 10, B. . . took sixteen grams of pure extract of hashish in a cup of black coffee on an empty stomach. A half-hour later, in place of the *excitement* that I was awaiting, a very peculiar state appeared. B. . . fell imperceptibly into a gentle laziness, a sort of reverie that resembled the mental repose of ecstasy. He felt the need to rest his limbs. Lying on his bed, his eyes half closed, several words whose meaning I could not grasp fell from his lips, which were half opened in a perpetual smile. He stayed almost twenty minutes without responding to our questions. Finally he cried that he could see the windows of the Tuileries. A magnificent ball was taking place, women glittering with diamonds were at the windows, etc.

About two hours later, B. . . fell fast asleep. I left him until the next morning. The manic excitement had abated. He again heard the voice that had pursued him for so long. During the night, shortly after retiring, B. . . leapt out of bed. He called Jacques! Jacques! Since that moment the voice continued to importune him.

B. . . remained in the condition I have just described. He was sometimes deeply irritated by the voice; he replied to it, questioned it, and threatened it. One day he threw his wooden shoe at a window through which he thought the voice was coming. But he never regressed to his first manic delirium.

F. . . , age forty, was born at Falaise and is a merchant. He was admitted to Bicêtre on July 7, 1842, and was discharged as cured on September 1, 1843. F. . . was in his third attack, which occurred in 1826. His family history, the part concerning him, could not have been worse. His mother had been mentally ill for many years; his father had been struck with a cerebral congestion and a hemiplegia, with little effect, however, on his mind. F. . .'s childhood was devoid of severe illness. F. . . attended school and showed great aptitude for work, but his personality was strange, troubled, and disturbed. In business, early in life, he encountered many misfortunes; he attempted to do too much at a time and lacked perseverance in his enterprises. F. . . always wanted to have his own way and never paid any attention to the advice of others.

In 1836, having suffered financial reverses, he became sad, anxious, and depressed; he attempted suicide. He was sent to Bicêtre and remained there three months, after which his wife signed him out, although the physician declared that he was not completely cured. Shortly after, F. . . , in the hope of reestablishing his fortune and in spite of all attempts to detain him, left for New Orleans, with wife and two young children. A few months had scarcely passed when his sadness, his habitual moodiness, gave way to a deep indifference for his affairs and then to an irrelevant gaiety. Soon a violent manic delirium struck, with rage, grandiose ideas, and so forth. Placed in a hospital, his *excitement* subsided after five or six months. He returned to Paris early in 1842. In March of the same year, another attack occurred, exactly like the first one. When F. . . was brought to Bicêtre, the excitement was not very acute. Delirium was general with grandiose ideas; F. . . was a prince, an emperor; he ruled the world; he had come down from heaven; he was the son of God; he was God. . . . After a month and a half of rest, after several bleedings, after the application of leeches to the nape of his neck and of vesicants to his legs, the excitement disappeared almost completely. But his exaggerated ideas had not disappeared at all, and they were all the more obvious because his speech was less incoherent. F. . . paid no attention to his appearance; he was filthy, dirty, tore his clothes, left them in the middle of the courtyard, or even threw them in the toilet. Sometimes he behaved in a most bizarre manner covering himself with ribbons or strips of colored cloth or reshaping his straw hat. He wandered hither and yon in the courtyard, collecting all kinds of refuse. He often stood with his arms crossed, staring at the sun.

With few changes such was the situation until July 1843, the time at which I gave him twelve grams of hashish (pure extract) in a cup of coffee, on an empty stomach. More than an hour and a half later,

F. . . felt no effect whatsoever except perhaps for a sharp appetite. He demanded his lunch immediately. I prescribed a cup of strong coffee, in the hope of accelerating the effects of the medication. A good half hour later, I saw him sitting beside his bed, his head in his hands, laughing heartily but soundlessly and without waking his neighbors. I asked him why he was laughing. He did not answer, indicating with his finger a patient beside him, and then he began to laugh even more. I asked the flute player whom I have already had occasion to mention to come close. Hardly had he tried some old brisk and lively airs when F. . . , ceasing to laugh, appeared to be listening very attentively. Then he darted suddenly into the middle of the room and began to dance, singing the airs played by the instrument. At my behest, the musician played something like a military march. F. . . immediately began to keep step, his eyes shining. He moved his arms as if he were holding a sabre or a rifle and stamped the ground with his feet. The excitement increased rapidly and in a few minutes it reached the degree of acuteness that we had observed at the onset of the illness. I was not alarmed; I knew a sure way to calm this great excitement. The music had caused the damage; it could correct it. In fact, his calm re-appeared with the first notes of an air full of sadness and melancholy. The patient, whose expression was suddenly grave, returned to the foot of his bed, and soon he burst into tears. I left him in this condition. In the evening, complaining of being very tired, he wished to retire earlier than usual. During the night he did not utter a word. The next day the condition of the patient did not appear to have changed noticeably: the exaggerated ideas were the same; the incoherence of ideas, general excitement, and irritability were even a little more pronounced.

On the ninth of that same month, I administered hashish in the same dosage as the first time. Like the first time, there occurred general excitement, irrepressible laughter, and inexhaustible chatter, followed by fatigue, by a feeling of stiffness throughout the body and, finally, by a prolonged, deep sleep.

It was not until the end of August that F. . . really seemed to begin to recover. His absurd ideas had not completely disappeared, but he spoke no more of them; he actually refused to discuss them with us. He returned to Saint Anne, where he applied himself diligently to the work that was required of him. I saw him again five or six days later.

From that point on, F. . . could be considered cured. He was on the verge of quitting the hospital when he was struck with an intense ophthalmia of the right side that delayed his discharge.

Q. . . (Adolphe), age thirty-five, was born in Paris, He was a self-styled tailor and gold worker. For about ten years, Q. . .'s life had been characterized by strange vicissitudes. He was interned alternately in prisons and asylums; Q. . . was subject to an intermittent mania. The attacks did not break out suddenly but reached their peak after a few hours or days. The affliction had its onset with an extremely mild excitement, hardly noticeable, even to those who knew the patient best, and with a remarkable instability of thoughts and plans, an urgent need to move, to change from one occupation to another. Q. . . gradually changed from the gentle, peaceful, sober, and orderly person that he was usually to a quick-tempered, irritable, quarrelsome individual, a regular customer of houses of prostitution and taverns. In this state of mind, in which he hardly seemed to be himself, Q. . . yielded easily, or rather irresistibly, to all kinds of influences. Any fairly strong will could take over his own. And on two occasions, despite the honorable traditions of his family, despite his own previously irreproachable behavior, Q. . . succumbed to the urgings of some rascals whom it had been his misfortune to encounter and committed several thefts.

In 1833 he was sentenced to seven years in prison and was sent to Poissy. The first month he experienced an attack of mild manic delirium, from which he rapidly recovered. From then on he led an exemplary life in prison. At the expiration of his sentence, he suffered a new attack of madness much more violent than the first, for which his mother arranged his admission to Bicêtre Hospital. Thought to be cured, he was discharged after four or five months. He had hardly regained his freedom when he stole a carriage. Arrested almost immediately, he was sent to Gaillon for five years. During this interval he suffered two manic attacks. Released from prison, Q. . . fell back into the excited state I mentioned above. He was placed under police surveillance and was sent to Saint-Pelagie prison for having broken his probation. They brought him to Bicêtre from there.

Hereditary predispositions (his father had become manic following a cerebral congestion), epileptiform convulsions in his childhood, and later chronic excessive masturbation seem to have been the principal causes that so deplorably warped Q. . . .

Upon admission to the hospital, Q. . . . showed all the symptoms of an acute manic agitation, such as incoherence of ideas, confused gestures, constant anger, and outbursts at the help. After a few days, the agitation subsided, but the mental disturbance continued. He was completely harmless with the other patients; however, he had to be kept in a strait jacket because he tore his clothing to shreds. In July 1842, the patient's state had worsened. His delirium seemed to have lost some of its original acuteness; a mild excitement persisted. Q. . . spent entire days singing near his bed or on a step in the staircase. He was heard to mutter incoherent words. He laughed like a person stunned when asked a question. Whenever he could escape surveillance, he scrounged all kinds of refuse, including excrement, and smeared it on his face. His physical health was excellent, and he was obviously gaining weight. In short everything suggested a chronic state and, eventually, incurability.

On September 17, Q. . . took about fifteen grams of pure extract of hashish. It was 11 o'clock, and the patient had not eaten since four o'clock the day before. The action of the medication was prompt and vigorous. As always, it began with uncontrollable laughter that lasted ten or twelve minutes. Gradually the patient became animated and strongly agitated. At times he seemed to be dreaming and wrapped up in himself. When questioned, he quickly turned his head toward the questioner, as if he had been suddenly shaken, first answered accurately enough, and then delivered, at times with hesitation and with a little stuttering, a torrent of incoherent words. Soon he went into an active pantomime, which left no doubt that he was the subject of numerous visual and especially auditory hallucinations. He seemed to affect certain bizarre poses that required a great exertion of muscular strength. Presently he remained motionless, his eyes fixed on the ceiling, listening attentively and appearing to point at something with his finger. After a sudden burst of laughter, he began jumping, prancing, and running about the room. His face was quite animated. His pulse was 80 to 85. After two hours, the agitation began to subside. Q. . . sat on his bed, visibly tired. His thoughts seemed to take a new direction; from time to time he interrupted his laughter by bursting into tears.

That night the patient appeared to sleep no more than two or three hours. Toward three o'clock in the morning, the agitation recurred with violence. He had to be maintained on his bed in order to prevent him from getting up. Moreover, he was a little obstreperous. At visiting time, we found Q. . . in the yard, very agitated and ranting wildly. It was impossible to capture his attention and to calm him for a moment.

No change occurred until the end of November, when the patient gradually became more calm and less turbulent; he began to take better care of himself and to speak more rationally. A few days later he was convalescing.

His mother, fearing, with reason, that her son might find himself again exposed to the bad influence of his former acquaintances, obtained a position for him at Bicêtre as an orderly. Q. . . himself requested the same favor, distrustful as he was of himself and afraid, in his words, of following once more the bad instincts that had caused him so much trouble.

For nearly eleven months we have been seeing our former patient daily. His mind is as lucid as his behavior is above reproach.

D. . . (Louis), age thirty-three, born in Soissons, was a hairdresser living in Paris. One of his cousins, on his mother's side, has been at Bicêtre for several years as a mental patient. D. . . spent five years in the military service. He was discharged after an attack of madness (mania with fury), that lasted only a few days. His general health was good; he did not drink; he led a clean life; he was happy and jovial. Then he began to suffer from severe headaches, buzzing in the ears. His personality changed so much that his wife barely recognized him and feared the worst. Finally, in December 1841, after a successful speculation, D. . . became extravagantly happy; his hopes, his pretentions, his vanity had no limits. He thought he was a rich man and behaved like one; he bought expensive articles, including hunting dogs and guns. He took himself for a genius, a first-rate poet; he called himself the poet-hairdresser. "Rest assured," he would tell his wife, "I will become famous." He covered the walls of his room with words, with incomplete and incoherent sentences that he claimed to be such fine poetry as to make Racine and Corneille die of spite, were they still alive. D. . . was taken to Bicêtre on February 16, 1842. There was little change in his condition until the end of March.

However, the excitement had gradually subsided. D. . . scribbled all day and his writings as well as his continuous chatter betrayed the disorder of his mind. The orderlies were constantly after him to prevent him from wearing the most extravagant disguises or from discarding his clothes. Prolonged baths, leeches on the nape of his neck, and purgatives, were all used to no avail.

On June 5 I gave D. . . , and another patient on whom I will report later, about thirty grams of *dawamesc*.

The first effects, excessive hilarity and immoderate laughter, appeared after an hour and a quarter. D. . . was under the influence of illusions and hallucinations whose nature we were not able to learn since the patient paid no attention to what we were saying, completely absorbed as he was by his own ideas. He was taken to the music room. The sound of a flute and other instruments affected him immensely. D. . . was very excited, danced, stamped his feet, or else stopped suddenly, lay down, kneeled, joined his hands and turned his eyes to the sky, wept, moaned, according to the variations of the music that dominated him and was alternately serious, lively, religious, or sad. When the music stopped, his excitement subsided. D. . . sat quietly on a bench and seemed to be ready to fall asleep. But he only appeared to be sleeping because a light touch, a few words whispered in his ear, sufficed to make him shake his head and look around him; his eyes half-open; the movements of his lips, his gestures, his energetic facial motions revealed clearly that his mind was far from being inactive as it would be were he sleeping soundly. He appeared to be in a state of somnambulism, totally absorbed in the contemplation of fantastic objects.

Toward evening there was no longer a trace of the symptoms that we have just described. D. . . dined with his usual appetite. Until he went to bed, he remained perfectly calm, not chattering as he had done previously but speaking irrationally and refusing to describe what he had experienced after eating the sweets I had given him. He affirmed that he could remember nothing except feeling a great contentment and laughing a great deal. He slept quietly, almost without dreaming. The next day, the patient's general condition was quite obviously improved. His speech was less incoherent. His nights became generally quieter. Pride and vanity were still at the root of everything he said, but he showed more reserve and less assurance and did not become irritated when contradicted. A few days later, he was sent to the farm at Saint Anne, where manual labor promptly contributed to his recovery.

Dr. L. . . . , age thirty-nine, was born in England. He was a surgeon. We have only vague information concerning the history of the patient. His father and mother were still living, and both enjoyed good health. He told us himself that he had been very dissipated in his youth, that he sought venereal pleasures and contracted gonorrhea several times but had never been treated with mercury. Five or six years before admission, romantic sorrows caused him to lose his mind and brought an acute manic agitation for which he spent two years in Bedlam. The agitation subsided and was replaced by a simple excitement. Dr. L. . . . , after repeated requests, obtained his discharge from the hospital. However, since he was only partially cured and since his behavior caused some anxiety they were soon talking of turning him back to Bedlam. Dr. L. . . . , frightened, resolved to flee to the continent. He came to Paris without even dreaming of having to earn a living, at least for the first months of his stay. Happily, he found a hospitable pharmacist of his acquaintance, who greeted him warmly despite his all-too-evident state of excitement. Dr. L. . . complained bitterly about his mother in particular, who "under the pretext of madness" had had him confined to a hospital. A little while later, the excitement increased to a point where it became necessary to isolate him.

When Dr. L. . . was brought to Bicêtre (January 19, 1842), the manic excitement had suddenly given way to a deep depression, or rather to a silence that no question, no request, could break. His expression, the manner in which he posed before us, his haughty airs and disdainful ways, indicated clearly that he was dominated not by sorrows or fanciful fears but rather by prejudices, defiance, and angry feelings. After exhorting him in vain, I tried to conquer his stubborn mutism with a shower. I had to give up. Diet proved more successful. Pretending to regard him as very ill, I forbade any nourishment except bouillon in the morning and at night and two pots of herb tea. The next day, Dr. L. . . summoned me briskly when I passed his bed and asked me why I had placed him on a diet. Then he complained that they had confined him to a general hospital like a beggar; if he was sick, as they seemed to believe, they should have placed him in a private clinic; he was wealthy enough for that. On January 23, a state of acute excitement appeared suddenly. Leeches were applied to the nape of his neck; vesicants were applied to his legs; and he was given lemonade emetic and baths.

In February the condition was the same. Excitement was increasingly acute; he was extremely talkative; there was little or no coherence in his ideas; and he was restless. Always active and always busy, the patient never ceased to come and go, to hold conversations with one or another. Soon a violent manic excitement occurred: incoherent thoughts, cries, screams, and outbursts. Dr. L. . . tore his clothing to shreds; he had to be restrained in a strait jacket. This condition persisted until the middle of March. Then the excitement we had confirmed at the time of his arrival imperceptibly reappeared, but with notable changes. Dr. L. . . recognized several persons of his acquaintance among the other patients and attendants. He showed a warm friendship toward some of them and aversion toward others. He greeted the chief attendant in his ward with the title of "Majesty", pretending that he was Louis Philippe in disguise. He behaved very warmly toward a young patient whom he said was his son. In short, he was surrounded only by friends, parents, illustrious personalities, spies, policemen, and so forth. Dr. L. . . still seemed to be under the influence of erotic instincts which were often expressed in filthy words or obscene gestures.

By June 5, the situation of the patient was unchanged. A dose of approximately thirty grams of *dawamesc* was given. Immediately thereafter he took a cup of strong coffee. The usual effects of hashish were slow to appear. Almost two hours passed without any change in the usual state of the patient except for a little anxiety, a vague inexplicable uneasiness. Dr. L. . . stopped talking. It seemed, however, that his silence was not purposeful but that he did not know how to say what he meant. He never finished his sentences, and he thought about a thousand subjects at once. He hesitated in the pronunciation of certain words, as a result of a light tremor of the lips, almost invisible but still easy to notice. Imperceptibly, the patient drifted into a kind of reverie and half-sleep, occasionally interrupted by shrieks of laughter. Dr. L. . . sometimes stared with a stupefaction that was clearly reflected in his expression, at his hands and at his feet, which he shook violently as though he wanted to get rid of something he was afraid of. I had him moved to a room in which music was being played. He seemed to pay no attention to it and continued his silent pantomime for nearly an hour. The following night was spent quietly. Contrary to his custom, the patient did not utter a word until five in the morning, when this *excitement* reappeared.

Until July 1, there was no appreciable improvement. The patient even seemed to acquire bad habits. He had become indifferent and apathetic. On July 2, a new thirty-gram dose of *dawamesc*[viii] was given with two cups of coffee, one before and one after. This time the action of the medication was more overt, stronger, and also more lasting. There was even a veritable manic agitation for five or six hours that suggested the earlier agitation in all its forms. A calm night followed with deep sleep. From July 3 to 25, the *excitement* diminished noticeably, the patient took better care of himself, and he was obviously headed toward cure. On the following September 14, he left the hospital in perfect health.[ix]

[viii] Note the high dosage of *Cannabis* extract given to his patients by Moreau (from 8 to 60 grams) assuming 1% THC content—this would amount to 80 to 600 mg of the active ingredient.

[ix] Moreau's book ends quite abruptly without the usual conclusion. It seems that Moreau was competing for a prize awarded by the French Academy of Medicine and had to submit his published work by a certain date. However, he was not awarded the prize by the Academy, and never elected into its membership. Only a few hundred copies of his book were printed, and it was never reissued until the present English translation.

APPENDIX

Andral, Gabriel (1797–1876). French physician, Professor of Internal Medicine at the University of Paris. He wrote the first textbook in internal medicine and the first comprehensive textbook of pathology, originated the terms "anemia" and "hyperemia" (1827), and advocated examination of blood in disease (1843) and thermometry in hospitals.

Aubert–Roche, Louis (1808–1878). French physician who traveled extensively in the Middle East and Egypt where he practiced medicine between 1833 and 1838 at the same time as Moreau was visiting that country. They both shared the same eager interest in studying hashish intoxication. Aubert–Roche wrote a pamphlet in 1840 titled "The Use of Hashish in the Treatment of the Plague."

Baillarger, Jules Gabriel François (1806–1891). French neurologist, on the staff of La Salpetrière Hospital. He was the founder of *Annales Medico-psychologiques,* and he described white bands found in the large pyramidal cell layer of cerebral cortex.

Bichat, Marie François Xavier (1771–1802) Professor of anatomy, University of Paris Medical School. His seven-volume treatise on anatomy revolutionized descriptive anatomy and marked him as the founder of modern histology and histopathology. The first to show that body organs are composed of tissues, he distinguished 21 different tissues by such methods as dissection and putrefaction. He believed that all disease is caused by tissue changes.

Bonnet, Charles (1720–1793). Swiss philosopher and student of biology.

Brain syndrome associated with systemic infection. Organic reaction occurring as a complication of the acute or convalescent stages of such disorders as pneumonia, typhoid fever, rheumatic fever, scarlet fever, malaria, influenza, small pox, and typhus; also known as infective-exhaustive psychosis, acute toxic encephalopathy, acute toxic encephalitis, and acute serous encephalitis. The chief types of reaction, which occur mainly in children, are delirious, epileptiform, stuporous or comatose, hallucinatory, and confusional. The most common form is the toxic delirium. (From *Psychiatric Dictionary,* Fourth Edition by Leland E. Hinsie and Robert J. Campbell, Oxford University Press, New York, 1970.)

Cabanis, Pierre Jean Georges (1757–1808). French physician, philosopher, and political figure, most prominent during and after the French Revolution. He reorganized French Medical Schools and medical teaching. "Medicine and Morals" said Cabanis, "must be based on a common foundation: that of the physical understanding of human nature. It is in the knowledge of Physiology that they must seek the solution for their problems and the basis for their aphorisms."

Calmeil, Juste Louis (1798–1865). French psychiatrist and pupil of Esquirol. He believed, as did Moreau, in the physical basis of mental illness. He was the first to show that mental changes and speech disturbances of general paralysis (a late form of neurosyphilis) were related to lesions of the central nervous system.

Cannabis sativa, botany of. *Cannabis sativa,* source of marihuana, is one of the oldest plants grown by man. From Central Asia, where it originated and was cultivated 5,000 years ago, it has spread all over the temperate and tropical zones of the globe. It is used for the fiber in its stem, the edible oil in its seeds, and the intoxicating substances in its flowering tops. *Cannabis sativa* is a single "unstabilized species," with many variants due to genetic plasticity, environmental influences, and human manipulations. The botany of the genus has not been well understood, and there may be several other species—*Cannabis indica* and *Cannabis ruderalis*—even though the tendency has been to recognize only one.

Two main types of *Cannabis* plants have been defined according to the concentration of the biologically active substance (delta-9-THC) contained in the flowering tops. The fiber-type plant with low delta-9-THC content (less than 0.2%) and the drug-type plant with a high delta-9-THC concentration (3.4 to 4.8%). Concentration of delta-9-THC in the plant is a function of genetic and environmental factors. The genetic factors appear to be predominant under stable environmental conditions for one to three years. The fiber-type marihuana is widely disseminated and grows spontaneously throughout the central plains of the United States in areas adjacent to former plantations where it was once cultivated as a fiber crop. Drug-type marihuana with 3.4 to 4.8% delta-9-THC occurs spontaneously and is cultivated from Mississippi to New Hampshire.

The intoxicating substances prepared from *Cannabis* will vary considerably in potency according to the nature of the plant (fiber or drug type), according to environmental factors, according to the varying mixtures of different parts of the plant, and according to the techniques of preparation. As a result, the psychoactive properties of *Cannabis* cover a very wide range of activity from nonexistent for the fiber type to hallucinogenic for the well-prepared nonextracted drug type. Such a basic botanical fact has been overlooked by physicians and educators who have spoken and written about marihuana as though it were a simple, single substance, or "a mild intoxicant," similar to wine, beer, or tobacco which uniformly yield a low concentration of toxic substances. All of the botanical features of *Cannabis* show the unusually wide variability of this plant.

Delirium. An acute organic reaction consisting of alteration of consciousness and attention (the patient alternates at various times between preoccupation and coma) ; impaired orientation and (especially recent) memory, which give rise to illusional falsifications and hallucinations of dreamlike scenes; delusions which are fleeting, unsystematized, and illogical because they are often secondary to the hallucinatory experiences; emotional lability and incontinence; and marked restlessness and agitation. The most common causes are intoxicants, drugs, infections, avitaminoses, metabolic disturbances (such as diabetes, uremia, and hyperthyroidism) , and trauma; but a delirious reaction can occur in the course of any organic brain disorder.

Delirium at one time was used in a general way to indicate insanity, psychopathy, and almost any psychopathologic manifestation; now obsolete, such usage explains such appellations as depressive delirium (melancholia) , persecutory delirium (paranoia) , touching delirium (compulsive touching) . (From *Psychiatric Dictionary,* Fourth Edition, by Leland E. Hinsie and Robert J. Campbell, Oxford University Press, New York, 1970.)

Delusion. A false belief, born of morbidity. A belief engendered without appropriate external stimulation and maintained by one in spite of what to normal beings constitutes incontrovertible and 'plain-as-day' proof or evidence to the contrary. Further, the belief held is not one which is ordinarily accepted by other members of the patient's culture or subculture (i.e., it is not a commonly believed superstition) .

Like hallucinations, delusions are condensations of perceptions, thoughts, and memories and can be interpreted much the same as hallucinations and dreams. Delusions are misjudgments of reality based on projection. (From *Psychiatric Dictionary,* Fourth Edition, by Leland E. Hinsie and Robert J. Campbell, Oxford University Press, New York, 1970.)

Dementia. Absence or reduction of intellectual faculties in consequence of known organic brain disease.

In years gone by, the term dementia has had various meanings. It was once synonymous with madness, insanity, and lunacy; in the early part of the 17th century it was synonymous with delirium. Nowadays, however, in recognition of the fact that many psychotic persons possess very keen intelligence, the term is not used sweepingly for all psychiatric states. It is often limited to those who show primary memory loss due to disorders in brain tissue, and as used today the term stresses the irreversibility of the intellectual defects, whatever their origin. The term 'deterioration' also refers to progressive loss of intellectual faculties, but without intimating a specific cause and without stressing the permanency of the change. (From *Psychiatric Dictionary,* Fourth Edition, by Leland E. Hinsie and Robert J. Campbell, Oxford University Press, New York, 1970.)

Depression. In psychiatry, depression refers to a clinical syndrome consisting of lowering the mood-tone (feelings of painful dejection), difficulty in thinking, and psycho-motor retardation. The general retardation, however, may be masked by anxiety, obsessive thinking, and agitation in certain depressions, especially those of the involutional period ('involutional melancholia').

Depression is '. . . a pathological state of conscious psychic suffering and guilt, accompanied by a marked reduction in the sense of personal values, and a diminution of mental, psycho-motor, and even organic activity, unrelated to actual deficiency' (Nacht, S., and Racamier, P. C., *International Journal of Psycho-Analysis*, XLI, 481, 1960).

As used by the layman, the word depression ordinarily refers only to the mood element, which in psychiatry would more appropriately be labeled dejection, sadness, gloominess, despair, despondency, etc.

Depression, even as defined above, may occur in the course of any psychiatric disorder although it is most commonly seen in the psychotic group, particularly in the manic-depressive reactions, the involutional psychoses and the chronic brain disorders associated with senile, circulatory or metabolic disease. (From *Psychiatric Dictionary*, Fourth Edition, by Leland E. Hinsie and Robert J. Campbell, Oxford University Press, New York, 1970.)

Esquirol, Jean Etienne Dominique (1772–1840). Pupil of Pinel and teacher of Moreau (who dedicated the present book to his memory). Esquirol, the founder of modern neuropsychiatry, contributed a classical description of paresis in 1838. He promoted Pinel's theories on the origin of mental disease in pathological changes in the brain; he emphasized the role of emotions as a source of mental disturbances, and supported his views with statistical tabulations. An able administrator, he founded 10 asylums in France and had them built unrestricted according to his own plans, not like prison buildings, but with wide open grounds.

Guillot, N. (1809–1881). French physician who studied the organization of the central nervous system in different vertebrates.

Horeau, Hector (1801–1872). French architect, pioneer in iron constructions, sometimes with oriental motifs, but mostly with a decoration considered strict at a time when twisted ornaments were modern; another traveler in the Orient. Horeau during the Commune in 1871 was offered the position as Chief Architect of Paris, but he was later arrested, put in prison and died under tragic circumstances.

Lelut, F. (1804–1876). French physician and psychiatrist of the Salpetrière Hospital. He was mainly interested in relating the morphology of the brain and cranium to the behavior of animals and man.

Leuret, François (1797–1851). French psychiatrist, contemporary of Moreau, chief physician of Bicêtre, author of *Psychological Fragments on Insanity* (1834). He was the main proponent of the "Moral Treatment for the Insane" which consisted in making them retract their delirious statements using intimidation and punishment such as a cold shower. Moreau became one of the main opponents of Leuret's opinions and methods.

Melancholia, melancholy. A morbid mental state characterized by *depression* (g.v.). 'The distinguishing mental features of melancholia are a profoundly painful dejection, abrogation of interest in the outside world, loss of the capacity to love, inhibition of all activity, and a lowering of the self-regarding feelings to a degree that finds utterance in self-reproaches and self-revilings, and culminates in a delusional expectation of punishment. This picture becomes a little more intelligible when we consider that, with one exception, the same traits are met with in grief' (S. Freud, *Collected Papers*, Vol. 4, tr. by J. Riviere, Leonard and Virginia Woolf, and The Institute of Psychoanalysis, London 1924–25). The one exception is the loss of self-esteem, which is not seen in grief of normal mourning. (From *Psychiatric Dictionary*, Fourth Edition, by Leland E. Hinsie and Robert J. Campbell, Oxford University Press, New York, 1970.)

Mania. 1. *Obs.* Any mental disorder, "madness," especially when characterized by violent, unrestrained behavior. 2. When used as a suffix, a morbid preference for or an irrepressible impulse to behave in a certain way, such as *kleptomania* (q.v.). 3. One of the two major forms af manic-depressive illness; see *psychosis, manic-depressive.*

The manic-form of manic-depressive psychosis is characterized by (a) an elated or euphoric, although unstable, mood; (b) increased psychomotor activity, restlessness, agitation, etc.; and (c) increase in number of ideas and speed of thinking and speaking, which in more severe forms proceeds to *flight of ideas* (q.v.), often with a grandiose trend.

In mania, the main disturbances in the ideational sphere are: *overproductivity, flight of ideas,* that is, a rapid shifting from one topic to another; of which *distractibility* is a part, the patient changing from topic to topic in accordance with the stimuli from without and from within; the shifting may be occasioned by what is called *clang association*—stimulation of a new train of thought by some external sound; *leveling of ideas,* that is essentially all topics have about the same value to the patient; *ideas of importance, grandiose ideas,* the patient expressing delusions of greatness perhaps in all fields; the feelings of well-being are expressed also in the sphere of *physical excellence.* Often the ideas are reproductions of those relating to *infantile sexuality.*

The principal modifications in the emotional field are: exaggerated feelings of gaiety, well-being, extreme happiness—in consonance with the ideas expressed.

The expression *psycho-motor overactivity* refers to physical overactivity. In extreme states it is incessant throughout the waking hours; the patient attempts to motorize, that is, to put into physical execution all the ideas that occur to him; this tendency, therefore, leads to a shifting of physical activity paralleling that in the mental sphere.

Depending upon the degree of mania, there are three types: *hypomania,* which is a less intense form; *mania,* which is presumably the common or usual type; *hypermania,* or a more intense expression of the manic reaction.

Some authors use the term *acute mania* synonymously with *mania,* and *hypermania* is often referred to as *delirious mania, Bell's mania, typhomania, delirium grave,* or *collapse delirium,* with partial or complete disorientation as the rule.

When a patient has a succession of manic attacks the condition is known as *recurrent or periodic mania.* When manic and depressive episodes alternate, the condition is called *alternating or circular psychosis or insanity.*

Periodic mania is to be distinguished from *chronic mania,* a form described by Schott in 1904 in which manic symptoms continue uninterruptedly for an indefinite number of years (in Schott's series, for 30,

25, 21, and 17 years) . In all such cases which have been reported, the particular episode which becomes chronic has begun after the age of 40.

A patient in a manic phase may not talk; his state is then known as *unproductive* or *stuporous mania;* he is said to be in a condition of *manic stupor.*

When a patient presents the symptoms of mania, but does not move, his condition is called *akinetic mania.* Follow-up studies suggest that akinetic mania and manic stupor and all of Kraepelin's 'mixed' or 'intermediate' states are really schizophrenic. (From *Psychiatric Dictionary,* Fourth Edition, by Leland E. Hinsie and Robert J. Campbell, Oxford University Press, New York, 1970) .

Monomania *(rare).* Partial insanity, in which the morbid mental state is restricted to one subject, the patient being of sound judgment and appropriate affect on all others.

In older psychiatry there were such expressions as *intellectual monomania* (e.g., paranoia) ; *affective monomania,* which corresponded with *manie raisonnante,* characterized by emotional deviation; *instinctive monomania,* which in general is the equivalent of the compulsive-obsessive syndrome of modern psychiatry.

When monomania or partial insanity was associated with depressive states, Esquirol suggested that the term *lypemania* be used, to distinguish the monomania with exaltation of mood. (From *Psychiatric Dictionary,* Fourth Edition, by Leland E. Hinsie and Robert J. Campbell, Oxford University Press, New York, 1970.)

Mute-mutism. The state of being mute, dumb, silent; voicelessness without structural alteration and with psychic causes. It is silence due to disinclination to talk . . . the individual can but will not speak. Mutism is not uncommonly observed among psychiatric patients as a result of psychogenic causes. It is common among patients in a state of stupor; indeed, the term "stupor" is (in use, at least) often a synonym for mutism. The condition is frequently observed in the catatonic form of schizophrenia, in the stupor of melancholia, and in states of hysterical stupor. (From *Psychiatric Dictionary,* Third Edition, by Leland E. Hinsie and Robert J. Campbell, Oxford University Press, New York, 1960.)

Paranoia, paranoea. Although paranoia in the sense of mental derangement, delirium, occurs in Aeschylus (Theb, 756), Euripides, Orestes, 822, Plato, Laws 928E and elsewhere, i.e., the term is even pre-Hippocratic, credit is generally given to Vogel for having introduced or reintroduced the term in medicine in 1764.

Following this, the term was inconsistently applied to a great number of diverse conditions until 1883, when E. C. Spitzka, a New York psychiatrist, defined paranoia as it is known at the present time. Kahlbaum was among the first to use the term in the way in which it is generally used today, to refer to gradually developing, systematized delusional states, without hallucinations but with preservation of intelligence, and with emotional responses and behavior that remain congruous with and appropriate to the persecutory or grandiose delusions. (From *Psychiatric Dictionary,* Third Edition, by Leland E. Hinsie and Robert J. Campbell, Oxford University Press, New York, 1960.)

Pinel, Philippe (1745–1826). French mathematician and physician, one of the founders of modern psychiatry, and the first director of the Bicêtre Hospital for the Insane where Moreau later worked. In his *Treatise on Mental Alienation,* Pinel advocated humane treatment for the mentally ill and the elimination of forcible restraints.

Rochoux, J. A. (1798–1862). French physician, specialized in internal medicine, and attending physician at Bicêtre Hospital.

Stupor. A state in which the sensibilities are deadened or dazed and the subject has little or no appreciation of the nature of his surroundings. The term is commonly synonymous with *unconsciousness,* in an organic, not in a psychic sense.

Further, in a second meaning that has no relationship with the condition of the sensorium, stupor is synonymous with *mutism.* For example, a patient may possess all the characteristics of the manic or depressed phase of manic-depressive psychosis, save that of talking; he is said to exhibit a manic or a depressive stupor; there need not be any essential disorder in intellectual or sensorial clarity. In the condition known as catatonic stupor the patient is ordinarily well aware of the nature of his surroundings. (From *Psychiatric Dictionary,* Third Edition, by Leland E. Hinsie and Robert J. Campbell, Oxford University Press, New York, 1960.)

LIST OF PUBLICATIONS OF J. J. MOREAU

De l'influence du physique relativement au désordre des facultés intellectuelles et en particulier dans cette variété de délire désignée par M. Esquirol sous le nom de monomanie. Thèse de doctorat. Paris, 1830.

Des facultés morales considérées sous le point de vue médical; de leur influence sur les maladies nerveuses, les affections organiques, etc. 1 vol. in-8°. Paris, 1836.

De la folie raisonnante envisagée sous le point de vue médico-légal. In *l'Esculape,* 1840.

Études psychiques sur la folie. Broch. in-8°. Paris,. 1840.

Traitement des hallucinations par le datura stramonium. In *Gazette médicale de Paris,* octobre 1841.

Recherches sur les aliénés en Orient. Notes sur les établissements qui leur sont consacrés à Malte (Ile de) au Caire (Égypte), à Smyrne (Asie-Mineure), à Constantinople (Turquie). In *Annales médico-psychologiques.* 1843, t. I.

Attaques d'épilepsie. Embarras de la langue. Aura epileptica dans la main gauche. Chute sur le côté gauche. A l'autopsie, kyste volumineux situé à la partie antérieure du lobe droit. In *Ann. méd. psych.* 1843, t. I.

Lettres médicales sur la colonie d'aliénés de Ghéel. In *Revue indépendante,* 1843 et *Annales médico-psychologiques,* 1845, t. V.

Revue médico-légale des journaux judiciaires pour tous les faits se rapportant à l'aliénation, à l'épilepsie à la surdi-mutité, etc. In *Ann. Méd-psych.* Années 1844–1845–1846.

Du hachisch et de l'aliénation mentale. Études psychologiques. 1 vol. in-8. Paris, 1845.

Influence des inspirations éthérées sur les affections convulsives. In *Union médicale.* 1847, n° 13.

Deux mots sur cette question: Les individus soumis à l'éthérisation sont-ils susceptibles de ressentir la douleur, comme dans l'état ordinaire? Est-il exact de dire qu'ils perdent simplement le souvenir de leurs souffrances? In *Union médicale.* 1847, n° 21.

Quelques inductions physiologiques concernant la monomanie suicide, tirées de *l'action de la vapeur d'éther sur la sensibilité générale.*In *Union medicale.* 1847, nᵒ 105.

De l'emploi du hachisch dans le choléra-morbus. In *Union médicale.* 1848, nᵒ 124.

De l'action de la vapeur d'éther dans l'epilepsie. In *Gazette des hôpitaux.* 1847, nᵒ du 1ᵉʳ avril.

Paralysie épileptique traitée par la strychnine. In *Gazette des hôpitaux.* 1848, nᵒ du 13 novembre.

Un chapitre oublié de la pathologie mentale. In *Union médicale.* 1849, nᵒˢ 146, 149 et 152, 1850, nᵒˢ 6, 7, 12, 15, 18, 21, 30 et 33.

De la paralysie générale des aliénés. In *Gazette médicale* de Paris, 1850, nᵒ du 11 mai.

Lettre à M. le Dʳ Amédée Latour, sur la dualité humaine. In *Union médicale.* 1851, nᵒ 28.

Mémoire sur les prodromes de la folie, lu à l'Académie de médecine dans sa séance du 22 avril 1851. In *Annales médico-psychologiques.* 1852, 2ᵉ série, t. IV.

De la prédisposition héréditaire aux affections cérébrales. Existe-t-il des signes particuliers auxquels on puisse reconnaître cette prédisposition? Mémoire présenté à l'Académie des sciences, dans la séance du 15 décembre 1851. In *Union médicale,* 1852, nᵒ 48.

De l'emploi du hachisch dans le traitement de la rage. In *Union médicale.* 1852, nᵒ 84.

Du traitement de l'épilepsie par l'oxyde de zinc. In *Union médicale,* 1852, nᵒˢ 144, 145 et 146.

Mémoire sur les causes prédisposantes héréditaires de l'idiotie et de l'imbécillité, lu à l'Académie de médecine, dans la séance du 26 octobre 1852. In *Union médicale,* 1853. nᵒˢ 15, 16, 17 et 18.

Particularités symptomatiques de l'œil dans la paralysie générale. In *Union médicale,* 1853, nᵒ 78.

Notes sur les établissements d'aliénés de Siegburg, Halle, Dresde, Prague, Berlin et Vienne. Réflexions sur la médecine psychiatrique en Allemagne. In *Union médicale.* 1853, nᵒˢ 151, 152, 154 et 155.

De l'étiologie de l'épilepsie et des indications que l'étude des causes peut fournir pour le traitement de cette maladie. In *Mémoires de l'Académie de Médecine,* t. XVIII. Paris, 1854.

De la folie au point de vue pathologique et anatomo-pathologique. In *Annales médico-psychologiques.* 1855, 3ᵉ série, t. I.

De l'identité de l'état de rêve et de la folie. In *Ann. méd. psych.* 1855, 3ᵉ série, t. I.

Cas d'empoisonnement et de folie aiguë par un cosmétique renfermant plusieurs substances toxiques. In *Union médicale,* nᵒ du 12 juillet 1855.

Hallucinations, troubles de l'intelligence, état chloro–anémique. Emploi de la belladone et des topiques. Guérison. In *Gazette des hôpitaux.* 1856.

Impulsions insolites sans désordre, de l'intelligence. In *Gazette des hôpitaux.* 1856.

Manie intermittente. Inefficacité du sulfate de quinine. Guérison par l'emploi de l'arsenic. In *Gazette des hôpitaux.* 1836.

La Psychologie morbide dans ses rapports avec la philosophie de l'histoire ou de l'influence des névropathies sur le dynamisme intellectuel. 1 vol. in-8º. Paris, 1859.

Quelques mots sur la colonie de Ghéel. Communication à la Société médico-psychologique, dans la séance du 28 avril 1862. In *Ann. méd.-psych.* 1882, 3e série, t. VIII.

De la folie hystérique et de quelques phénomènes nerveux propres à l'hystérie convulsive, à l'hystéro-épilepsie et à l'épilepsie. Études cliniques. In *Union médicale,* 1865.

Traité pratique de la folie névropathique (vulgo hystérique). 1 vol in-148. Paris, 1869.

SELECTED BIBLIOGRAPHY ON *CANNABIS* *

BOOKS

Bejerot, N. (1970). *Addiction and Society.* Charles C Thomas, Springfield, Ill.

de Felice, P. (1936). *Poisons Sacrés, Ivresses Divines.* Editions Albin Michel, Paris.

Joyce, C. R. B., and Curry, S. H. (1970). *The Botany and Chemistry of Cannabis.* J. & A. Churchill, London.

Kaplan, J. (1971). *Marihuana—The New Prohibition,* World Publishing Company, New York.

Marihuana: Chemistry, Pharmacology and Patterns of Social Use (1971). Ann. N.Y. Acad. Sci., Vol. 191, pp. 1–269.

Marihuana and Its Surrogates (1971). *Pharmacological Reviews,* Vol. 23, pp. 263–389.

Moreau, J. J. (1845). *Du Hachish et de l'Alienation Mentale, Etudes Psychologiques.* Libraire de Fortin, Masson, Paris (English edition: Raven Press, New York, 1972).

Nahas, G. G. (1972). *Marihuana—Deceptive Weed,* Raven Press, New York.

Wilson, C. W. M. (1968). *Adolescent Drug Dependence.* Pergamon Press, Oxford.

Wittenborn, J. R., Brill, H., Smith, J. P., and Wittenborn, S. A. (1969). *Drugs and Youth.* Charles C Thomas, Springfield, Ill.

PAPERS

Agurell, S. (1970). Chemical and pharmacological studies of cannabis. In *The Botany and Chemistry of Cannabis,* C. R. B. Joyce and S. H. Curry (eds.). J. & A. Churchill, London, pp. 175–191.

Asuni, T. (1964). Socio-psychiatric problems of *Cannabis* in Nigeria. *Bull. Narcotics,* 16:17–28.

Ball, J. C., Chambers, C. D., and Ball, M. J. (1968). The association of marihuana smoking with opiate addiction in the United States. *J. Crim. Law Criminol. Pol. Sci.,* 59:171–182.

Boyd, E. S., Boyd, E. H., Muchmore, J. S., and Brown, L. E. (1971). Effects of two tetrahydrocannabinols and of pentobarbital on cortico-cortical evoked responses in the squirrel monkey. *J. Pharmacol. Exp. Ther.,* 176:480–488.

---

* Prepared by Prof. G. G. Nahas

Cameron, D. C. (1969). Drug dependence and the law: A medical view. In *Drugs and Youth,* J. R. Wittenborn, H. Brill, J. P. Smith, and S. A. Wittenborn (eds.). Charles C Thomas, Springfield, Ill., pp. 219–228.

Campbell, A. M. G., Evans, M., Thompson, J. L. G., and Williams, M. J. (1971). Cerebral atrophy in young *Cannabis* smokers. *Lancet,* 7736:1219–1224.

Carlin, A. S., and Post, R. D. (1971). Patterns of drug use among marihuana smokers. *J. Amer. Med. Ass.,* 218:867–868.

Carlini, E. A. (1968). Tolerance to chronic administration of *Cannabis sativa* (marihuana) in rats. *Pharmacology,* 1:135–142.

Carstairs, G. M. (1954). Daru and bhang: Cultural factors in choice of intoxicant. *Quart. J. Studies Alcohol,* 15:220–237.

Chopra, G. S. (1969). Man and marihuana. *Int. J. Addictions,* 4:215–247.

Chopra, G. S. (1971). Marihuana and adverse psychotic reactions. *Bull. Narcotics,* 28:15–22.

Christozov, C. (1965). L'aspect marocian de l'intoxication cannabique d'après des études sur des malades mentaux chroniques: 1ere partie et 2eme partie. *Maroc. Med.,* 44:630–642; 866–899.

Clark, L. D., Hughes, R., and Nakashima, E. N. (1970). Behavioral effects of marihuana: Experimental studies. *Arch. Gen. Psychiat. (Chicago),* 23:193–198.

Colbach, E. (1971). Marijuana use by GI's in Viet Nam. *Amer. J. Psychiat.,* 128:96–99.

DeFarias, C. (1955). Use of maconha *(Cannabis sativa* L.) in Brazil. *Bull. Narcotics,* 7:5–19.

Delay, J. (1965). Psychotropic drugs and experimental psychiatry. *Int. J. Neuropsychiat.,* 1:104–117.

Dhunjibhoy, J. E. (1930). A brief résumé of the types of insanity commonly met with in India with a full description of "Indian hemp insanity" peculiar to the country. *J. Ment. Sci.,* 76:254–264.

Doorenbos, N. J., Fetterman, P. S., Quimby, M. W., and Turner, C. E. (1971). Cultivation, extraction and analysis of *Cannabis sativa* L. *Ann. N.Y. Acad. Sci.,* 191:3–15.

Dornbush, R. L., Fink, M., and Freedman, A. M. (1971). Marijuana, memory and perception. *Amer. J. Psychiat.,* 128:194–197.

Ferraro, D. P., Grilly, D. M., and Lynch, W. C. (1971). Effects of marihuana extract on the operant behavior of chimpanzees. *Psychopharmacologia,* 22:333–351.

Foltz, R. L., Fentiman, A. F., Jr., Leighty, E. G., Walter, J. L., Drewes, H. R., Schwartz, W. E., Page, T. F., Jr., and Truitt, E. B., Jr. (1970). Metabolite of (−)-*trans*-Δ-tetrahydrocannabinol: Identification and synthesis. *Science,* 168:844–845.

Forney, R. B., (1971). Toxicology of marihuana. *Pharmacol. Rev.,* 23:279–284.

Frankenheim, J., McMillan, D., and Harris, L. (1971). Effects of 1-Δ⁹-and 1-Δ⁹-*trans*-tetrahydrocannabinol on schedule-controlled behavior of pigeons and rats. *J. Pharmacol. Exp. Ther.,* 178:241–252.

Freedman, I., and Peer, I., (1968). Drug addiction among pimps and prostitutes in Israel. *Int. J. Addictions,* 3:271–300.

Gourves, J., Viallard, C., LeLuan, D., Girard, J. P., and Aury, R. (1971). Case of coma due to *Cannabis sativa*. *Presse Med.*, 79:1389.

Halikas, J. A., Goodwin, D. W., and Guze, S. B. (1971). Marihuana effects. A survey of regular users. *J. Amer. Med. Ass.*, 217:692–694.

Haney, A., and Bazzaz, F. A. (1970). Some ecological implications of the distribution of hemp (*Cannabis sativa* L.) in the United States of America. In *The Botany and Chemistry of Cannabis*, C. R. B. Joyce and S. H. Curry (eds.). J. & A. Churchill, London, pp. 38–48.

Hardman, H. F., Domino, E. F., and Seevers, M. H. (1971). General pharmacological actions of some synthetic tetrahydrocannabinol derivatives. *Pharmacol. Rev.*, 23:295–315.

Harris, L. S. (1971). General and behavioral pharmacology of Δ^9-THC. *Pharmacol. Rev.*, 23:285–294.

Hollister, L. E. (1970). Tetrahydrocannabinol isomers and homologues: Contrasted effects of smoking. *Nature*, 227:968–969.

Hollister, L. E. (1971a). Marihuana in man: Three years later. *Science*, 172:21–24.

Hollister, L. E. (1971b). Action of various marihuana derivatives. *Pharmacol. Rev.*, 23:349–358.

Isbell, H., Gorodetsky, G. W., Jasinski, D., Claussen, U., Spulak, F., and Korte, F. (1967). Effects of (—) delta-9-*trans*tetrahydrocannabinol in man. *Psychopharmacologia*, 11: 184–188.

Isbell, H., and Jasinski, D. (1969). A comparison of LSD-25 with (—) delta-9-*trans*-tetrahydrocannabinol (THC) and attempted cross tolerance between LSD and THC. *Psychopharmacologia*, 14:115–123.

Jones, R. T. (1971). Marihuana-induced "high": Influence of expectation, setting and previous drug experience. *Pharmacol. Rev.*, 23:359–370.

Kaplan, H. S. (1971). Psychosis associated with marijuana. *N.Y. State J. Med.*, 71:433–435.

Kaplan, J. H. (1971). Marihuana and drug abuse in Vietnam. *Ann. N.Y. Acad. Sci.*, 191:261–269.

Keeler, M. H., Ewing, J. A., and Rouse, B. A. (1971). Hallucinogenic effects of marijuana as currently used. *Amer. J. Psychiat.*, 128:105—108.

Keup, W. (1970). Psychotic symptoms due to *Cannabis* abuse. *Dis. Nerv. Syst.*, 31:119–126.

Klausner, H. A., and Dingell, J. V. (1971). The metabolism and excretion of Δ^9-tetrahydrocannabinol in the rat. *Life Sci.*, 10:49–59.

Kolansky, H., and Moore, W. T. (1971). Effects of marihuana on adolescents and young adults. *J. Amer. Med. Ass.*, 216:486–492.

Kornhaber, A. (1971). Marihuana in an adolescent psychiatric outpatient population. *J. Amer. Med. Ass.*, 215:1000.

Kubena, R. K., and Barry, H., III. (1970). Interactions of delta-9-tetrahydrocannabinol with barbiturates and methamphetamine. *J. Pharm. Exp. Ther.*, 173:94–100.

Lambo, T. A. (1965). Medical and social problems of drug addiction in West Africa. *Bull. Narcotics*, 17:3–14.

244   *HASHISH AND MENTAL ILLNESS*

Lemberger, L., Axelrod, J., and Kopin, I. J. (1971). Metabolism and disposition of delta-9-tetrahydrocannabinol in man. *Pharmacol. Rev.,* 23:371–380.

McIsaac, W. M., Fritchie, G. W., Idanpaan-Heikkila, J. E., Ho, B. T., and Englert, L. F. (1971). Distribution of marihuana in monkey brain and concomitant behavioral effects. *Nature,* 230:593–594.

McMillan, D. E., Dewey, W. L., and Harris, L. S. (1971). Characteristics of tetrahydrocannabinol tolerance. *Ann. N.Y. Acad. Sci.,* 191:83–99.

Magus, R. D., and Harris, L. S. (1971). Carcinogenic potential of marihuana smoke condensate. *Fed. Proc.,* 30:279.

Mann, P. E., Cohen, A. B., Finley, T. N., and Ladman, A. J. (1971). Alveolar macrophages. Structural and functional differences between nonsmokers and smokers of marijuana and tobacco. *Lab. Invest.,* 25:111–120.

Manning, F. J., McDonough, J. A., Jr., et al. (1971). Inhibition of normal growth by chronic administration of delta-9-THC. *Science,* 74:424–426.

Manno, J. E., Kiplinger, G. F., Haine, S. E., Bennett, I. F., and Forney, R. B. (1970). Comparative effects of smoking marihuana or placebo on human motor and mental performance. *Clin. Pharmacol Ther.,* 11:808–815.

Manno, J. E., Kiplinger, G. F., Scholtz, N., and Forney, R. B. (1971). The influence of alcohol and marihuana on motor and mental performance. *Clin. Pharmacol. Ther.,* 12:202–211.

Mechoulam, R., Shani, A., Edery, H., and Grunfeld, Y. (1970). Chemical basis of hashish activity. *Science,* 169:611–612.

Melges, F. T., Tinkelberg, J. R., Hollister, L. E., and Gillespie, H. K. (1970). Marihuana and temporal disintegration. *Science,* 168:1118–1120.

Miras, C. J. (1969). Experience with chronic hashish smokers. In *Drugs and Youth,* J. R. Wittenborn, H. Brill, J. P. Smith, and S. A. Wittenborn (eds.). Charles C Thomas, Springfield, Ill., pp. 191–198.

Mirin, S. M., Shapiro, L. M., Meyer, R. E., Pillard, R. C., and Fisher, S. (1971). Casual vs. heavy use of marihuana. A redefinition of the marihuana problem. *Amer. J. Psychiat.,* 127:1134–1140.

Nahas, G. G. (1972). *Cannabis sativa,* the deceptive weed. *N.Y. State J. Med.,* 72:856–868.

Nakazawa, K., and Costa, E. (1971). Metabolism of D9 tetrahydrocannabinol by lung and liver homogenates of rats treated with methylcholanthrene. *Nature,* 234:48–49.

Petrzilka, T. (1970). Synthesis of (−)-tetrahydrocannabinol and analogous compounds. In *The Botany and Chemistry of Cannabis,* C. R. B. Joyce and S. H. Curry (eds.). J. & A. Churchill, London, pp. 79–92.

Podolsky, S., Pattavina, C. G., and Amaral, M. A. (1971). Effect of marihuana on glucose tolerance test. *Ann. N.Y. Acad. Sci.,* 191:54–60.

Renault, P. F., Schuster, C. R., Heinrich, R., and Freeman, D. X. (1971). Marihuana: Standardized smoke administration and dose effect curves on heart rate in humans. *Science,* 174:589–591.

Rolland, J. L., and Teste, M. (1957). Le cannabisme au Maroc. *Maroc. Med.,* 387:694–703.

Scher, J. M. (1970). The marihuana habit. *J. Amer. Med. Ass.*, 214:1120.

Schultes, R. E. (1970). Random thoughts and queries on the botany of *Cannabis*. In *The Botany and Chemistry of Cannabis*, C. R. B. Joyce and S. H. Curry (eds.). J. & A. Churchill, London, pp. 11–38.

Seevers, M. H. (1970). Drug dependence and drug abuse. A world problem. *Pharmacologist*, 12:172–181.

Solursh, L. P., Weinstock, S. J., Saunders, C. S., and Ungerleider, J. T. (1971). Attitudes of medical students toward cannabis. *J. Amer. Med. Ass.*, 217:1371–1372.

Soueif, M. I. (1967). Hashish consumption in Egypt with special reference to psychological aspects. *Bull. Narcotics*, 19:1–12.

Soueif, M. I. (1971). The use of *Cannabis* in Egypt: A behavioural study. *Bull. Narcotics*, 33:17–28.

Stearn, W. T. (1970). The *Cannabis* plant: Botanical characteristics. In *The Botany and Chemistry of Cannabis*, C. R. B. Joyce and S. H. Curry (eds.). J. & A. Churchill, London, pp. 1–10.

Talbott, J., and Teague, J. (1969). Marihuana psychosis. *J. Amer. Med. Ass.*, 210:299–303.

Tennant, F. S., Jr., Preble, M., Prendergast, T. J., and Ventry, P. (1971). Medical manifestations associated with hashish. *J. Amer. Med. Ass.*, 216:1965–1969.

United Nations Conference for the Adoption of a Single Convention on Narcotic Drugs (1961). Vols. I and II. United Nations, New York.

W.H.O. Scientific Group (1971). *The Use of Cannabis*. World Health Organization Technical Report Series No. 478. Geneva.

Williams, E. G., Himmelsbach, C. K., Wikler, A., Ruble, D. C., and Lloyd, B. J., Jr. (1946). Studies on marihuana and pyrahexl compound. *Public Health Rep.*, 61:1059–1083.